D0765326

PRINCES OF
DARKNESS

PRINCES OF DARKNESS

The Saudi Assault on the West

LAURENT MURAWIEC

Translated by

GEORGE HOLOCH

ROWMAN & LITTLEFIELD PUBLISHERS, INC.

Lanham • Boulder • New York • Toronto • Oxford

ROWMAN & LITTLEFIELD PUBLISHERS, INC.

Published in the United States of America
by Rowman & Littlefield Publishers, Inc.
A wholly owned subsidary of The Rowman & Littlefield Publishing Group, Inc.
4501 Forbes Boulevard, Suite 200, Lanham, Maryland 20706
www.rowmanlittlefield.com

PO Box 317
Oxford
OX2 9RU, UK

Distributed by National Book Network

Princes of Darkness is a translation of *La Guerre d'apres*, first published in 2003 by Editions
Albin Michel S.A., Paris, France. Published by arrangement with the author.

Copyright © 2003 by Editions Albin Michel S.A.
First Rowman & Littlefield translation 2005

British Library Cataloguing in Publication Information Available

Library of Congress Cataloging-in-Publication Data

Murawiec, Laurent.
[Guerre d'après. English]
Princes of darkness : the Saudi assault on the West / Laurent Murawiec ; translated by
George Holoch.
p. cm.
Translation of: La Guerre d'apres, first published in 2003 by Editions Albin Michel
S.A., Paris, France.
Includes index.
ISBN 0-7425-4278-5 (hardcover : alk. paper)
1. Saudi Arabia—Politics and government. 2. Al Sa' ud, House of. 3. Saudi
Arabia—Kings and rulers. 4. Islamic fundamentalism—Saudi Arabia. 5.
Wahh ab iyah—Saudi Arabia—History. 6. Terrorism—Religious aspects—Islam. 7.
Petroleum industry and trade—Saudi Arabia. 8. Saudi Arabia—Foreign relations—
United States. 9. United States—Foreign relations—Saudi Arabia. 10. Saudi Arabia—
Foreign relations—Europe. 11. Europe—Foreign relations—Saudi Arabia. I. Title.
DS244.63.M8713 2005
953.805'3—dc22

2005009053

Printed in the United States of America

♾™ The paper used in this publication meets the minimum requirements of American
National Standard for Information Sciences—Permanence of Paper for Printed Library
Materials, ANSI/NISO Z39.48–1992.

To Claudia, this as well as everything else.

Contents

Acknowledgments   ix

Introduction   xi

1   The Arabia of the Al-Sauds   1

2   Wahhabis, Princes, and Apartheid   9

3   Wahhabism Takes on the World   23

4   Seizing Control of Islam   29

5   The Saudi Multinational   43

6   The Historic Rival   55

7   The Saudi Islamintern and Its Feats   67

8   The Chain of Terror   81

9   "Islamists of All Countries, Unite"   95

10   The Export of Terrorism   107

11   Washington on the Auction Block   119

12   Self-Interested Friendships   129

13   The Rags of the Emir   145

14   Arabs Made in Britain   161

15   1939: Hitler and Ibn Saud   173

16   State Anti-Semitism and Global
     Expansionism   185

17   The Oil Weapon   199

18   Buying Palaces and Countries   211

Conclusion: Taking the Saudi Out of Arabia   227

Epilogue   245

Notes   269

Index   297

About the Author   305

Acknowledgments

There have been many individuals and organizations that have contributed, in one way or another, to this book. They are too many to list, but I would like to single out the fine and influential works by Yossef Bodansky, *Bin Laden: The Man Who Declared War on America* (1999); Steven Emerson, *American House of Saud: The Secret Petrodollar Connection* (1985); and Sandra Mackey, *The Saudis: Inside the Desert Kingdom* (1987). They made my job in reporting this important story a bit easier.

Introduction

"The Saudis are active at every level of the terror chain, from planners to financiers, from cadre to foot soldier, from ideologist to cheerleader."
—Briefing by the author on July 10, 2002,
to the Defense Policy Board of the Pentagon

On July 10, 2002, I mounted the broad white stone staircase leading to the south gate of the Pentagon. A senior policy analyst at the Rand Corporation, the noted research institute that works chiefly for the Defense Department, I was coming to give a briefing with the provocative title: "Taking Saudi out of Arabia."

I was going to speak to the Defense Policy Board, whose role is to suggest new strategic ideas off the beaten track, an assembly of about thirty members, former defense secretaries, armed forces chiefs, senators and representatives, and strategists. The recommendations of the Board go directly to Defense Secretary Donald Rumsfeld.

I came at the request of the head of the Board, Richard Perle. During the Reagan administration, he had played an essential role in the victory over the Soviet Union. In 2002, he was among the leading figures in Washington, one of the strategists in what President George W. Bush has called the "war on terror."

That day, I intended to do some spadework in an important area. Within the small circle of advisers and influential men who made up the Board, the briefing was intended to launch a debate that had long been blocked. In Washington, Saudi Arabia was still a taboo subject.

I began—the briefing included twenty-four slides projected on a large screen. The ensuing debate was serious and lively, as befits a group of that caliber. "If you're right, what should be done? How can all this be put into practice? What will be the consequences for our relations with one country or another?" After an hour and a half of presentation and discussion, coffee and cookies were welcome.

A French citizen, and a recent immigrant to the United States, I felt honored by the occasion, as I had when I testified before a congressional committee. I left with the feeling that I had contributed, to the extent that I could, to the politics of my adopted country.

Soon thereafter, I flew off for a vacation in Europe, my mind at rest, with the feeling that I had done my duty. After a few weeks devoted to Shakespeare in England, to my family and friends in France, and to my fiancée's family, I returned to the oppressive heat of early August on the banks of the Potomac. A few days later, the thunderbolt struck: the *Washington Post* printed on the front page the contents of my briefing under the resounding headline: "Briefing Depicted Saudis as Enemies, Ultimatum Urged to Pentagon Board." The author, Tom Ricks, a respected journalist, a specialist in defense questions, summed up the matter at the beginning of his article: "A briefing given last month to a top Pentagon advisory board described Saudi Arabia as an enemy of the United States, and recommends that U.S. officials give it an ultimatum to stop backing terrorism, or face seizure of its oil fields and its financial assets invested in the United States." The conclusions had not respected diplomatic niceties: to stimulate debate, what could be better than a straight argument without circumlocutions? Calling the briefing "explosive," the *Post* reporter quoted this sentence from it: "The Saudis are active at every level of the terror chain, from planners to financiers, from cadre to foot soldier, from ideologist to cheerleader." In the ensuing days and weeks, I would indeed recognize the "explosive" nature of my statement.

For two or three weeks, there was a frenetic media circus, sometimes suggesting a school of piranha that had tasted blood, sometimes a swarm of flies falling on a jam pot. All the American media jostled each other for an interview, an appearance on a talk show, a debate. The networks, the major cable networks, small stations, dailies, radio stations, committees, and commissions, all wanted a piece of the action. My office at Rand was under siege. I referred all calls to the public affairs office, because the management had asked me to maintain silence.

The affair was turning into a scandal. I had committed a crime of lèse-majesté. Like the little boy in Andersen's fairy tale, I had shouted: "The emperor has no clothes!"

But nothing in what I had said was radically new. Others had presented the facts and often made the same analyses, long before. But their questions had never made it into the public arena. The debate, that had until then been confined to seminars for specialists, became widespread, and all kinds of people got involved. The comedian Jay Leno took it up on The Tonight Show: "The government and the Rand Corporation, the think tank, have figured out that the Saudis are our enemies. And you know what gave them the clue?"—pause for comic effect—"the hijackers." And the whole country laughed in agreement, already persuaded of the truth of the statement.

Anger had been growing, and a crisis brewing in the country since September 11. Chance and circumstances precipitated a national and international debate on the Saudi question. The "explosive" remarks, the location—the Pentagon—the status of the audience, and the leak that revealed its content to the public changed the game. As the expression goes, the story had legs.

In the following days, the uproar was deafening. After the daily press and the electronic media, the weeklies entered the fray. I was made a target of public condemnation: "a foreign resident," said one with dubious emphasis, "a French-Jewish-Polish strategist," snorted another, with even viler insinuations, "an unrepentant extremist," "an ignorant pontificator," "an obscure figure," "Dr. Strangelove." The list of insults was long and not lacking in variety. Some reporters added new details to my biography: one claimed I was born in Poland, another told of my exotic adventures. One or another episode in my life was examined under a distorting microscope. One reporter's stupid remarks were instantly repeated and amplified by others. I understood the contemptuous remark of the Austrian writer Karl Kraus: "No ideas and the ability to express them: that's a journalist."

An experienced observer of the Washington scene confessed his surprise to me: "In my career of twenty-five years, I have never seen the propaganda machine get moving so quickly and with so much fury. You've really hit a sore spot."

Then Secretary of State Colin Powell thought it necessary to call his Saudi counterpart, Prince Saud al-Faisal, to tell him that my briefing represented neither the opinion of the president nor that of the administration, and to "reiterate the traditional position of the government of the United States concerning the close ties uniting the two countries and to emphasize that nothing had changed in the strength of their relations." If we are to believe the press release from the Saudi embassy datelined Jeddah, this is exactly what Foreign Minister Saud himself said.[1] He had even called my remarks "fiction pure and simple."

Things did not stop there. According to the official periodical *Saudi Arabia*, President Bush in person had picked up the phone, called Crown Prince Abdallah, and "emphasized that he rejected the content of the briefing presented by Laurent Murawiec of the Rand Corporation to the Defense Policy Board on July 10 in which he described the kingdom as an enemy of the United States." President Bush praised the strength of relations between the two countries and regretted the "irresponsibility" of the media coverage given to the baseless views of Mr. Murawiec on the friendly relations between the two countries, reflecting neither the reality of the ties nor the strength of bilateral relations. These ideas "will have no effect on friendship and cooperation, deeply rooted for decades, even in current circumstances." The last clause leads one to wonder: What circumstances was the president referring to? September 11?

The Saudi Crown Prince, for his part, was very pleased, according to the official organ.[2] Less voluble, Defense Secretary Donald Rumsfeld merely said, truthfully enough, that the briefing "does not reflect majority opinion in my department," which was hardly a ringing endorsement of the Saudis. His irritation was principally directed at the "leak" and its source or sources. His spokeswoman, Victoria Clarke, nonetheless reflected the "party line" adopted in Washington: "Neither the briefing nor the comments of the members of the Defense Policy Board reflect the official views of the Defense Department. Saudi Arabia is an old friend and ally of the United States. The Saudis are fully cooperating in the global war against terrorism, for which the administration is deeply grateful." She might have added that the Saudi dynasty was the official sponsor of Santa Claus.[3]

The dynasty was furious and made relentless efforts to dampen the crisis that had erupted. The same Prince Saud, former foreign minister, boldly stated that my views "are distracting attention from the war against the terrorism that poses a true threat to the United States, Saudi Arabia, and other peaceful nations of the world."

Despite violent official denials, the *Washington Times* pointed out that "the briefing hit a sore spot." At the very time that Crown Prince Abdallah was visiting President Bush at his ranch in Crawford in April 2002, the Israeli army discovered extensive documentation demonstrating the funding of Palestinian terrorism by Saudi Arabia; a telethon had collected $50 million for the "families of Palestinian martyrs"; the kingdom, moreover, was singularly lacking in vigor in its cooperation in the fight against terror; countless articles in the press had pointed to the Saudi nationality of fifteen of the September 11 hijackers; and a good half of the Guantanamo prisoners were Saudis. The *Washington Times* reporter quoted his own paper as having "reported last spring that one of the religious leaders of the kingdom had delivered incendiary remarks on Saudi television against Jews in general, and in the same breath had violently attacked Western culture, Europe, and the United States."

While reporting the negative, not to say disagreeable, comments made about me, the article, like many others, took the opportunity to present the essential elements of my briefing: "The only way to deal with Saudi Arabia is to warn it that by continuing to support terrorism it would force the United States to occupy the oil fields...this strong strategic recommendation is one of a long list that includes getting rid of Saddam Hussein and establishing a friendly government in Iraq, capable of guaranteeing oil supplies and reducing Western dependence on Saudi Arabia." Several class action suits were filed by families of September 11 victims against Saudi funders of terrorism, and an FBI investigation is also following that trail.[4]

"Extremely provocative" complained CNN, going on to say that the leak had "caused a diplomatic earthquake."[5] And David Ignatius, associate editor of the *Washington Post*, proclaimed: "Now, the Saudis surely need to reform their government—for their sake more than ours. But for all their faults, the Saudis don't deserve the sort of sneering, slapdash insults in Murawiec's briefing."[6] The columnist Robert Novak, echoing the State Department, attacked Richard Perle in the guise of taking me on.[7]

On the right, Arnaud de Borchgrave, editor at large at UPI, attacked me twice, repeatedly pointing to the fact that I was a "foreigner." In 1992, when Saudi Arabia acquired UPI, he had played an important role.[8] He passionately defended Saudi friendship and the Saudi alliance. He violently attacked the "Gallic plan to put the Middle East to fire and the sword." On the left, the online magazine *Slate* got part of the text of my briefing from the Pentagon and put it online, along with a pseudo-biography drawn from a hasty Google search. All of this was worthy of the habits of the press described in his time by Balzac.

I was informed from Paris that the French foreign minister had also been intent, although nothing obliged him to do so, on calling Saud al-Faisal to tell him that this reckless Frenchman did "not at all" represent the policy of France. To be sure, the frightful Murawiec had been a consultant to the defense ministry in Paris, but that "in no way" influenced French policy toward the Saudi kingdom, full of friendship, respect, etc.

On Meet the Press on August 11, 2002, the half-way presentable Saudi Adel al-Jubeir, adviser to the foreign minister, expressed nothing but indignation and a clear conscience. In Saudi Arabia itself, with the elegance characteristic of the kingdom's media, the large-circulation Saudi daily *Okaz* explained that the Pentagon was "full of Jews and allies of the Zionists," and everything could be laid at the feet of plots and conspiracies against Islam conducted by the "forces of Evil." And on August 31, the Saudi daily *As-Sharq Al-Awsat*, owned by Prince Khaled bin Sultan, served up the same refrain: "What is this Zionist strategy adopted by [Richard] Perle and his associates?... By giving Laurant [sic] Murawiec his orders and supervising his analysis—which discovered that Saudi Arabia is an enemy of the United

States—Richard Perle, who conspires against and is guilty of treason against his country, is merely implementing a Zionist conspiracy. This conspiracy consists precisely of pushing America into a war against the Muslims of the entire world. What proves [Richard Perle's] propensity toward aggression is the fact that he is one of the principal advocates of an American war against an Arab-Muslim nation," wrote a certain Zainil-Abdin al-Rikabi, with no concern for logic.

In the English-language Beirut *Daily Star*, the Saudi journalist Jamal Khashoggi, offspring of a wealthy and well-known Saudi family, launched a torrent of abuse: Murawiec is guilty of "cheap intellectual prostitution."[9] In Egypt, the semi-official daily *Al-Ahram* complained: "Although the [American] administration promptly disclaimed any responsibility for the briefing, Murawiec's ideas, it is said, are shared by eminent members of the administration, including Vice President Dick Cheney, Defense Secretary Donald Rumsfeld, and his deputy Paul Wolfowitz. The publication of the principal elements of the briefing calls into question the basis of the Saudi-American relationship, oil for protection."[10]

Embarrassed denials had served no purpose.

The United States Muslim Student Association showered me with insults and threats, and all sorts of Islamic websites made me their whipping boy.

In Washington, the "association of the friends of Saudi Arabia" went into action. A former Deputy Director of the CIA, who had briefly been Secretary of Defense before becoming head of the Carlyle Group, the large and powerful investment company, an essential link in the Saudi political and business presence in the United States, led the charge. In concert with his Saudi clients and friends, he attributed my briefing to the pernicious influence of Israel. Granted that he had good reasons to resent me: the Bin Laden family had been among his investors, and other Saudi giants among his partners. And, a troubling detail, he was a member of the board of trustees of the Rand Corporation, which I was forced to leave a few weeks later.

None of my critics seriously discussed the argument of the briefing. To discredit the message, discredit the messenger: "He's a madman," "he knows nothing about it," "he has a dubious past." It was as though the great goodness and angelic purity of Saudi Arabia and its leaders were self-evident; as though the Saudi-American partnership were gospel truth; and almost as though nothing had happened on September 11 and afterward.

Fortunately, public opinion came out strongly in my favor. In the course of a few days, I received several hundred e-mails. Ninety-eight percent of them congratulated me for my stance: "Bravo! Finally someone speaks the truth in Washington!" "You're my new hero!" wrote a pastor in Wisconsin. "We should have dealt with them seventy-three years ago when I was twelve," wrote a retiree who had worked in Saudi Arabia. "I admire the courage you have shown," said an engineer from California. "Hang in there! Don't let the volley of abuse get you down!" Soldiers and officers who had served in the Arabian peninsula told me of their misadventures with anger and bitterness. Relying on a Gallup poll, a commentary by the pro-Arab Zogby International was forced to recognize soon thereafter that 75 percent of Americans thought that Saudi Arabia could not be trusted and 63 percent that it was a hostile power.[11]

My e-mail came from Africa and Asia, India and Pakistan, and also from Arab countries. An Arab friend called me from London to say: "Two thirds of the Arabs I talk to congratulate you: finally someone who tells the truth in Washington. It's about time!" Another, hostile to me and to English spelling, inveighed against me: "You dimented [sic] fascist pig." But that was an exception. My argument had touched a sensitive chord.

There were also favorable newspaper articles, several of which touched me and brought me welcome support in the storm. "I find no fault with the Rand analysis as an intellectual product. Murawiec is a precise thinker," wrote James Robbins on August 8 in the conservative *National Review*. The next day, an article by the African-American columnist Deroy Murdock appeared online: "Overthrow the house of Saud (they are worse than Saddam)." Building a strong indictment, he concluded: "If it's necessary, let's overthrow Saddam Hussein. But the expert from Rand is right: the Bush team should stop pretending that Saudi Arabia is Holland with sand dunes."[12] In the online edition of *U.S. News & World Report*, Michael Barone found in my briefing the essential outlines of the analysis he had himself formulated earlier. "An intellectual speaks truth to power" was certainly the sentence that comforted me the most.[13]

The most favorable result was the importance taken on by the debate. Editorials and opinion pieces proliferated. All aspects of the Saudi problem were opened up for discussion. The impunity and immunity that Saudi Arabia enjoyed in Washington were coming to an end. In the public at large there was one conviction: the arrogance, the vulgar ostentation, the intolerance of the Saudi leaders, taken together with the nationality of the September 11 assassins, left no room for doubt. Things moved more slowly in Washington, where the inertia of established interests and received ideas holds back change. One does not break from one day to the next with habits inherited from fifty years of experience, especially when a war is impending, the one against Iraq, or rather against Saddam Hussein.

A month after the "leak" to the *Washington Post*, I left the Rand Corporation.

Despite the distress it had caused me—it is unpleasant to be dragged through the mud by some of the media—the "affair" had had its virtues: it had enabled a national and international controversy that had long been stifled to come to the front of the stage; it had indicated to many people—including families of the victims of September 11—that they were not alone in seeing the Saudi kingdom as the heart of the problem; it had given a great kick to the ants' nest of Saudi-American business dealings; my name was now spelled and even pronounced correctly.

Finally, the "affair" had given me the impetus to write this book. All things considered, the outcome was positive.

The Arabia of the Al-Sauds

Neither a nation nor a state, the Arabia now called "Saudi" is an empire only recently forged in rivers of blood. Between 1902 and 1932, the Al-Saud clan annexed to its family estates the formerly independent territories of Asir, Hijaz, and Shammar. The Kingdom of Saudi Arabia—"Arabia of the Sauds" in Arabic—is thus younger than either the Soviet Empire or the Yugoslav Federation (both born of World War I) before their collapse.

Today's Arabia is the joint offspring of the internal combustion engine; the shifting positions of British imperial policy; the efforts of a clumsy amateur—an American philanthropist with a passion for diplomatic intrigue; a pro-Nazi Englishman converted to Islam; an American geological engineer with a penchant for archeology; an eighteenth-century visionary preacher with a good head for business; and a succession of buccaneers with a taste for power and a gift for strategy.

Conquered by the sword, the Empire displays the weapon on its banners: on the Saudi flag is not only the *shahada*, the profession of faith—"There is no God but Allah and Mohammed is his prophet"—and the palm tree, but above all the sword. "In the Middle East," an Egyptian politician used to say, "there are no nations but only tribes with flags." Monopolized by the Al-Saud clan, this Arabia is not a state, but a family business, the only one in the world with a seat in the United Nations.

Even though it sends its ambassadors with deep pockets to capital cities around the world, "this is a land of silence," as one diplomat put it.[1] Behind the scenes, on the other side of those windowless walls, the country is ruled surreptitiously but implacably. The local media are servants hired to produce propaganda. Foreign media are rarely admitted, and then only after passing through a succession of filters to verify that they have the right attitude, as in the old Soviet Union. "It is as though a veil of silence covered most of the country," as though the true Saudi Arabia could only appear swathed from head to foot in an *abaya* or a black *hijab*.

Yet this archaic system is shown reverence by deferential diplomats, obsequiousness by the rare journalists allowed into the kingdom, and benevolence by oil companies. Bankers speak of Saudi Arabia in respectful tones, industry looks to it with hope. In Washington, London, and Paris, when arms dealers think of their profits, they turn their faces toward Mecca, or rather toward Riyadh, the capital. Civil servants dream of career prospects, generals of their missions, the elite of the police force imagine future jobs. As for politicians, they consider how their next election campaign is going to be financed.

The Al-Sauds are flattered for their wisdom and they daily hear "your royal highness" more often than anyone since the Sun King. This goes even for the scheming entrepreneurs, Mister ten percent, or twenty, or thirty, who, despite their big bellies, pass for playboys in the pages of ingratiating glossy magazines. Each age enjoys the glamour it can afford. No one scoffs at petrodollars.

The Romans used to say money has no odor. It is like natural gas, and it is equally toxic. Money also talks, and its voice is loud and compelling, and highly persuasive. Since the House of Saud orchestrated soaring oil prices through OPEC, in 1973 and 1974, and again in 1978 and 1979, the Saudi Treasury has raked in the almost unimaginable sum of two trillion dollars, that is, an average of nearly $80 billion each year, the equivalent of the yearly GDP of a country like Colombia or Malaysia. They say in France that a good reputation is worth more than a gold belt, but you can buy one with the other.

These sums of money fall like manna: fortunes are made without effort, without work, without investment, without scientific research, without technological innovation. All of that is imported. Riches are acquired as in a Bedouin raid, by abduction, a monstrous ambush that has taken the world economy hostage and exploited a transitory monopoly to extract the ransom. And what has been achieved with this unearned fortune? To the thirty thousand members of the reigning Al-Saud family, it has provided unlimited incomes. They have built palaces by the hundreds, run up monstrous shopping bills in the supermarkets of the West—an orgy of luxury consumer goods—edible and sexual, including alcohol (the Al-Saud dynasty counts a remarkable number of drunks in its ranks). They have bought everything and anything that was for sale. In London, Paris, Marbella, Geneva, and New York, they have acquired palaces and residences, filled and refilled the horns of plenty: Rolex watches by the thousand, champagne by the truckload, and untold quantities of perfumes and luxury automobiles. And they have opened countless bank accounts in Geneva, Zurich, Luxembourg, Nassau, and the Cayman Islands.

And what about the rest? In 1974, oil and its byproducts accounted for 91 percent of Saudi exports. In the year 2000, the figure was 91.4 percent. *In a quarter of a century, during which the country was saturated with oil revenues, nothing had changed.* No industrialization took place. It is the six million immigrants who do the work—Americans, Europeans, Indians and Pakistanis, Filipinos, Egyptians and Palestinians, Yemenites, Koreans, all mercenaries deprived of their basic rights, virtual slaves who keep the machines running, who assemble, repair, manage, and construct. From the economic point of view, it is a total loss: the riches produced throughout the entire world, extorted by a monopoly, and poured into this country, have produced absolutely nothing.

A mere façade of modernity has been stuck onto the desert kingdom; it is a gold-plated realm. Under the gilded surface lies nothing but sand and oil. What is missing is the work ethic, the effort to produce, the desire for science and innovation. What it lacks is a human infrastructure and an organization of the society and its values that would allow for creativity and production. The kingdom consumes: it is a veritable "black hole," as they say in astronomy. Resources come in from everywhere and disappear into sheer nothingness. Just as the Bedouin despises the peasant and his life of labor, preferring the vainglory of caravans and rifle fire—signs of "virility"—the Saudi likewise despises those who produce. To the mind of the idle rich and the Bedouin, wealth is not created but confiscated. The world is a zero-sum game: you have to take from Peter to give to Saud. "[C]amel-breeding Bedouin were considered [by themselves] the noblest representatives of the human race[compared to settled people]... Craftsmen were even more despised in Arabian society than were the 'lower' tribes," according to one historian.[2]

Since 1973, this has been the way of the world. The oil kept on flowing, bringing in millions of dollars of royalties. All was for the best in the best of all possible bank accounts: the United States and the entire Western world have used Saudi Arabia as a gas station. Sometimes it was necessary to protect the pumps from the swarms of predators in the neighborhood: the Ayatollahs' Iran in 1979, and in 1990, Iraq under Saddam Hussein.

It is true that the regime practices a multifaceted apartheid toward inferior races and species: foreigners, Shiites, Christians, Jews, and women. It is true that you can find yourself in jail for the slightest reason or no reason at all. Torture is widely practiced: whipping, stoning, amputation, decapitation. There are fifty thousand mosques—one for every hundred male adults—and fifty thousand *imams* who direct prayers. Their sermons, and the schoolbooks, newspapers, radio, and television, all official and rigidly controlled by the regime, are filled with calls to hate and murder Westerners. All this in the name of Islam.

Other than the "right" conferred by their conquest, what title can the Al-Sauds claim, those pirates on the seas of sand? The religion they profess, Wahhabism, is a strange mixture of paganism, provincial narrow-mindedness, and rhetoric borrowed from Islam. Hardly a generation ago, the Al-Saud family religion was considered by the Islamic world as a weird distortion of Islam by exalted visionaries: the backward religion of ignorant and crude Bedouins. For the educated Arab from Cairo, Damascus, or Beirut, for the refined Persian or the Muslim from the Indian subcontinent, the religion of Riyadh (60 percent of the population are not professed Wahhabis) was the object of disdain and condescension: the kind of bigotry you would expect from camel drivers and goat breeders.

In thirty years, miraculously, the status of Wahhabism has progressed from the obscure and distant orbit of Pluto to the central, majestic position of Jupiter. Yesterday consigned to the outer edge, the reigning family has now spread its credo over the whole Muslim world. Islamic centers financed by Riyadh, mosques and Koranic schools where only the Wahhabi doctrine is taught, obscurantist universities, missionaries with money to burn and large goals who preach from Morocco to Indonesia, from Nigeria to Uzbekistan, the international press in Arabic monopolized by rich Saudis, international Arab organizations, all converge to produce a single picture. The Al-Sauds have used the enormous power and wealth that came from oil to buy countries, consciences, political parties, celebrities, and mercenaries.

And not only in the Muslim world. Saudi corruption has played a large role, especially in the Middle East. But the Al-Saud family has been smart enough to extend its purchases beyond the Muslim world: the rot has also reached Europe and the United States. The fantastic arms purchases, made by a kingdom that does not have one tenth of the qualified soldiers required to put the high-tech systems into action, have enabled the kingdom to gain untold influence in the West. The smell of petrodollars is very enticing.

To bring the honeymoon to an end, Khaled Almihdhar, Majed Moqed, Nawaf Alhazmi, and Salem Alhazmi had to board a Boeing 757, American Airlines flight 77, and Satam M.A. al-Suqami, Waleed M. Alshehri, and Abdulaziz Alomari had to board a Boeing 767, American Airlines flight 11, and the others. It took all the horror of Manhattan's Twin Towers, and the south side of the Pentagon, and three thousand dead. Only when it turned out that fifteen of the nineteen September 11 hijackers were Saudi citizens, was the question posed: could Saudi Arabia, our friend, our ally, be in fact our enemy? It was from then onward that the nationality of Osama bin Laden, his accomplices, his supporters, his financiers, his propagandists, and ultimately those who gave the orders, began to be viewed in a new light: the light blackened by the smoke, debris, and dust of September 11, 2001.

The question of trust has been posed and must be elucidated. If Saudi Arabia is not our friend but our enemy, we have to treat it accordingly. In order to do this, we must closely scrutinize the country, its regime, the reigning family, its oil, and its history. We will see how the oil-induced gangrene has infected a tribal society. We will see how Riyadh has purchased huge armies of mercenaries. Those who work, those who produce, those who defend: none of them, or almost none, are Saudis. We will listen to what the princes, the *imams*, the propagandists are saying in Riyadh, in Mecca, in Medina.

We will examine the "conquest" of the Muslim world by the money of Saudi outsiders over the last thirty or forty years. We will see Wahhabism seep into the heart of Islam, the Saudi Bedouins establish themselves as masters and judges of the world: often hated, often feared, never respected, but always flattered, always present. We will see societies penetrated by Wahhabi ideology and Saudi money tremble and sometimes collapse, in Pakistan, Algeria, and Egypt.

We must look at half a century of influence in Washington: how, starting out from the famous oil firm Aramco (Arabian-American Oil Corporation), a real lobby developed—one of the most powerful, best positioned, most insidious mechanisms of influence in a capital that boasts so many. We will see that lobby weigh on, influence, alter decisions made and directions taken, even at the highest levels. We will observe the greed for profits of a variety of people, presidents and senators, businessmen and bankers, academics and journalists. We will see men of influence, advertisers, and lobbyists, conducting their dance to sell the Saudis to decision makers in Washington and the rest of the country.

And that, as we shall also see, is what explains American blindness in front of the rising storm. The countless links between the Saudi elite and international terror, that so many analysts and observers had established before and after September 11, 2001, should have been perceived, revealed, attacked, unraveled by all available means. Now we have to go back to the source, beyond the mere overthrow of the dictatorial regime of Saddam Hussein.

What is to be done? There is no point in drawing up an indictment if there is no remedy. We must, in conclusion, ask: What is to be done about Saudi Arabia? Should we take the "Saudi" out of Arabia? And if so, how?

CHAPTER 2

Wahhabis, Princes, and Apartheid

On November 20, 1979, the first day of the fifteenth century according to the Muslim calendar, fifteen hundred well-armed and well-organized attackers seized the huge building complex of the Grand Mosque in Mecca. The *mujahedin* were led by a former captain in the National Guard (or "White Guard"), headed by Saudi Crown Prince Abdallah, an offshoot of the *Ikhwan* (the Brotherhood of Bedouins recently converted to Islam that had been the spearhead for the founder of the dynasty, Ibn Saud, in his conquest of Arabia). The extremists had a Saudi core, but included in their ranks Egyptians, Kuwaitis, Sudanese, Iraqis, and Yemenis, among others. The attackers had received military and tactical training in Libya and South Yemen from East German, Cuban, and Palestinian (members of the Popular Front for the Liberation of Palestine) instructors, along with a contingent of apprentice terrorists trained in Iran.

The event shook the royal family to its foundations. Coming after Ayatollah Ruhollah Khomeini's revolution in Iran, that had disparaged and challenged the Islamic legitimacy of the Al-Sauds, the eruption of a fundamentalist challenge in the heart of their fortress was a terrible shock. Khomeini's Iran was Shiite: its violent opposition could always be attributed to Persian hatred of the Arabs and to the heresy of the Shiite "schismatics," who were not even Muslims in the eyes of the Wahhabis. The Mecca assailants were Sunnis, Saudis, and Wahhabis. Made up of members of the Shammar, Harb, and Utaiba tribes, adherents of an extremist Wahhabi sect, Al-Mushtarin, members of the Muslim Brotherhood from Hejaz, and soldiers of the National Guard, they were not some marginal figures, but came from the tribal core that was heavily favored by the regime, and they had made their preparations in urban areas under the noses of the authorities. The magnitude of active and passive complicity in the attack began to come to light.

Juhaiman al-Utaibi, the leader of the attackers, presented his confederate Muhammad al-Qahtani as the *Mahdi*, the Muslim Messiah. He came from one of the tribes involved in the *Ikhwan* revolt a half-century earlier. His own grandfather had died in the fight against Ibn Saud.

His alter ego, a colonel in the National Guard, had organized the supply of arms and equipment. The trucks that had carried weapons and ammunition, and huge quantities of water and provisions for the attackers came from the National Guard and from the large multinational construction firm close to the royal family, the Bin Laden Group. Juhaiman harangued the huge crowd of now trapped worshippers. His sermon violently denounced the corruption of the royal family and its extravagant and frenetically wasteful way of life, and he called for its overthrow in the name of a purified Islam. All of Saudi Arabia echoed with fiery sermons, and processions of extremists took place as the news spread. The holiest place in Islam, the one that contained the *Kaaba*, "the cube," which in turn is built to host the *hajaru l-aswad*, the black stone, which is as the geometric center of Islam, was occupied by these rebels. Bombs exploded in front of palaces and official buildings.

The siege lasted for two weeks and caused several hundred deaths. The incompetence of the Saudi police and soldiers was such that the regime called on French special forces (who acted out the role of instant pseudo-converts to Islam in order to be allowed to get in) to defeat the insurgents, who demonstrated excellent tactical abilities and strong fighting spirit.

The instinctive and immediate reaction of the royal family was to close women's hair salons, to dismiss female announcers from television, and to prohibit girls from continuing their education abroad.[1]

Three weeks after the siege of the Grand Mosque, the Soviet army invaded Afghanistan. The Al-Sauds now had a better opportunity than closing hair salons to refurbish their tarnished image. With Wahhabi extremists in command, the Iranian ayatollahs could no longer sow doubts about the purity of Riyadh's Islam.

The survival instinct is the most prominent shared talent of the Al-Saud family. Their only science is the science of power, or the science of survival. The five most powerful princes in the kingdom: Fahd, Abdallah, Sultan, Salman, and Nayef, are nicknamed "the five illiterates." The five sons of King Abdulaziz Ibn Saud were sent to the best English and American universities. With all the family's money and influence, the most that Muhammad could manage was a bachelor's degree from Menlo Park College in California; Khaled's biography makes no mention of any degree from New College, Oxford. Saud's economics studies at Princeton seem to have fared no better, nor those of Abdulrahman at the Sandhurst military school in Britain, or Turki's studies at the University of London.

Consider the hair-raising tale of the education of the sons of King Saud and of Crown Prince Khaled in the 1960s. A dozen teachers, mostly Egyptians, along with a few Saudis, were in charge of sixty or seventy princelings, who arrived by limousine at eight thirty in the morning, driven by their individual private drivers. Each prince was accompanied by fifteen to twenty servants, bodyguards, and various attendants, five or six of whom accompanied the young highnesses into class. They stayed as long as their protégés, usually not very long.

The official curriculum consisted of geography, English, history, physical education, science, mathematics, Arabic, and religion. The princes showed up "fairly regularly," but "classes had to be shortened because of the students' gradual loss of interest and the difficulty of imposing any discipline on the young princes."[2] An attendant had to "fetch a glass of water, sharpen the prince's pencils, and perform other minor tasks . . . if the royal student had had enough for the day, he ordered his *khawi* [bodyguard] to gather up his things and take him from the school." All the work had to be done in school because the teachers had not been able to impose the idea of "homework." The crown prince took his many sons hunting, on vacation, or on trips for two or three weeks at a time. "One of the worst problems encountered by the teachers came from the *khawis*. There was a kind of competition between the two groups to win the favor of the princes. . . . They say that the *khawis* undo in the afternoon what the teachers have done in the morning. The *khawis*, they say, supply alcohol to their young princes and, in some cases, there is a strong suspicion of homosexual relations between princes and escorts."[3]

Education, as we can see, is not the family's strong point. Let me repeat: the science of the Al-Sauds is the science of power, their principal art is the art of wasting. They have shown exceptional talent in both areas.

According to one scholar, "The royal family itself formed a supreme coalition of twenty thousand members."[4] It includes from five to eight thousand adults, all "princes," descendants of Ibn Saud and his sons and brothers. Ibn Saud had thirty-six sons and two hundred sixty grandsons and great-grandsons (and an equal number of girls). The growth of the family was exponential. The Austria of the Hapsburg Empire, it was said, grew through marriage; Saudi Arabia through pregnancy. There are also the younger branches and the allies of the Al-Sauds, the Al-Saud Al-Kabir, Al-Jilowi. Al-Turki, and Al-Farhan families, and the "aristocratic" families that have intermarried with the Al-Sauds, the Al al-Sheikh (the family of Abd al-Wahhab, of whom King Faisal was a direct descendant), the Al-Sudairis (one of whose representatives produced seven sons for Ibn Saud, that is, three of his successors since 1953, and the coming ones as well).

This extended family, this caricature of a tribal clan, operates as a collective body made up of autonomous units, subunits, and sub-subunits, all welded together by oil, money, and power. All or almost all important ministerial and managerial positions, posts as provincial governors, and in the religious hierarchy go to this collective body. It is as though we were witnessing the progress of a dense mass of bacteria of the same species, a water ballet with the bacteria moving in the same direction and responding to the same imperatives.

This tentacular family functions as a formative element of Saudi society, analogous to the role played by the Communist Party in the former Soviet Union. It is the body that controls the wealth, directs its distribution, and makes all decisions affecting the economy, society, religion, domestic and foreign policy, education, the media, and everything else. At the top are one hundred who make the decisions: they govern Saudi Arabia, they constitute "the highly privileged tribe that permeates the entire country," as the full-page advertisement purchased by the Saudi authorities in the April 25, 1983, *New York Times* ingenuously phrased it. *Al shaykuh abkhas*, "the royal family knows [better]," is commonly heard, as one used to hear "the Party is always right."

The fact is that the Saudi state is only superficially a modern state or even a state at all. Loyalties are not directed toward abstract institutions. *Al-dawla*, the government, is a cold and disembodied entity, while *Al-hukuma*, on the other hand, represents "the chiefs," who are very real. People identify with them through personal ties and in no other way. One is a liegeman, not a citizen. It is also true that the tribe-party is above the laws and that it is so large that its privileges, exempt from ordinary law, deconstruct the entire society.

As in traditional Bedouin societies, the control of the (oil) wealth and its distribution ensures the supremacy of the leader of the collective body. Around each group and sub-group extend in concentric circles the networks of relatives—uncles, cousins, relatives by marriage—and clients clustering around the "spigots" of wealth represented by the groups closest to the core of the royal family.

Obviously, the cohesion of the structure depends on the constant infusion of huge quantities of dollars, a dependence increased by the accelerated demographic growth of the royal family, which is driven by an irresistible, uncontrollable impulse to continually create the conditions enabling it to perpetuate this constant infusion.

In symmetry with the superiority of the tribe-caste-party, the order over which it presides is a multifaceted apartheid: women, Shiites, and foreigners are pariahs, inferiors, the sub-humans of the Wahhabi system. Without rights, persecuted, and oppressed, they are the hidden face of the regime.

In the justice system, Islam accords the testimony of a woman only half the value of that of a man. On the essential matter of women's social status and their place in the universe, the Koran is unambiguous: "Men are superior to women because of the qualities through which God raised men above women . . . Virtuous women are obedient and submissive," says verse 38 of the fourth *sura* ("Women").[5] The sacred Book merely reiterates, in essence, and makes holy the tribal mores of its time and place, softening and "modernizing" some customary practices, particularly with respect to divorce and inheritance.

Saudi Arabia, for its part, has modernized nothing. It was in 1957—and not in the seventh century—that King Saud issued an edict forbidding women to drive. In the name of Islam, the Saudi-Wahhabi regime has worsened the position of women. Sequestration inside the walls of home, the requirement to wear an *abaya* showing only the eyes, illiteracy and the virtual impossibility of exercising a profession, the prohibition of pursuing education abroad, all is horribly summed up in a recent affair, the fire on Friday, March 15, 2002, at a girls' school in Mecca. These "privileged" girls, allowed to study, did not take the privilege with them to paradise. Here is the report of events given by the BBC:

> The Saudi religious police prevented schoolgirls from leaving a burning building because they were not wearing Islamically correct clothing, according to the Saudi press. The Saudi media, permitting themselves rare criticism of the powerful religious police, the *mutawiyin*, accused them of having prevented the rescue of fifteen young girls who died in the fire last Monday. Eight hundred students were in the school in the holy city of Mecca when the tragedy occurred. According to the daily *Al-Eqtisadiah*, the firemen clashed with the police when they drove the girls back into the building because they were wearing neither veils nor *abayas* as required by the strict interpretation of Islam that prevails in the kingdom.
>
> A witness says that he saw three policemen "hitting girls to prevent them from leaving the school because they were not wearing *abayas*." The *Saudi Gazette* presented statements from witnesses according to which the religious police—known as the "Office for the Promotion of Virtue and the Suppression of Vice"—had blocked men who were trying to help the girls by warning them that "it is a sin to get close to them." According to the father of one of the victims, the custodian of the school even refused to open the gates to let the girls go out. "Lives could have been saved if [the efforts of rescuers] had not been stopped short by the members of the Office," the newspaper concludes.
>
> The families of the victims are furious. Most of the victims were crushed in the panic while trying to flee the flames. The school was locked at the time of the fire, a normal practice intended to ensure the complete segregation of the sexes.
>
> The religious police is greatly feared in Saudi Arabia. Its members patrol the streets to enforce respect of the dress

code and the segregation of the sexes, and to enforce the times of prayer. Whoever refuses to obey them is often beaten and sometimes jailed.[6]

It is better to lose lives—the lives of little girls, of course—than to sacrifice "modesty." The murderous *mutawiyin* were only following the law, custom, the norm of the Saudi kingdom. A woman is, by law and in reality, a minor. Her entire existence needs permission from a male—her father, her uncles, her brothers, her husband, her sons. She lives in the shadow of the male and in submission. This is the implacable logic of polygamy. A woman cannot leave home alone or without her male "guardian." This is why Saudi Arabia has five hundred thousand foreign drivers for a total indigenous population of fifteen million. A woman cannot possibly drive a car, a sign of and way to personal autonomy. Even if, because of inheritance or a dowry, a woman is rich, she is divested of the tools allowing her to exercise her financial power. She cannot go to a bank, and Saudi banks refuse to deal with women or to honor their checks without the approval of their husbands. It is reported as a sign of emancipation, although it is not easy to confirm or deny, that 40 percent of the financial assets of Saudi Arabia are held by women. This may be true but, in order to evaluate it, it is well not to forget that many men in the royal family nominally transferred assets to their wives in order to avoid certain prohibitions concerning property decreed in his time by King Faisal. Royal, princely, and rich women wear fashionable haute couture clothing under their *abayas* and take off their black "women's sacks" as soon as they get home or are on board a plane that has left Saudi soil. The hypocrisy is consummate. Antoine Basbous, an attentive observer of the region, quotes the man who was for almost half a century the supreme authority on questions of Saudi morals, Abdulaziz bin Baz: a woman can risk going out, in male company, of course, "showing her eyes or only one eye, to thoroughly conceal her face, because she needs to see the way in order not to get lost . . ."[7] Another Wahhabi cleric "decreed that women should part their hair in the middle; a part to the right or the left was not in conformity with Islamic law . . ."

What is a woman who is barely or not at all educated, who is denied the possibility of any productive or creative activity in society, and who is cut off from the slightest personal autonomy? Her only function, the one to which she is reduced, is reproduction, with its ancillary tasks of nursing and socializing the children. Mares are given reins, ornaments, and trimmings, little ribbons and earrings, they are stroked and pampered, but they wear blinders, and they are whipped whenever they wander off the straight and narrow path. Woe to her if she kicks over the traces. Why on earth would one ever educate a mare? Make her pregnant, she makes babies, and then you start over again. Anyone thinking of educating a mare must have lost his mind.

The unprecedented boldness of forty-seven Saudi women from good families, who took it into their heads, during the period when American troop strength in Saudi Arabia was growing, before the active phase of the 1991 Gulf War, to take the wheel of a car with the ubiquitous guardian in the passenger seat, were appropriately punished. These sluts, as the Grand Mufti, the priceless Bin Baz, called them, were arrested. The language used to denounce them was eloquent: "Whores and prostitutes," "advocates of vice," "filthy secularists," said the fundamentalist sheikhs. Bin Baz had previously ruled that "an unveiled woman [is] one of the great evils and patent sins" and a leading cause of "general depravity."[8] The "shameless drivers" became a target of systematic opprobrium in the sermons of all the mosques in the kingdom.

Women obviously do not have the right to vote, but in fact they share that fate with men: no one votes in Saudi Arabia, a sad state of equality.

The situation of women in Saudi Arabia is comparable to that of the "inferior" races in apartheid South Africa, promised "separate development," meaning in fact underdevelopment. But at least this can be said in favor of the old South Africa: a large number of the representatives of the "races" in question were able to receive an education, including a university education, and in time, they were able to exercise all sorts of liberal professions and to occupy managerial posts. This is not the case in Saudi Arabia.

Other victims of official apartheid are the Shiites, who perhaps represent 80 percent of the population of the eastern oil province of Hasa and of the southwestern province of Asir bordering Yemen, making up in all between 18 and 20 percent of the Saudi population. In the eyes of the Wahhabis, beginning with their founder, Shiism is the worst abomination. On the ladder of creation, the Shiites are located beneath Christians, Jews, and pagans. Or, as Wahhabi theorists assert, Shiism was in fact invented by a Jew who had pretended to convert to Islam, in connection with a conspiracy intended to destroy Islam. That explains everything. The furious hatred of the Wahhabis against the Shiites was unleashed on many occasions, with the capture and sacking of the holy city of Karbala in 1802 as one of the bloodiest examples.

With the conquest of the Shiite territories in the 1920s, the Wahhabis fell on their victims with ferocious cruelty. The conquest was punctuated with countless massacres. The obstacles put in the way of the extermination of Shiites by Ibn Saud (who preferred subjects to corpses) were among the complaints extremists made against the king. In the eastern province, the police, the National Guard, and the army are quick on the trigger whenever Shiites show any inclination to protest.

What is the situation today? Wahhabis enjoy a complete monopoly in education, which excludes Shiism from teaching, schoolbooks, or any other pedagogic material. In universities,

Shiism is presented as a perverse deviation and a Jewish plot. An iron-clad segregation is maintained in employment: No Shiite, whether Jaafari, Ismaili, or Zaidite, can be appointed as a judge, an *imam*, a teacher of religion, the director of a school, a minister, a diplomat, and so on: in short, a second class subject can never accede to the first rank. All judges come from Najd and must be Wahhabis. Of all the schools of Muslim law, only Hanbalism, from which Wahhabism derives, is authorized; the others—the Shaafi, Maliki, and Hanafi schools, not to mention Shiism—are banned.

Shiites are excluded from religious institutions, the Senior Ulama Council, the High Council of Justice, the Council of Fatwas, the Ministry of Islamic Affairs and Foundations, the Ministry of the Hajj, and so on. Shiites are forbidden to publish books and newspapers, or to speak on radio and television. They are virtually forbidden to build mosques. Over the past twenty years, in fact, a dozen existing Shiite mosques have been confiscated by the authorities. The large Shiite community of Medina, for example, saw its mosque confiscated, was forbidden to assemble, and its leader, the ninety-year-old Sheikh Muhammad Ali Al-Amri, was arrested on numerous occasions.[9]

Officially, none of that exists. "Shiites are not subject to any discrimination. They are Muslims and citizens of Saudi Arabia. Discrimination has never been acceptable in Saudi Arabia, from the very foundation of the state, nor is it acceptable today," explained the assistant minister of Islamic affairs, Tawfiq al-Sediry, as persuasive as a Soviet minister explaining the superior form of democracy prevailing in his country.[10] Prince Talal bin Abdulaziz has conceded that "the Shiite minority is suffering and consider that they are second class citizens, which is true. They are deprived of their rights." The Wahhabi *ulamas* are definitive: "Shiites are the principal enemy. But victory will always be ours because God is on our side." The Shiites are apostates, a crime punished with death in Islam. The Shiites in the city of Qatif, in

Hasa province, galvanized by the events in nearby Iran, demonstrated in 1979–1980 and were shot down like flies; the Saudi government ordered the old city to be demolished. In May 2000, seventeen Ismaili Shiites from Najran were sentenced to death—you don't treat apostates with kid gloves—for having protested against the closing of their mosque on government orders. International pressure forced the king to commute their sentences in December 2002.

One hundred twenty-five years ago in Qatif, a local sheikh acquired a 90-hectare strip of land on the shore of the Persian Gulf and bequeathed it as a community foundation to the inhabitants of the village of Awamiya in the form of a *waqf*, a common Muslim form of permanent endowment. In 1996, one of King Fahd's brothers seized the land unceremoniously and sold it to a private promoter. Protests by the villagers were put down with violence and arrests. The official world claims that the villagers had never held legal title. The villagers are Shiites. Saudi Arabia has refused to sign the Universal Declaration of Human Rights, because man has no rights and God has all, through the intermediary of his favored creatures, who turn out to have Saudi passports.

"Bas Saudi! Bas Saudi!" "Not Saudi!" say the natives when they cut ahead of foreigners patiently waiting in line. The foreigner—Ibn Saud himself said so—is the source of all evil. "[T]he Saudi Arab is convinced of the superiority of his own culture over that of the West . . . He believes that he can acquire and use whatever the West has to offer in the way of material goods and technological methods, and at the same time reject the culture which produced them," writes J. B. Kelly. "[T]he educated and semi-educated members of the population take it for granted that the most advanced technology in the history of mankind is at their disposal for the mere asking—to serve their needs and sustain them in their ease without their being required to understand, let alone to adapt to, any of the philosophical attitudes and cultural values which brought this technology into being."[11]

Already in the nineteenth century, Bedouins willingly used rifles while violently hating their manufacturers. The intense xenophobia of the Saudis is tied to "an innate sense of spiritual and racial superiority," which produces arrogance and hostility to foreigners. Bedouins look down on others because they are the summit of creation. Their God has revealed it to them and their *ulema* has confirmed it. Shored up by oil wealth, this pride has not changed.[12] We recall that already in the eighteenth century, the "Wahhabis considered all Muslims of their time who did not share their credo as polytheists even worse than in the time of *jahiliyya* [pre-Islamic barbarism]; whoever had heard their preaching and had not rallied was a *kafir* [an unbeliever]." There are "us," the pure, and "them," the accursed. The contact between the internal tribal world and the external world can come only by submission of "them" to "us" or through aggression by "us" against "them."

We can see the extent to which the religious factor is inseparable from political realities: Saudi and Wahhabi are Siamese twins. As the royal family knows, separating them would mean killing them. It is this close union that guides and directs everything the country does.

CHAPTER 3

Wahhabism Takes on the World

It is better to speak directly to the Good Lord than to His saints. To understand contemporary Wahhabism, let us consult the Grand Mufti of Saudi Arabia, the man who, until his death in 1999, was its inspiration. A blind man, he resembled the Grand Inquisitor in Verdi's *Don Carlo*: he would kill you for a trifle. One quality lacking in the cruel character in the opera distinguished him, although it was involuntary. His *fatwas* were considered infallible. They outline a map of the mental universe of the contemporary Wahhabi of the upper sociopolitical strata.

The incessant and multifarious obsession with woman, embodiment of all perversities, temptress, instrument of Satan, leaps out for anyone who examines the religious and legal decrees and commentaries, the *fatwas*, issued by the Mufti: he thinks of nothing but that, with a feeling of panic and violent hatred. Consider these examples.[1]

A believer asks him what rewards women will have in paradise (the question–answer model is a great producer of *fatwas*): "Allah will re-create the old women and make them virgins again. Similarly, he will re-create the old men and make them young again," the virginity of men not seeming to be a priority for the Allah of Bin Baz. He is on the other hand seriously concerned with menstruation and babies' vomit (does it dirty an item of clothing so that one cannot pray with it on?). The age of marriage? As young as possible for girls, even if the husband is thirty or more years older. Did the Prophet not take Aisha as his bride when she was six or seven and he was fifty-three, and consummate the marriage when she was nine? As long as the husband is pious, says the Mufti.

Woman, always woman. Can a Christian marry a Muslim woman? Certainly not. The marriage is invalid. Any children would be the offspring of fornication. A woman must wear a *hijab* in the presence of almost all men, her husband excepted. But if a man who is in the presence of a woman is blind, then says the *fatwa*, she can take off her *hijab*. Do women, he is asked, have a deficit in reason and religion? Is that really the case? "Yes, men in general are superior to women in general." Women, he goes on, "are the place for the fulfillment of the desire of men." A famous *hadith* is quoted in support: "A man is never alone with a woman without Satan also being present." Obviously, danger lurks everywhere, it oozes out of woman by nature.

The words are not extreme. Another *fatwa*, issued by his associate, Sheikh Ibn Osaimin, answers the question: "Is the discharge from a woman's vagina pure or impure?" The answer: "The faithful know that everything that comes from the private parts is impure, except for one thing, which is pure, namely, sperm." Why are we not surprised? Can women teach young prepubescent boys in elementary school? No, answers the old man. Satan would be in charge, and the consequences of such a mixture of the sexes would be devastating. Let us separate. "The preservation of our religion depends on it." Can one then employ a non-Muslim female servant? It would be a disaster for the children, a "source of evil and immorality."

The unbeliever, quite obviously, is Satanic in essence. A woman believer asks: "My brother-in-law prays only rarely. I live with my husband's family. What should I do?" Boycott him, answers the fearless Mufti. "Whoever does not pray cannot be made comfortable. It is not at all forbidden to kill him if he is turned over to the authorities and does not repent."

Is singing allowed? "It is forbidden to listen to music and to sing. No doubt touches this prohibition. . . . Singing develops hypocrisy [read: "unbelief"] in hearts," says Ibn Osaimin. You must not sing at a birthday party. Besides, birthday parties "are an innovation," that is, a heresy. You should not participate in them. And putting photographs or paintings on the wall? "It is not permitted to have a portrait of any creature that has a soul," animals included. Another *hadith* is quoted: "Those who will be punished the most harshly on the Day of Judgment will be those who make images." Identity photographs, however, are a regrettable necessity.

Let us summarize: it is forbidden not to forbid. Narrow-minded, limited, provincial, the conception of the world expressed here is a product of pathology. Satan the tempter infiltrates everywhere. It is appropriate to establish a dictatorship over behavior, hearts, and minds to prevent those infiltrations.

In 1963, King Faisal expressed his most authoritative opinion: "The [school and university] curricula in Moslem countries were infiltrated with malicious and dangerous trends which dissuaded the sons of Moslems from studying the history of their religion or making any research about it or about its rich heritage, or from carrying out any deep and thorough scientific investigation about the Moslem Sharia Code as it really is. . . . What does man aspire to? He wants 'good.' It is there, in the Islamic Sharia. He wants security. It is there also. Man wants freedom. It is there. . . . He wants the propagation of science. It is there. Everything is there, inscribed in the Islamic *Sharia*."[2] Education thus has "the duty of acquainting the individual with his God and his religion and adjusting his conduct to the prescriptions of religion, the satisfaction of the needs of society, and the realization of the objectives of the nation." If we add Stalin or Hitler or Mao and subtract God, this is a perfect replica of the totalitarian indoctrination of children.

Social control is total. As Antoine Basbous correctly notes, "In Saudi Arabia, whoever does not belong to the royal family finds his behavior dictated in the smallest details by the clerics. From the age of seven, children are taught to watch their parents and denounce them if they do not perform their five daily prayers in the neighborhood mosque or if they break the Ramadan fast."[3]

The good king's science was made explicit shortly thereafter by his favorite Mufti, Bin Baz. The great *ulama* in fact acquired a degree of celebrity by proclaiming in an infallible *fatwa* that the earth does not move: "Hence I say the Holy Koran, the Prophet's teaching, the majority of Islamic scientists and the actual fact all prove that the sun is running in its orbit, as Almighty God ordained, and that the earth is fixed and stable, spread out by God for his mankind and made a bed and a cradle for them, fixed down firmly by mountains lest it shake."[4] The most extreme penalties were provided for those who held otherwise. Those deniers would, in fact, be attacking the words of the Prophet himself, that is, the word of Allah.

Bookstores, video clubs, printing presses, and advertising agencies are strictly supervised by government authorities and the religious police, "to insure that standards of taste and ethical practices are maintained."[5]

What role does Saudi mathematics play in the international scientific community? Where are the Saudi physicists, astronomers, chemists, biologists, neurologists, doctors, zoologists, botanists, and computer scientists? Not to mention artists and musicians, where are the novelists, playwrights, and other writers? Where are the great sociologists, psychologists, and economists who would bring fame to the country?

The question is often fiercely debated as to whether the Al-Sauds can "liberate themselves from the Wahhabis." Are they only "giving guarantees to religious extremists"? The Al-Sauds are prisoners in a jail that they themselves have built, of guardians that they themselves appoint, of a prison system that is their mirror image. In fact, no one can any longer dissociate one from the other, the Al-Sauds from Wahhabism: they have been married to one another for 250 years. Abdulaziz Ibn Saud brought forth a monster, the *Ikhwan*. He thought he could use it at will, crush his enemies and his victims thanks to it, and put it back in the closet, so to speak, once its mission was accomplished. But the *Ikhwan* and its values stick to the skin of Saudi Arabia as the tunic of the centaur Nessus stuck to the skin of Hercules and consumed him, inseparable unto death.

Wahhabism embodies the tribe-party of the Al-Sauds. Their ascendancy and their power are inconceivable without the ideology they convey. And this totalitarian religious ideology is intrinsically destructive. Islam is a religion, Wahhabism an ideology which, like the incubus in stories of witchcraft, has entered the body of the bewitched victim. Wahhabism is as corrosive as an acid. It corrodes and dissolves the nation to the benefit of the tribe, below the level of the nation, and above the level of the nation, at the level of the *umma*, the imaginary, formless, worldwide community. "The nationality of the believer is his doctrine"[6] (just as the proletarians had no country).

Saudi Wahhabism destroys religion through extremism, rigidity, hardness of heart and spirit. It destroys the state, or prevents its formation, by favoring networks of relatives and clients, by making institutions mere screens for those networks, and by institutionalizing corruption. It destroys the social bond by reducing the people to nothing but fragmented and unorganized plebeians, dependent on the handouts distributed by the princes.

CHAPTER 4

Seizing Control of Islam

The Soviet Union operated on the international stage on three separate levels. There was the state with its ceremonies, the flag, the national anthem, embassies, and armed forces. This was the official level. Then came the Communist International (Comintern), later replaced by the International Department of the Central Committee of the USSR, supposed to act "without any contact" with the government. It controlled communist parties throughout the world and directed their policies. Finally came the secret services, the KGB and military intelligence (GRU), which often concealed their operations under the respectable costumes of embassies and often used the resources of communist parties and "mass" organizations created and controlled by the apparatus, the "peace movement" and movements for women, youth, intellectuals, unions, teachers, and so on.

For this threefold structure to function harmoniously, it was essential that appearances be preserved and that on the surface the three levels seem separate and distinct. That allowed Western embassies to close their eyes and Lenin's cherished "useful idiots" to claim to see nothing. "No, of course not. The Soviet government is not responsible for what the Communist Party does." The nasty work could quietly proceed on all levels, official, unofficial, and underground.

Saudi Arabia uses the same recipes. It functions like a state, through embassies: it sends representatives to the UN, to UNESCO, to the specialized organizations of the international community, and ambassadors to foreign capitals. It also operates through front organizations, that function like an "Islamintern," an Islamic International subject to Saudi-Wahhabi control. The front organizations in turn engender myriad specialized bodies and movements for the most varied populations. Saudi Arabia also has several intelligence services. But most important, it has three assets of which the USSR made very little use: religion, international finance, and tribal bonds.

Controlling Mecca and Medina, masters of the *hajj*, the Saudis occupy a central position in Islam. King Ibn Saud used and abused this position in order to establish his legitimacy. King Faisal used it to launch his grand design: control and subordination first of the Arab world and then of the Muslim world. The Wahhabi devastation, consolidated domestically, set out to conduct its ravages abroad.

Whereas the Comintern was a mechanism in which orders circulated in a bureaucratic manner, the Saudi-Wahhabi International uses family, clan, and tribal ties to transmit its orders. This can be clearly seen in the countless Islamic banks and financial companies in which the bonds of tribal relations can always be discerned behind the surface appearances of multinational enterprises. Saudi Arabia functions like a parasitic shareholder in the international economic and financial system; it profits from the market while violently rejecting its principles. The parasite knows how to use the interstices of the system, whereas the USSR never went very far down that path. Under the three-piece suit, the *jellaba* always peeks out.

How does the Saudi Islamintern operate? Recall what King Faisal thought of the transfer to the outside world of ways of action specific to the Saudi domestic realm: "Faisal believed it possible to transfer into the international arena the domestic principles on which the Saudi state was based. Islam provided stability, security, purpose, and discipline at home—so why not abroad as well?"[1]

Domestically, the king holds court, as one may imagine the last Merovingian kings receiving members of their extended family, clients, debtors, petitioners, and beggars: this is the *majlis* or weekly "council." It is an essential locus of power, where many ties of loyalty and vassalage are maintained and confirmed. There is an internal *majlis* reserved for close associates and devoted to matters that should not see the light of day, and an external *majlis*. The king entrusts the execution, and often the development, of decisions made, or rather announced, in the *majlis* to his close associates. This is the most opaque and hermetic inner circle, the brothers, half-brothers, uncles, cousins, and nephews. In turn, each important member of the family group and of the clientele holds his own *majlis*, assembling his own networks, and so on, with the enormous royal family playing the role of a "party" traversing the society. It resembles a series of nested fractal images in which the lower levels reproduce the structure and functions of the higher levels.

Great fortunes in Saudi Arabia all come from a single source, proximity to the royal family; the closer they are to the fountain, the more they are watered and the more they are implicated. The heart of the system, of course, consists of the five branches of the royal family, to which should be added the "aristocratic" families from which the princes select the mothers of their children: the Al-al-Sheikhs, descendants of Ibn Abd al-Wahhab, and the al-Sudairis. The friends and companions of the kings are in the first rank: doctors, notably Khashoggi and Pharaon, who came from Syria in 1936 and whose sons became millionaires; Kamal Adham, whose half-sister married King Faisal, and who headed the secret services before turning to finance; the naturalized Syrian Akram Ojjeh; Suleiman Oleyan; the fabulously wealthy Yemenite families from Hadramaut; Al-Amudi, Bin Laden, Bin Zagr,

Baroum, Bin Mahfouz; the merchants and bankers, Saleh Kamel and the Al-Qosaibis, of which Ghazi Al-Qosaibi, the former industry minister, for a time passed for a "modernizer," before repenting and writing, in his London ambassador's residence, poems in praise of terrorist murderers.[2]

This crowd of debtors, courtiers, and profiteers, this demimonde of middlemen and shady entrepreneurs, swindlers, procurers, moneychangers, and flatterers, forms the concentric circles surrounding the kernel of the royal family. They all have their own networks of relatives and clients. They are the favored intermediaries for the impulses that come from the king, the princes, and the royal family.

Domestically, the Bedouin dynasty buys the tribes. One buys loyalty as one acquires a camel, with less constancy, however, on the part of the one who is bought—we might call it a leased loyalty. One takes the daughter of the head of a tribe as one's fourth, or following divorces, nineteenth wife, in order to cement a political alliance. People are co-opted by the offer of a position, a job, a payoff, land, an import monopoly, a large contract. The dynasty flatters, entices, palavers, and smiles. In case of repeated failures, it intimidates, threatens, confiscates, harasses, imprisons, tortures, kills, and massacres.

It is thus not necessarily the Saudi "state"—if the concept has any meaning as a description of this tribal hodgepodge, this mass of family fiefs—that is at work. External action can just as well be the work of the families of the merchant "commoners," enriched exclusively through their proximity to the royal family, who head almost all of the large companies in the kingdom. The charitable organizations that recycle the *zakat* (religious tax) that they pay, headed by their representatives and by the *ulamas* of the regime, also play a role. Moreover, a royal edict of 1984 strictly forbids any collection of funds without government authorization. One might as well say that nothing important is done outside the range of vision of the Saudi totalitarian system.

At all levels of operation, everyone has his own networks, domestic as well as international. Whether it involves a group, the nation, or a sect, activity carried on outside the kingdom is more or less based on domestic modes of activity. Conduct abroad, with appropriate adaptations and precautions, mirrors conduct at home, sometimes with more coarseness, sometimes with more restraint. In its principle and its forms, the international activity of the Saudi-Wahhabi sect resembles its domestic activity: it projects onto the world's screen the tribal theater of Saudi Arabia.

The comparison between the Saudi Islamintern and the Soviet Comintern, between the Fifth and the Third Internationals, is not fortuitous: in both cases a police state, controlled by a dictatorial ruling stratum, developed an expansionary policy with worldwide ambitions. External action reflected domestic character. A single totalitarian cause produced very similar effects.

Let us recapitulate: The first Saudi empire had no intention of limiting its conquests to the Arabian peninsula, as evidenced by the countless raids launched against towns and countryside in the Levant and Mesopotamia. Steeped in the parallel between the warriors of the Prophet and their own banditry, the Wahhabis intended to impose their "reform" of Islam on the entire *umma*. Too limited and too ignorant of the external world, they overestimated their strength and underestimated that of the enemies they provoked. It took desert bumpkins to challenge the sultan of the Ottoman Empire, and they were easily defeated. The second Saudi empire had neither the time nor the resources to set out to conquer the world, or even the Muslim *umma*, as it struggled to conquer a few oases. The third empire, founded with cunning by Abdulaziz Ibn Saud, was from the outset an enterprise of imperialist expansion, both messianic and predatory. Not a single one of the neighboring countries escaped from attack or threat of arms by the Saudis. Kuwait was besieged in 1922, Yemen attacked and despoiled in 1932–1934, the territories of Bahrain, Qatar, and Oman claimed or nibbled at by force of arms, and Transjordan and Iraq were the victims of bloody raids. But Ibn Saud had one superiority over his accomplices in the Ikhwan: faced with a superior force, he knew how to avoid a losing battle, to end a war, and to accept a compromise. As long as the regional power of the sultan remained dominant, he paid tribute to the Ottoman Empire, remaining constantly on the lookout for associates able to form a counterweight to Istanbul: he found them in the English, useful one day to betray the Turks, betrayed a little later for the benefit of the Americans.

Once the empire had been established, stabilized, and enriched by the first flow of oil wealth, his son and second successor Faisal launched the second phase of the Saudi-Wahhabi Reconquest. As we have seen, in 1962–1963, he laid the groundwork for his worldwide offensive, which took off in 1967–1969. In 1973, he finally acquired the means to accomplish his aim of seizing control of Islam.

For a long time, "[t]he most common subject of editorials [in the Saudi press] was Saudi Arabia's Herculean efforts in the defense of Islam, and the second was condemnation of the policies and practices of Western countries. . . . [T]he newspapers," according to Sandra Mackey, "continue to run a wide range of stories about Western culture which they juxtapose against bitter anti-Western editorials. . . . [T]hey have become more strident in their claims about the superiority of their own culture, a culture they assert the West does not understand." The journalist concludes by pointing to "the [Saudi] media's unceasing drive to present the West in the worst possible light. . ."[3]

In this Manichaean world, it was truly incumbent on the heroes of the true God to fight Evil with all possible means. The aim, as Gilles Kepel summarizes it, was to "make Islam a factor in the forefront on the international stage, substituting it for defeated nationalism, and reducing the pluralistic forms of expression of the religion to the credo of the lords of Mecca." In this context, he continues, "religious allegiance becomes a key for the distribution of their aid and subsidies to the Muslims of the world, the justification for their preeminence, and the means of dissipating greed . . ."[4]

First, the royal family had to defend its realm from the ambitions of the Arab national-socialist regimes. In Egypt, Gamal Abdel-Nasser proclaimed to anyone who would listen: "Arab oil [should go] to the Arabs," which offended the Al-Sauds' ideas about property. Other Arab nationalist dictators, the Syrians and the Iraqis, held similar views. To defend itself, the Saudi monarchy developed a toolkit—international and multistate organizations, NGOs, newspapers, and other media—which would be just what was needed when they had to defend their Islamic credentials against the vengeful gibes of Ayatollah Khomeini. Once the defense of the kingdom had been ensured, they gathered up the remnants of their exhausted challengers who were searching for patrons and support.

The history of the worldwide spread of Wahhabism offers a striking parallel with that of the Third International. Lenin's Communist International won over the most heterogeneous groups, movements, and individuals: rebels, left-wing society ladies, despairing workers, extremist theoreticians, rebellious soldiers from the trenches, revolutionary anarchists, disaffected socialists, blasé or declassed intellectuals, and what Marx called the *lumpenproletariat*. A new star had just appeared in the galaxy of the international left: it attracted all the remaining fragments of the socialism that had been demolished by the Great War. What Western admirers of Lenin took for the October Revolution was the triggering event, the catalyst of this reorientation of political movements.

In the case of Saudi Arabia, it was money that brought about the realignment. The great pan-Arab experiments had failed miserably. The historic crisis of the Arab countries was at its height. Countries and identities, ideologies and individuals were destabilized. With the use of money and power, the Wahhabi force of attraction became incomparable. Since Islam was the "default" ideology of the Arab world, the most basic fallback identity, the offer of an Islamic identity presented by Saudi Arabia became credible. The tribal spirit, however, distinguishes the Saudi-Wahhabi International from the rigid bureaucracy of the Communist International: the Bedouin chief forms a coalition with his allies, even when they are temporary. The Islamist International operates in the form of coalitions, not according to strict Leninist hierarchy.

Under the aegis of oil wealth, there was a gradual coming together—a federation rather than a merger—among several Islamist movements whose common characteristics, beyond apparent doctrinal divergences, were the "return" to the "pure" Islam of the origins: a literal reading of the Koran; the utopia of a perfectly homogeneous society in which conflict would be impossible; openly displayed hatred of the West and Westernization; and an aggressive missionary program expressed through *jihad*. There was a convergence between Wahhabism and all these movements: the Deobandi of the Indian subcontinent; the Tablighi from the same region, who went door to door throughout the Muslim world and beyond spreading their message of a return to pure Islam; the Salafists (from *salaf*, venerable predecessors); and the movements around the Muslim Brotherhood from Egypt. Wahhabism, rich in oil, became the unifying and homogenizing element, engendering "unexpected cross-fertilizations, grafts, and hybrids" among these "fundamentalist" Islamists now joined together in the Wahhabi embrace."[5]

The militant preaching of the first Saudi empire had attracted the attention of the Muslim world. In the early nineteenth century, it had drawn disciples from pilgrims from distant lands. "The denunciation of idolatry and of the cult of saints, the opposition to *bida* [innovation], the holy war against the 'polytheists' and 'infidels,' a combination of class and egalitarian slogans—all these elements of the Wahhabi belief-system and practice found acceptance in countries with different socio-political structures and were adapted to local requirements. Wahhabism penetrated as far as India, Indonesia, and Africa."[6] In India, the politician and preacher Said Ahmad Barelwi, converted to Wahhabism in Mecca in the 1820s, declared *jihad* against the infidel shortly after his return to India. Setting out from Patna in 1826, his forces invaded Punjab and began slaughtering Sikhs. In 1830, he seized Peshawar and established there an ephemeral *jihadi* state—a Taliban state before the fact—before being killed in the following year. His disciples, who were active in Bengal and in northern India, declared a *jihad* against the English. "The hatred which some Indian Moslems bore towards the English—fanned into flames by seditious preachers who promised them deliverance or paradise—now became the text of every sermon," according to a nineteenth-century writer.[7] The Wahhabis were to play an important role in the 1857–1859 insurrection against the British, in which Muslim action was decisive. The English managed to eliminate the last hold-outs only many years later, and the Wahhabis remained a continuing danger for the Indian Empire.

The Deobandi movement, for its part, came into existence in 1867 in Deoband, north of Delhi. The *maulana* Abul Qasim Nanotvi set up a *madrasa* there called *Darum Uloom*, "The House of Knowledge," with the aim of training new generations of scholars who would be able to bring about a rebirth of Islam, the old foundations of which in India had just been violently shaken. The *sharia* was at the center of their efforts at intellectual renewal. Twelve years after its foundation, twelve *madrasas* were operating in India. In the centenary year of 1967, there were nine thousand in South Asia, and there are fifteen thousand today. The movement flourished most strongly in the newly established Pakistan. The Deobandi founded the *Jamaat-i Ulema Islami* (JUI), a religious movement that later became a political movement of a radically populist stripe, based on opposition to American imperialism and on social "progressivism." This Deobandi movement was the source of the Taliban who ravaged Afghanistan.

By publishing thousands of *fatwas* dealing with the slightest aspects of everyday life, the Deobandi created a kind of parallel universe, removed from present reality. With the establishment of Pakistan in 1948, they made their great reentry into the world. The movement began to "take over the state": they "ask for constantly greater resources to finance their schools . . . and want the state to guarantee jobs for their graduates, whose only training is in religious subjects. . . . For this purpose, they agitate for the Islamization of the laws, the administration, and the banking system . . . which would make it possible to use the skills of their pupils, to guarantee their employment, and eventually to establish them in positions of power."[8]

The compatibility of the Deobandi with Wahhabism is striking: hatred of non-Islamic cultures and, within Islam, hatred of everything but the most literal interpretations. Deobandi teaching requires the confinement of women and the wearing of the veil; since women are by nature less intelligent than men, there is no reason to educate girls beyond the age of eight. In *madrasas*, that boys enter at five and where they stay until the age of twenty-five—the narrowness of the mental universe created in these conditions is easy to imagine—science is banned as being "non-Islamic." Reading and recitation of religious texts predominates. Computers are allowed, but not the internet. Television news is permitted but films prohibited, although many *madrasas* completely prohibit newspapers and television.

Graduates of Deobandi *madrasas* in the thousands head other schools throughout South Asia. Originally less violent and aggressive than the Wahhabis, the Deobandi rapidly converged with them, as evidenced by their enthusiastic support for the Taliban in Afghanistan, many of whose leaders came from their mills for fanatics. When the Taliban destroyed the celebrated statues of Buddha in Bamiyan in March 2001, *Darum Uloom* warmly supported them. After September 11 of the same year, this house of a rather particular knowledge issued a *fatwa* claiming that the Jews had carried out the attack.

One of the most significant thinkers in the galaxy of Islamic fundamentalism also came from India, the journalist Sayyid Abul-Ala Mawdudi (1903–1979). In his 1927 *Jihad in Islam*, he explained: "Islam is a revolutionary doctrine and system that overturns governments. It seeks to overturn the whole universal social order . . . and establish its structure anew. . . . Islam seeks the world. It is not satisfied by a piece of land but demands the whole universe. . . . *Jihad* is at the same time offensive and defensive. . . . The Islamic party does not hesitate to utilize the means of war to implement its goal."[9] In 1941, he founded *Jamaat-i Islami*, one of the breeding grounds of modern fundamentalism. When Saudi Arabia set up the World Muslim League (WML), Mawdudi become one of its leading figures.

Here is a sample of what he had to say: "The *Shariah* is meant for those who are brave and courageous like the lions, determined to face all oppositions and turn the tide in their own favor. They regard the will and pleasure of Allah over and above every other thing, and struggle to make the world submit to the will of Allah. A Muslim is not meant to adopt the ever-changing patterns of the world, he is supposed to change the world according to the will of Allah . . ." To grasp the fact that the course of events can be changed, the contemporary believer should put himself in the place of the Prophet in the seventh century: "Was not the entire world dominated by infidelity and pantheism? Did not despotism and oppression rule supreme? Was not . . . mankind torn and split into various classes? Were not . . . ethical values overshadowed by lewdness, sensuality, feudalism, capitalism, and injustice?" He then argues that "revolution or evolution, it has always occurred as a result of force, and force always moulds others, but is not moulded itself. It does not bow before others, but makes others to bow before it. Revolutions are never brought about by cowards and the imbecilic."[10]

The enthusiasm of the Saudi-Wahhabis is easy to understand: he was the first recipient of the King Faisal Prize for services to Islam.

Egypt, one of the epicenters of Islam, produced Hassan al-Banna and his organization the Muslim Brotherhood. They probably had the most decisive influence in the "return to Islam" in the modern period, at least in the Sunni world. "The Koran is our constitution" was their slogan, to symbolize their rejection of the modern world corrupted by the West. Expressing the passionate unease created by the uprooting and dislocation of identity prevalent in Arab and Muslim countries,[11] the Muslim Brotherhood, founded in 1928, not only recruited many disciples among both the lower classes and the elites of Egypt, but succeeded in establishing the first Muslim International.

The credo of its founder Hassan al-Banna (1906–1949), brooked no disputes, based as it was entirely on answers, not questions: "(1) Islam [is] a total system, complete unto itself, and the final arbiter of life in all its categories; (2) [it is] an Islam formulated from and based on its two primary sources, the revelation in the Koran and the wisdom of the Prophet in the Sunna; and (3) an Islam applicable to all times and to all places."[12] This was a total, indeed a totalitarian Islam in the full sense of the word, directed toward creating al-Nizam, a New Order. One can hardly be surprised at the links between the Egyptian Muslim Brotherhood and the secret services of the Third Reich.

In one of the writings most representative of his thought, Al-Banna asserted that "the provisions of Islam and its teachings are all inclusive, encompassing the affairs of the people in this world and the hereafter. . . . Islam is a faith and a ritual, a nation and a nationality, a religion and a state, spirit and deed, holy text and sword . . ."[13] Al-Banna and his mentor, Rashid Rida, were enthusiastic supporters of Wahhabism.

Nor should we be surprised by the importance of *jihad* in the objectives of the Muslim Brotherhood or by the impressive series of political assassinations it committed after Al-Banna's call in October 1947 for the immediate preparation of a *jihad*. Two prime ministers—including Ahmad Mahir Pasha, who had just announced that Egypt was declaring war on the Axis Powers—a former finance minister, an important judge, and the Cairo chief of police fell beneath the bullets of the Brotherhood's assassins, while bombs destroyed movie theaters and other dens of vice, large stores owned by foreigners, and so on. The political police responded by assassinating Al-Banna, and the government outlawed the Brotherhood. Since then, periods of brutal repression have alternated with a certain degree of cooperation between the Muslim Brotherhood and government authorities.

In the 1950s, fleeing harsh repression by Gamal Abdel-Nasser, hundreds of members of the Brotherhood sought refuge in Saudi Arabia. Despite dogmatic and political divergences, the kingdom opened its arms to them. This influx highlighted the Islamic haven that the kingdom represented. In addition, Saudi Arabia was suffering from an acute shortage of primary and secondary school teachers, with an illiteracy rate of approximately 85 percent: the Muslim Brotherhood arrived at the right time. The royal family, in effect, gave them an entire university as a gift, the University of Medina.[14] Not only did the Brotherhood train thousands of Saudi and international leaders in their doctrine, but the cross-fertilization that resulted contributed to the convergence between the Wahhabis and the Brotherhood. In addition, many of the Brotherhood's members who had settled in Saudi Arabia participated in the oil boom and were able to make fortunes and then return to Egypt at Nasser's death and invest their money there.

To confront the revolutionary call following the Iranian revolution and the attack on the Grand Mosque, Wahhabis and the Brotherhood agreed on the need to protect the kingdom: the al-Sauds authorized the members of the Brotherhood to stay in Saudi Arabia provided they remain discreet. In return, they would help the Saudi authorities by participating in and supporting the activities of the World Muslim League, maintaining for Saudi benefit contact with all kinds of Islamic groups. "The Egyptian Brothers . . . thus had a voice in the distribution of Saudi support" to the Islamist galaxy. One of the principal founders of the League was Said Ramadan, the son of Hassan al-Banna.

A level of social development incomparably superior to that of Saudi Arabia and a rich tradition of Islamic studies made the Egyptian Muslim Brotherhood the essential providers of a ready-made ideology for the Arab-Islamic world. Populist, puritan, and messianic, as Olivier Roy describes them, the Muslim Brotherhood constantly reiterated simple slogans that provided answers to everything.[15] Consider as an example Sayyid Qutb, hanged by Nasser in 1966, whose works were translated into Farsi by Ayatollah Seyed Ali Khamenei, supreme guide of post-Khomeini Iran. In his book *Milestones*, a mixture of frenzied prophecy, breathless imprecations, and fierce hatred, this extremist among extremists places *jihad* at the center of the Muslim's life: *jihad*, he asserts, is not at all defensive, but offensive. Islam has no other vocation than to conquer the world. Individuals should be divested of everything that might come between them and submission to Islam.[16]

CHAPTER 5

The Saudi Multinational

What this has produced is a joint venture that considerably extends the international reach of the Wahhabi regime. Saudis acquire, at least temporarily, huge international networks useful for propagating their views, but they also operate through their embassies and their own transnational organizations: the World Muslim League (WML), the Organization of the Islamic Conference (OIC), and the World Association of Muslim Youth (WAMY). Since the 1980s, it seems, the estimated amount of funds transferred around the world in this context has reached the staggering figure of $70 billion.

Saudi embassies all have an "attaché for Islamic affairs," who combines the role of political commissar with those of secret agent and missionary. Sometimes, as in the Washington embassy, a royal prince occupies the post. According to Antoine Basbous, in this way Saudi Arabia has sent out eight hundred "missionaries" with a more or less diplomatic status. There are between ten and forty in a large number of Latin American countries, for example, a dozen in Albania, and even three in Japan.[1]

The World League, *al-Rabitat al-alam al-islami*, was established in 1962 as a NGO for the worldwide diffusion of Wahhabism; its central office is in Riyadh where it enjoys quasi-official status. "It functions as the world headquarters for extremist Islamist networks," according to an analysis by the Supreme Islamic Council of the United States, a vigorous opponent of the Saudis.[2] Along with millions of copies of the Koran and millions of copies of Wahhabi writings, the League disseminates the cultural and doctrinal model of Wahhabism. It is like a trawler catching potential recruits in its nets. In every region of the world in which Muslims are found, the League opens offices, "plays the role of scout, makes an inventory of associations, mosques, and programs." As a nongovernmental organization (NGO), it joins its efforts to those of the private sector: "An ad hoc association would prepare a proposal in support of [its] plan [to build a mosque] . . . then . . . seek a 'recommendation' from the local office of the League for a generous donor," usually a Saudi.[3] Here is a perfect example of the Saudi method of operation: the League, a quasi-official body, organizes and sponsors Islamic and Islamist groups and organizations in the process of Wahhabization, and opens the financial spigot to them by giving its green light to those mysterious "rich Saudis" who are so quick to finance terror. The Saudi government? Not at all involved, of course. The secretary general of the League must, according to the by-laws, be a Saudi subject. With offices in one hundred twenty countries around the world, the League is a spider weaving its web in which are caught "Wahhabizable" Muslims, who are then selected and digested by the process of Wahhabization.

We should also note complementary initiatives such as the establishment of the House of Islamic Finance, a transnational network of "Islamic" financial institutions (that is, supposed not to make loans charging interest, characterized as "usury"), the *Dar al-Mal al-Islamiyya* (DMI), a subsidiary in part of the Faisal Islamic Bank of Geneva—whose CEO is Prince Muhammad al-Faisal, son of the former king and brother of Prince Turki, head of the Saudi secret services from 1975 to 2001; one of the purposes of the DMI is to finance Islamic proselytism. The U.S. Treasury Department froze the assents of a certain number of the League's organizations in connection with investigations for terrorism and support of terrorist activities. Its American offices were searched by federal agents on March 20, 2002, as were those of a branch of the League, the International Islamic Relief Organization (IIRO), which was already suspected of having links with a number of operations for logistic and financial support of al-Qaeda. The IIRO had called attention to itself by contributing a half-million dollars to the Palestinian Intifada, and $1,000 to the family of each "martyr."[4]

The League and the DMI have left traces in the international terrorist constellation of which al-Qaeda is a part, so that it is difficult if not impossible to distinguish "Islamic" from "Islamist" and extremists from terrorists. The same holds true for the Organization of the Islamic Conference (OIC), established in Rabat in 1969 on the personal and insistent initiative of King Faisal of Saudi Arabia.

The king brought together all factions of Islam: a new Zionist plot—because to his mind the world was nothing but a series of Zionist plots—had come close to destroying the mosque of Omar in Jerusalem. There could be no hesitation. No Arab leader, or almost none, could avoid his Islamic duty and refuse to go to the Rabat summit called by the king. From the outset, the basis for mobilization was affected by this paranoid state of mind: we were in the presence of an "assault against Islam." The twenty-nine founders deliberated solemnly. The purpose of the enterprise was to "promote Islamic solidarity among the member states," to consolidate cooperation in all areas, to "coordinate efforts for the preservation of the Holy Places," to support the struggle of the Palestinian people, and to strengthen the combat of all Muslim peoples.

The takeover bid launched by Saudi Arabia, Inc. for world Islam had taken a giant step forward. It was like a seizure of power in Islam, which brought an eccentric and previously marginal sect into the very heart of world Islam. What the fire of the Reichstag had been to Adolf Hitler in

January, 1933, the fire at the Mosque was for the Saudis, though, in fairness, they were not involved in setting it off, just in leveraging it to maximum effect. The plotters were Saudis, and it was not a bloody coup but one carried out with a checkbook. The OIC had the function of "institution-aliz[ing] a consensus around the views of Saudi Arabia,"[5] just as the Communist International in its time had been a zoo with Russian keepers and with foreign Communist Parties in the cages.

In 1975, the OIC set up the Islamic Development Bank, whose "purpose is to contribute to the economic develop-ment and social progress of member countries and Muslim communities, collectively and individually, in accordance with the principles of *sharia*, that is, Islamic law," according to its charter.[6] In twenty-eight years of activity, although it is richly endowed with capital (six billion "Islamic dinars," a nominal currency unit with a value equivalent to that of the IMF accounting unit, the Special Drawing Right, about one quarter of which was provided by Saudi Arabia), the bank has made no appreciable progress toward its declared goal with its fifty-four members. The bank's headquarters, it goes without saying, are located in Jeddah. Among the "banking" activities contributing to the noble motives cited above, some headings make one wonder: "Al-Aqsa Funds Unit" (mean-ing Jerusalem), and "Al-Aqsa Intifada Unit." There is a great lack of transparency around certain divisions of the group. The OIC also has, as an international "counter-society" by imitation, a counterpart to UNESCO, ISESCO, an Academy of Muslim Jurisprudence.

There is also the World Assembly of Muslim Youth (WAMY), a breeding ground for extremist leaders and front organizations enabling the Bin Laden galaxy to operate; a large number of them have been indicted in the United States and targeted by the United Nations report on the financing of terrorism, as we will see in detail.

The WAMY, founded in 1972, is headquartered in Riyadh. It extends through four hundred fifty Islamic youth and student organizations in thirty-four countries. Its charter conceals little, since the aims of the organization are defined in these terms: "To serve the true Islamic ideology based on the *tawhid*," that is, on Wahhabism for which this is the preferred term—the Wahhabis are reluctant to be designated by their name. Other objectives include: "To strengthen the factors of ideological unity" (meaning to terrorize and silence any non-Wahhabi voice in the Muslim world); to strengthen also "fraternal Islamic relations among Muslim youth," and then "to support organizations of Muslim youth around the world through coordination of their activities and aid in the realization of their projects."[7]

What does this mean? After the first attack against the World Trade Center in Manhattan in 1993, a manual for bomb makers was found in the apartment of one of the plotters; it had been published by the WAMY and printed in Saudi Arabia. The inspiration for the attack came from Sheikh Omar Abdel Rahman, a blind and violent cleric, who had long taught and preached in Riyadh.[8] That should be enough to complete the investigative file. There is more. Four of the September 11 hijackers are suspected of having had contacts with the American office of WAMY, located not far from Washington. Abdullah bin Laden had been president of WAMY, "which was alleged to have maintained relations with several members of the al-Qaeda network."[9] As early as 1996, the FBI had listed WAMY as an "organization suspected of terrorism."[10]

The Islamic Relief Organization, another "charity" implicated in terrorism, the Supreme World Council of Mosques, and the Complex of Islamic *Fiqh* (Jurisprudence) complete the panoply.

Alongside international organizations and NGOs, the Saudi royal family has also developed its subversive activities through the family's private and semi-public networks and operations. It is impossible to disentangle the web of the "private" and the "public" in a country in which the king on his own authority pockets ten percent of the annual oil revenues, a part of which it is up to him to distribute at his discretion. Saudi-Wahhabi "international aid" is not free, neither for the donors nor for the recipients.

From 1973 to 1993, according to the propaganda services of King Fahd, the kingdom devoted 5.5 percent of its GDP to "international aid." The Saudi Fund for Development, established in 1974, with a capital endowment of approximately $2.5 billion, since increased to $6 billion, is intended to link the beneficiary countries to Saudi Arabia. Political support is the necessary condition for the receipt of loans. Saudi Arabia has contributed more than a third of the OPEC Development Fund, roughly one billion dollars.[11] This generosity, made possible by the enormous revenues derived by Saudi Arabia itself from the beneficiary countries, enables it to strengthen political and diplomatic support for the kingdom at the UN, the Human Rights Commission, UNESCO, and other international organizations where majorities are automatic and votes are for sale, or else, for the most honest, for rent.

"International aid" and the rise of a "purified," that is, Wahhabized Islam require considerable resources. "It was only when oil revenues began to generate real wealth," according to ingenuous royal propaganda, "that the kingdom was in a position to satisfy its ambition to spread the message of Islam around the world . . .," and King Fahd was not the last to "attack the caricatures of Islam that are widely disseminated by some of the Western media and to unmask them. Islam is a religion of compassion . . ." The king intended to "counteract negative stereotypes. In this enterprise, King Fahd accomplished only a partial victory," we learn, but "prejudices against Islam, the tendency in certain places to establish an equivalence between Islam and fanaticism or even terrorism, persist and have not been completely eradicated from the minds of Western populations," says the document, whether written before or after September 11, we do not know.

"The amount of contributions granted by King Fahd in this area is astronomical and has to be counted in billions of riyals." Around the world, Saudi Arabia has financed all or part of two hundred ten Islamic centers, fifteen hundred mosques, two hundred ten Islamic secondary schools, and two thousand primary schools, according to the January 31, 2003, issue of *Ain-al-Yaqeen*, a semi-official Saudi paper, under the florid heading: "Projects of pride for the Islamic people and honorable accomplishments based on feelings of responsibility toward the nation. . . . The illustrious efforts of the kingdom in the area of the creation of Islamic centers, mosques, and institutes."

The Islamic cultural centers in Málaga, Toronto, Rome, Brasilia, and Rio de Janeiro were entirely paid for by Saudi Arabia. The same is true for Gibraltar, Mantes-la-Jolie, and Edinburgh. In Geneva, Brussels, Madrid, New York, and Zagreb, in Australia as in London, Lisbon, and Vienna, the "cultural" generosity of the Wahhabi monarchy has been manifested. The same thing occurred in N'Djamena in Chad and Khartoum in Sudan, one of the principal headquarters of combined Sunni and Shiite terrorism, and in Nigeria, where there are rumblings of a war of religion between Muslims in the north and Christians in the south. The track can be followed in Asia in Tokyo, Indonesia, and the Maldives. In the United States, there are the Islamic Centers of New York and Washington, the Big Mosque in Chicago, the mosque in Fresno, the Islamic Centers of Columbia, Missouri, and New Brunswick, New Jersey, the mosque of the Albanian community in Chicago, the Tida center in Maryland, an Islamic Center in Virginia, and a center in Toledo. Africa has had its share, with Gabon, Burkina Faso, Tanzania, and Senegal. Among the mosques and other institutions constructed in part from Saudi funds are those of Lyons ($3 million), Chad ($15 million), King Faisal University in Guinea (around $14 million), the Great Mosque in Senegal ($3 million), the Farou'e mosque in Cameroon ($4 million), the mosque of Zanzibar ($2.5 million), the mosque of Bamako ($5 million) with a great bridge over the Niger River bearing the name of a Saudi king, the mosque of Yaoundé ($5 million), and the renovations of the mosques at Al-Azhar University in Cairo, Bilal in Los Angeles, Omar-ibn-al-Khattab in Jerusalem, and Brent Central in London. In Canada, Calgary, Quebec City, and Ottawa have been endowed with millions of dollars.

In Europe, the kingdom spent $5 million for the Islamic Cultural Center in Brussels; the Islamic Center in Geneva receives the same amount annually; the Islamic Center in Madrid was given $8 million, the London center $6 million, and the one in Edinburgh $4 million. King Fahd has personally donated $50 million for the Islamic Center of Rome, including a mosque, a challenge to the Vatican, since not only is it forbidden to build a church in Saudi Arabia, but even holding a non-Islamic religious service is illegal and severely punished.

We should not forget the Wahhabi Islamic "academies" scattered around the world that train or indoctrinate high-ranking leaders. The Islamic Academy of Washington opened in 1984 with 1,200 students, half of whom were Saudis. In its first decade of existence, the costs assumed by the donor amounted to $25 million. The King Fahd Academy in London accepts 1,000 students. The King Fahd Academy in Moscow is charged with countering the anti-Islamic materialism of the former USSR and "reaffirming Arabic and Islamic culture." Inaugurated in 1995, it has 500 students and a mosque, at a cost of more than $7 million. An Islamic academy was erected in Bihac in Bosnia-Herzegovina, in connection with the considerable efforts made by the Wahhabis to take control of Islam in the Balkans.

University chairs in the West have been very richly endowed by King Fahd. As one of the most astute observers, the former English diplomat, John Kelly, explains, "the rulers of the Arab oil states are neither simple philanthropists nor disinterested patrons. . . . They expect a return upon their donations to institutions of learning and their subsidies to publishing houses; whether it be in the form of subtle propaganda on behalf of Arab or Islamic causes, or the preferential admission of their nationals, however unqualified . . . or the publication of the kind of sycophantic flim-flam about themselves and their countries which now clutters sections of the Western press and even respectable periodical literature."[12] The king's staff has explained the goal pursued: the expenditure of huge sums "further demonstrates the desire of King Fahd to encourage and develop communication between Islamic culture and other cultures, to encourage greater understanding of the true nature of Islam by clearly explaining the beliefs of Muslims and correcting false conceptions and caricatures, and to show that Islam welcomes knowledge with enthusiasm." It would be harder to state more clearly that this is a matter of propaganda covered by a light academic veneer.

There is thus an Abdulaziz Chair at the University of California at Santa Barbara endowed by the royal family in 1984; a King Fahd Chair at Harvard endowed by His Royal Highness himself; the King Fahd Chair at the School of Oriental and African Studies (SOAS) in London; and finally, a chair at the University of the (Persian) Gulf. Other academic institutes were established in Japan, Indonesia, Mauritania, Djibouti, and Ras al-Khema. The kingdom also provides funding to the Institut du Monde Arabe in Paris, American University in Colorado, Howard University in Washington, the Institute of History of Arab and Islamic Science in Frankfurt, the Middle East Institute in Washington—once nicknamed "the chorus of the friends of Aramco," because the company always financed this Washington think tank whose analyses are very difficult to distinguish from the kingdom's propaganda—Syracuse University, and Shaw University in North Carolina.

The prestigious Duke University, in Durham N.C., began to receive generous Saudi donations in 1977. It hosts the only university center in the United States entirely devoted to the Arabian Peninsula. It has become, according to one critic, "a de facto southern branch of the Saudi embassy," and serves as a central office for information, public relations, consulting services, the organization of bilateral exchanges, and Saudi propaganda. One Duke professor was unsparing in his criticism: "It is less a university activity than an activity in which certain members of the university serve as a go-between for Arab interests and major corporations."[13]

Royal propaganda is less forthcoming about the repeated scandals that have struck one of the objects of its solicitude, Georgetown University in Washington, which, among other things, trains career diplomats. It already had a flourishing department of Arabic language and literature when Saudi Arabia, Egypt, the United Arab Emirates, and the Sultanate of Oman offered to finance a Center for Contemporary Arab Studies (CCAS) . . . under certain conditions. The humorist Art Buchwald commented at the time: "I don't see why the PLO has to have a PR organization when Georgetown is doing all their work for them."[14] The university had just accepted nearly a million dollars from Colonel Mohmmar Qaddafi, which the president of the university would return with interest four years later. The Foreign Service School took in nearly $3 million in gifts from the gulf states. The price to be paid was negligible: it simply had to promote understanding and sympathy for the Arab point of view, a request fully compatible with academic standards. John Esposito, director of the CCAS, a university professor who had converted to Islam, has made it his specialty to attack those Western fanatics who have the temerity to associate, in one way or another, the Arab-Muslim world with terrorism.[15] His university center has become a center for propaganda in favor of extremist positions.

Oxford University received more than $30 million—an exceptionally large gift for a university—to endow its Center for Islamic Studies. It has become difficult to criticize certain countries and certain ideas at Oxford. *Sic transit gloria academica*. On the other side of the Atlantic, Martin Kramer, author of a harsh critique of the servility and intellectual mediocrity of Arab-Muslim studies in the United States, has commented: "Berkeley, Harvard? They are the last places to look for critical thinking. None of them has produced anything about opposition movements in Saudi Arabia. Why? Even if you have not yet collected, you are in line."[16]

CHAPTER **6**

The Historic Rival

The recruiting of intellectuals and the mobilization of academic institutions, or more simply the creation of bridges, of networks of vassals and friends, have all been institutionalized under the umbrella of the King Faisal Foundation (KFF). Every year it grants international King Faisal Prizes, in imitation of the Nobel Prizes, comparable to the Stalin (later Lenin) Prizes of the past.

The 2000 prize was given to Al-Azhar University in Cairo, the more than thousand-year-old Islamic educational institution with unequalled prestige in the Muslim world: Al-Azhar is the supreme authority on religious questions for Sunni Islam. "The prize was given to Al-Azhar University for services rendered to Islam in order to emphasize the role that it has played in the preservation of the Arab and Islamic heritage, in the confrontation undertaken against tendencies toward Westernization, and the propagation of Islam and the Arabic language."[1]

Al-Azhar, founded in 971 by the Shiite Fatimid dynasty that ruled in Cairo; it later turned into the bastion of Sunni theology, with its academy of Islamic research, fourteen faculties in Cairo and thirteen others elsewhere in Egypt, eight faculties for women, tens of thousands of students and graduates, and five to six thousand teachers, is a central institution in the Arab-Muslim world.[2] It also runs hundreds of primary and secondary schools (called the "Azhari institutes") where 1,530,000 pupils and students are enlisted (according to 2002 data).

The prize was the final step in a long Saudi campaign aimed at taking control of Al-Azhar. For the Al-Sauds, Egypt is the historic rival, the perfect example of the "Arabs of the cities" hated by the "Arabs of the desert." It was Egypt that crushed the first Saudi empire and humiliated the Wahhabis. Traditionally, the scholars of Al-Azhar, rich and proud of their ancient heritage, scorned the illiterate desert dwellers. Whoever wishes to dominate the Sunni Arab-Muslim world needs to have his authority legitimated by Al-Azhar, especially if that authority is usurped and questionable.

In order to get a sense of the results of Saudi influence on the venerable university, consider what the grand sheikh of Al-Azhar, Mohammed Sayed Tantawi, said in June 2000 to the Saudi newspaper *Ain al-Yaqeen* on receiving the prize:

Ain al-Yaqeen: "You have followed the violent campaign carried out against the kingdom of Saudi Arabia on the pretext that it does not respect human rights. What is the purpose of that campaign?"

Sheikh Tantawi: "The principal purpose of the campaign is to combat Islam. The campaign is unjust. Saudi Arabia leads the world in the protection of human rights because it protects them according to the *sharia* of God . . . If Saudi Arabia did not apply *sharia*, the family of the victim [of a murder] would disdain the state and take vengeance itself.

"Everyone knows that Saudi Arabia is the leading country for the application of human rights in Islam in a just and objective fashion, with no aggression and no prejudice."

Ain al-Yaqeen: "Some people think that Al-Azhar does not take the same position regarding those who make decisions [meaning: is Al-Azhar subject to the political authorities?]"

Sheikh Tantawi: "That is not true; we tell the truth whatever it may cost us. Doubt has always existed; there are people who doubt the unity of God and the message of the prophets."

The cat was out of the bag: with that statement, Tantawi had just publicly kowtowed to Saudi Wahhabism. The "unity of God" that he speaks of is the *tawhid*, the heart of Wahhabi doctrine. An informed Muslim reader could not fail to identify the confession for what it was: the university in Cairo was surrendering with no significant conditions to the powerful Saudis. Later in the interview, the sheikh might very well quibble about "the existence of some minor differences" in doctrine between scholars of Al-Azhar and Saudi *ulemas*, the submission was nonetheless complete. The interview concluded with a stirring eulogy for the late Grand Mufti of Saudi Arabia, Sheikh Abdulaziz bin Baz: "I never failed to see him whenever I went to Saudi Arabia."[3]

To sense the importance of the scene, it is necessary to be aware of the traditional submission of Sunni scholars and the scholars of Al-Azhar to the political authorities. Scholars always engaged in the most extraordinary contortions in order to satisfy the demands of the powerful that asked them for *fatwas* granting them carte blanche. Even though Gamal Abdel-Nasser "nationalized" the university in 1961, making its clerics civil servants, it was nevertheless before the Saudi empire of the Wahhabis that the sheikh prostrated himself.

In order to follow the process of purchase step by step, we will retrace the analysis of Abu El-Fadl, professor of Islamic jurisprudence at the University of California, himself a graduate of Al-Azhar, and the descendant of a long line of scholars from that university. The process began with the establishment of the World Muslim League in 1962. Over the four ensuing decades, he explains, the Saudis, with great perseverance, took control over the ideological direction of Al-Azhar. The beginnings were subtle: attractive offers of sabbatical study leaves for scholars in the Persian Gulf. "In six months of leave, they earned twenty years worth of salary." These contributions became habitual. The scholars became more and more eager to add them to their salaries of $40 a month. Through the League, the Saudis began to endow chairs and to finance entire departments. By the end of the 1990s, it had become difficult to find an Azhari who had not in one way or another benefited from Saudi generosity and who had not returned the favor in the form of studies or commentaries favorable to Wahhabism.

El-Fadl evokes certain turning points. When he began his studies at Al-Azhar, at the age of six (young boys memorize whole sections of the Koran, until they know it by heart at the age of twelve), a certain moderation was still the rule. Things changed imperceptibly. One of his teachers, Muhammad Jalal Kishk, had often mocked the characteristic obscurantism of Wahhabism. In 1981, he received the $200,000 King Faisal Prize and, in addition, the tidy sum of $850,000 for the King Fahd Prize. Thereafter, he published a pro-Wahhabi volume entitled *The Saudis and the Islamic Solution.*

Today, he explains, Saudi control of Al-Azhar is virtually fully accomplished. The Azharis who refuse to accept this supremacy are purged. When another of his teachers published a book in 1989 accusing the Wahhabis of justifying fanaticism and tarnishing the reputation of Islam, the Saudis financed the publication of seven books in two years to drag him through the mud. The pan-Arab press joined in when the daily *Al-Sharq al-Awsat,* owned by a Saudi prince, attacked him in turn.[4]

This is not merely an academic question. The decrees of Al-Azhar carry authority throughout the Muslim world. Everyone pays attention to them. They influence governments and elites and the *ulamas* throughout the *umma.* They help to shape public reactions far beyond Egypt. In 1990, the Saudi authorities, who were having difficulty securing support for the use of American forces and other infidels to defend the country against Saddam Hussein, appealed to Al-Azhar and "begged" it for a *fatwa.*

Consider the case of one of the most famous Azharis, Sheikh Mohammed Metawali Sharawi, who died in 1998 at the age of 97, who became the first television star of Islam, with an estimated audience for his broadcasts of 70 million viewers. Subsidized by Saudi Arabia, the telepreacher "played an essential role in changing Egyptian public opinion, shifting it from a liberal approach to medieval repressiveness." While fundamentalists intimidated, threatened, and killed, his work consisted of "terrorizing public opinion," to adopt the expression of the Egyptian writer Ubrahim Issa. The result was a "furtive Islamization" of society. Toward the end of his life, Sharawi boasted of not having read a book, apart from the Koran, since 1943. Servile toward the authorities, he wrote a poem deifying King Farouk, heaped praises on Nasser, and finally became a cabinet minister under Anwar al-Sadat. He had spent several long periods at King Abdulaziz University in Saudi Arabia. The Muslim Brotherhood mourned him deeply—he had been one of its founders along with Hassan al-Banna. His *fatwas* explained that women should not be appointed to government positions, in view of "their incomplete faith and minds." As for the Copts—the Orthodox Christian minority that settled in Egypt before Islam, probably representing more than 15 percent of the population—they are *dhimmis*, second-class citizens. Electricity? Contrary to divinely ordained human nature because it "changes night into day and makes people active at night." Organ donation? Blasphemy: "You do not have the right to donate an organ [from your body] because you are only the caretaker of a body that belongs to Allah." Narrow fanaticism, obscurantism, hatred: Saudi money was well invested.

Saudi strategy operates in many ways. Always using the basic lever of money, of which it has quantities that are, if not unlimited, at least out of the ordinary, it has used strategies of encirclement. International organizations are the webs, with radial and circular connections, and intersecting crossroads.

Islamic cultural centers are directed by Wahhabized elements and become relay stations for missionary, doctrinal, and political activity. The sermons in the mosques are Wahhabi as well as the doctrines that they propagate; their preachers have been trained in Saudi Arabia, in Wahhabi universities; the books that they use follow neither Maliki, nor Hanafi, nor Shafi traditions—the other principal schools of Sunni jurisprudence—but only Hanbalism, the most rigid school, the one from which Abd al-Wahhab hailed.

We must recognize the role played by improvisation and not see consistency where it does not exist. Everything occurs in a certain disorder. The large number of wealthy princes, of privileged merchant families, of affluent clerics, gives rise to a panoply of initiatives that are not necessarily coordinated or centrally organized. But they all go in the same direction, and that is what is important. This explains the strength of the Saudi model of subversion compared to the Soviet model; it is admirably suited to its target, the Arab-Muslim world. We must also recognize the role played by instinct: the Saudis instinctively do what their Bedouin ancestors always did. They buy loyalty with gifts and marriages, with alliances and the hope of booty and power. They acquire networks and absorb them as they are. Instinct does not necessarily bring about coherent organizational structures.

The model has great weaknesses: it depends closely on oil wealth and Saudi money. If they dry up or become scarce, the "watering" of the networks will become more difficult. There is, of course, some breathing room: in addition to oil revenue, there are the huge liquid assets accumulated less by the state—which is in chronic deficit and heavily indebted, to the tune of more than 100 percent of GDP—than by its owners, the royal family and its retinues of vassals, relatives, and clients.

Money buys consciences, but not hearts. There is great resentment among many of the "bought." The conduct of a wicked lord, the typical man of the Saudi royal family, provokes a good deal of suppressed hatred. If it finds outlets, favorable circumstances permitting a loosening of the vise, this hatred will explode in the faces of the complacent rulers themselves.

When dollars are no longer enough, there remains persuasion, for which it is necessary to guarantee media support wherever possible. In Saudi Arabia itself, television news is unintentionally comical, at least for someone not forced to endure it day after day. With the same dictatorial foolishness as television news in the old Soviet Union, it conducts indoctrination through boredom, recruitment by saturation. From one end of the year to the other, the news begins with a presentation of the heroic deeds accomplished that day by the sovereign, if he is capable of walking and talking, which has long not been the case for King Fahd, who suffered a stroke in 1995, and who "is not in possession of all his faculties," as the pious phrase goes. That is no obstacle. The heir apparent, His Royal Highness Prince Abdallah bin Abdulaziz, accompanied by His Royal Highness Khalid bin Abdallah, director of planning and head of the National Guard, and by His Royal Highness Prince Mitab bin Abdallah, assistant head of the National Guard, and by His Royal Highness . . . today inspected the new National Guard barracks in X. They were received by the governor of Y province, His Royal Highness Prince Z, by the head of the municipality of X, Sheikh W, accompanied by His Eminence Sheik Someone bin Someone. An endless static shot allows us to imbue ourselves with the handsome faces filing past; the news continues. His Royal Highness Crown Prince Abdallah bin Abdulaziz unfortunately conducted another inspection or inaugurated a shopping center today. Here we are again at the airport, contemplating the majestic descent to the runway, the warm handshakes, the caravan of official cars, the streets, the shopping center, a steady shot of the local dignitaries all in a row, and more handshakes. And so forth: after the number one in the royal hierarchy, the hit parade continues with the thrilling adventures of the heir to the crown prince, His Royal Highness Prince Sultan bin Abdulaziz, and so on. And there are days when we have to welcome His Excellency the minister of foreign affairs of Burkina Faso, himself accompanied by his minister plenipotentiary extraordinary, His Excellency the ambassador of the same Burkina Faso, who . . . Everything takes place against a musical background of Vivaldi. Isn't culture marvelous! (in defiance of strict Wahhabi doctrine—another frightful compromise with the modern world).

What you must know, what you must think today: in that Saudi television is no different from television elsewhere in the Arab world and in a large part of the third world governed by dictatorships. No news is good news. The written press follows the same line.

Taking over Al-Azhar meant taking control of Arab-Muslim minds "upstream." The press and other media in Arabic represent the "downstream," what touches minds not through immersion but through everyday impressions. Clearly, outside Saudi Arabia, the insipid menu served up by the Saudi media does not work. Control over the public means of expression in the Arab world has thus been established surreptitiously.[5]

Before the years between 1975 and 1980, there were two varieties of Arab press. Within each country, except for the haven of diversity that Lebanon had been, little local *Pravdas* ruled, faithfully parroting the line of the party in power, or the king, or the *emir*. There was also a pan-Arab press, often based in Beirut, which lacked neither pluralism, nor freedom of expression, nor, sometimes, sponsors. When Colonel Nasser wanted to sell an idea and did not want his domestic organ *Al-Ahram* to be the source, a Nasserite daily in Beirut took care of it. Nasserite, Baathist, and communist newspapers, supported by their respective financial backers, coexisted with "conservative" or "pro-Western" papers, often supported by Saudi Arabia.

Al-Hayat was the first pan-Arab daily. Its owner, a rich, cultured, and liberal Shiite, looked on pan-Arab nationalists with skepticism and strongly opposed Nasser. Saudi, American, and British funds were not lacking. He was assassinated in 1966, apparently by the Egyptian secret services, but his widow was able to keep control of the newspaper and of its English-language counterpart *The Daily Star* until the Lebanese civil war, which was a turning point. Beirut ceased being the capital of the pan-Arab press, which emigrated to Paris and London. With the first oil shock in 1973, the Lebanese press barons found new sponsors. *Ad Destour* and *Al-Watan al-Arabi* were financed by Iraq, and *Al-Hawadis* by Saudi Arabia. Its owner, who had harsh words for the Syrian dictatorship, was killed by the regime's secret services, who first soaked his right hand in a bath of sulfuric acid. The paper survived the murder, its retreat to London, and its return to Beirut, where it equitably sells six pages a week to Saudi Arabia and to other buyers.

It was in the 1980s that the Saudis, goaded by the invectives of the Khomeini regime, began to play a serious role. The Iran-Iraq war and the first Afghanistan war precipitated their intervention. Published in London and distributed around the world, the daily printed on green paper, *As-Sharq al-Aswat* ("The Middle East"), became the first pan-Arab information organ of the Saudis. Originally associated with two Saudi businessmen, Prince Salman bin Abdulaziz finally scooped up all the shares. The editorial board, first made up of expatriate Arabs, was gradually Saudi-ized. Offshoots appeared: the weekly *Al-Majalla* ("The Magazine"), *Sayyidati* ("My Lady"), a sort of Arabic *Elle* in which models appear without *hijabs* or *abayas*, and other specialized magazines for sports, automobiles, and the like. Should this be surprising? The group breathes devotion to Saudi Arabia but, intended for an international Arab public that is able and willing to make comparisons, *As-Sharq* has a flexible line and even publishes columns by Western commentators.

In Saudi Arabia, *As-Sharq* is treated like a foreign paper and subject to censorship.

Originally pro-Iraqi, with the drying up of funds from its sponsor, *Al-Watan* took a turning that led it on the road to Riyadh. This paper known for its scoops, well written and readable, has built up a well deserved reputation as the recipient of leaks from Arab secret services. *Al-Hayat*, which suspended publication for a time, reappeared: the son of the assassinated founder, a former reporter for *The Washington Post*, re-created the paper in London, using family funds to make it into an independent daily. His friend Prince Khalid bin Sultan, son of the defense minister, himself an air force general and head of the Saudi armed forces, joined the paper as a minority shareholder. Khalid, a potbellied forty year old, was caricatured by Gary Trudeau as Khalid the Helmet in *Doonesbury*. If we are to believe his own testimony, Khalid practically won the Gulf War single-handed. At first, the new *Al-Hayat* began as an Arabic *International Herald Tribune*. It was modern, and its solid network of correspondents around the world guaranteed it coverage of professional quality, including in Moscow and Israel—a major first; it even published Israeli columnists. What had to happen eventually did; the two brothers and associates of the owner received an offer that they could not refuse, and the Saudi prince found himself in control. The former owner who had been forced out was nonetheless able to keep the English-language counterpart, *The Daily Star*.

All the major printed pan-Arab press organs were now in Saudi hands. There remained the rapidly expanding electronic media.

The owners of the Middle East Broadcasting Corporation (MEBC), established in London for over a decade, are a group of Saudi financiers close to the royal family, including in particular Walid al-Ibrahim, brother-in-law to King Fahd, the most golden of Saudi golden boys, who never leaves his father's bedside. "Azzuz" has become the principal puppet master who is able to make the senile and comatose king speak. His mother is the sister of Walid al-Ibrahim: the family is sacred. MEBC recently emigrated to Dubai.

Based in Rome, a second satellite television network, Orbit, offers thirty channels in its package. It is also Saudi owned. The owner of ART, Arab Radio and Television, also based in Rome, is Sheikh Saleh Kamel, close to the royal family and often charged with financial and other missions.

The competition has been stiff, however, since Al-Jazira, the television station based in Qatar, began broadcasting.

It should be clear that even if the Saudi princes do not hold a monopoly on the news, they stand head and shoulders above others in the media oligopoly and make their "line" felt in editorial policies throughout the media. The pan-Arab media environment is preponderantly controlled by Saudi Arabia.

CHAPTER 7

The Saudi Islamintern and Its Feats

We have seen how the Muslim Brotherhood and the Saudi Wahhabis together have ravaged Egypt. Everywhere we look in the Muslim world, we witness the corrosive effects of Saudi money and Wahhabi ideology. A few terrible examples will illustrate this.

Algeria, as we know, was plunged into a long and atrocious civil war that caused between 100,000 and 150,000 deaths, demoralized the nation, and traumatized the population. In their thousands, educated professionals and intellectuals, particularly women, fled the country because they were the preferred targets of fanatical and bloodthirsty *mujahedeen*, while the military authorities took advantage of the situation to settle scores with these opponents of their total supremacy. This brain drain further weakened a country already enfeebled by corrupt military rulers who had shamelessly played the card of anti-imperialism, hatred of France, forced Arabization, and extreme Islamization.

The agents of Arabization and Islamization were for the most part clerics trained in Egypt by the Muslim Brotherhood. They were principally financed by Saudi Arabia. When popular rebellion against the regime broke out, the Islamic Salvation Front (*Front islamique du salut* or

FIS) was in a position to take over leadership of the movement. Its head, Abassi Madani, was the "Saudi's man," collecting, it was said, a million dollars a month from Riyadh: Youssef Abdelatif Jamil, a wealthy Saudi financier, paid the money to the FIS treasurer, Ahmed Simozrag. Even while repression of the FIS was raging, Madani kept up close ties with the "clerical and Arabophone wing of the FLN."[1] The Saudis were thus working both sides of the street, while the Algerians were slaughtering each other: by financing and encouraging Arabization and Islamization, they had helped to mobilize the hordes of the "bearded ones" that their men were leading, while they continued to maintain contact with the authorities.

The network of the Saudi International held both ends of the chain. The Algerian "Afghans" played the principal role in the transformation of the FIS into the GIA (Armed Islamic Group). In the course of the three final years of the Afghan conflict, the Pakistani embassy in Algiers had issued 2,800 visas to Algerians wanting to go to Pakistan for training as *jihadis*. Most of them had been recruited by a fundamentalist sect close to the Saudis, the Tabligh-i Jamaat, whose role in Pakistan we will examine in detail. The Algerian Tabligh was one of the four groups making up the FIS. Later on, Bin Laden and his organization infiltrated between 600 and 1,000 "Afghans" into Algeria, where they formed the kernel of the GIA.[2]

The kingdom did not even deny that initial support and financing for the FIS came from Saudi Arabia. On the contrary, after the dispute among Islamists provoked by the Gulf War, Prince Sultan bin Abdulaziz told a pan-Arab daily that "Arabia held out a helping hand on religious principles and with the aim of propagating the teachings of Islam, imbuing the masses with Islamic culture. But it turns out that Abassi Madani, along with Rashid Ghannouchi [Tunisian] and Hassan al-Turabi [Sudanese] . . . have exploited religion for political purposes. [They] have turned away from reality . . .

by supporting [Iraqi] aggression [against Kuwait] . . ." The helpful hand always ended up strangling others.

In 1994, an international arms shipment intended for the GIA was spotted and reported by the press. Its financing was provided by the Lugano branch of a Saudi bank located in Panama City, the Al-Taqwa Bank, later accused of having been an important link in the financing of the al-Qaeda network. Renamed NADA Management, it was placed in bankruptcy on December 31, 2001, although investigation into it is ongoing. Among its officers was the Swiss neo-Nazi and Islamic convert Ahmed Huber.[3]

The Saudi origin of the FIS and the outright assassins of the GIA was not only financial, but also theological. According to Antoine Basbous: "The *fatwas* of the GIA, which called all the opponents of Islamism *kaffirs* [infidels], and which proclaimed from London that sheiks Bin Baz, the mufti of Saudi Arabia, and Bin Athimayne, a member of the committee of the grand *ulama* of Arabia, two leading lights of Wahhabi Islam, were their inspiration, provoked a timid reaction from the two clerics, who openly condemned neither the principle nor the content of those *fatwas*." When his opinion was sought, Bin Athimayne had "refrained from condemning his self-proclaimed disciples. He [had] simply called for strict adherence to Koranic law before pronouncing such condemnations."[4] Remember that this was not a matter of some trivial theological details; these *fatwas* were death sentences for thousands of Algerians.

It was not until December 1997 that an authorized Saudi voice condemned the actions of the GIA: "Are these killers who cut off heads and limbs worthy of creating an Islamic state?" To judge the sincerity of the speaker, the heir apparent Prince Abdallah, we might wonder why those killers, and not the Taliban, not the Abu Sayyaf group in the Philippines, and not the Egyptian Gamaa Islamiya, killer of Copts, tourists, and many others, were the only ones to incur princely opprobrium; there are evidently some heads that it is good to cut off, and some of those doing the cutting act advisedly or in accordance with Wahhabi orthodoxy.

The ethnic cleansing unleashed in the Balkans by Slobodan Milosevic was to give the Saudis the opportunity to fish in troubled waters. The Islam of Bosnia is European and cosmopolitan, like Sarajevo, an intolerable crime in the eyes of the orthodox. From 1992 on, the Saudi High Commission had contributed not less than $600 million to the region.

On March 19, 2000, the Bosnian authorities seized a large quantity of documents in Sarajevo and Zenica that led to the indictment in Chicago of Enaam Arnaout, head of the "charitable" Benevolent International Foundation (BIF), and speculated to be a member of the Syrian network of Osama bin Laden, on a number of charges for association with a terrorist enterprise.

"Evidence of Saudi charitable institutions being used to advance terrorism was found early in 2002, in the offices of the Saudi High Commission for Relief to Bosnia-Herzegovina. Documents seized by the Sarajevo authorities revealed the scope of the Saudi-backed Wahhabi 'jihad' in the Balkans during the previous decade . . .[T]he Saudi High Commission had come . . . to take over local Islam."[5] In 2001, the same charitable-terrorist High Commission had received the King Faisal Prize for "services to Islam."[6] In the same year, the Bosnian police searched the offices of the Al-Haramayn foundation and found traces of transfers of funds from Saudi Arabia to al-Qaeda.

In return for their services and their money, the Saudis demanded that the mosques destroyed by the Serbs be rebuilt as Wahhabi mosques and that their credo be adopted. The long history, solid structure, and intellectual depth of Bosnian Islam ruined these plans.

The lunatic regime of Enver Hoxha had pulverized Islam in Albania, and the Tito regime had leveled it in Kosovo. In 1999, the SJRCK (Saudi Joint Relief Committee for Kosovo) had announced the training of fifty *imams* and *muftis* and the sponsorship of 328 missionaries. Free tickets were given to 300 Kosovars for the pilgrimage to Mecca in 2000. In February 2002, the authorities in Tirana confiscated the local assets of the Saudi financier Yasin al-Qadi.[7]

In both cases, the method was to exploit the distress and poverty of local Islam, bring in terrorists under the cover of fighting the enemies of Islam, recruit local forces, establish a fundamentalist and terrorist infrastructure, and change the nature of the religion practiced by the local Muslims.

Saudi expansionism is also visible in Central Asia. The Taliban are Saudis without oil, and the Saudis are Taliban with oil: the definition is as precise as it is accurate. We need to add that without Saudi Arabia there would be no Taliban.

From the outset, the Afghan *jihad* received the support of Riyadh, eager to restore its faded glory as the champion of Islam. Riyadh mobilized its religious networks, the World Muslim League, and the entire Salafi galaxy for the purpose. In Arabia itself, three organizations directed Saudi intervention: the secret services headed by Prince Turki al-Faisal, the ad hoc committee led by his uncle, the governor of Riyadh, Salman bin Abdulaziz, and the apparatus of the League.[8] The Pakistani party Jamaat-e Islami, which had been founded by Sayyid Abul-Ala Mawdudi, was "the preferred distributor of Arab financial aid to the resistance." It favored the Hezb-i Islami of the brutal psychopath Gulbuddin Hekmatyar, more concerned with veiling women, when he was not killing them, and persecuting modernists than fighting. In turn, the most favored faction of *mujahedeen* was that of Abdal Rabb-Sayaf, a notorious Wahhabi, who did little fighting against the Soviet forces on the ground but was a presence in the Wahhabi world. The Peshawar office of the World Muslim League declared that it had opened 150 "Koranic learning centers" and 85 "Islamic schools" thanks to $100 million in contributions. Prince Salman's committee contributed 539 million rupees.[9]

During the long war against the Soviet invasion, a large number of *mujahedeen* leaders were trained in Saudi *madrasas*. According to the journalist Ahmed Rashid, one of the most knowledgeable observers of the region, "Wahhabism began to exercise more and more perceptible influence in the region."[10] In addition, hundreds of Uzbek and Tajik forces were exfiltrated to Pakistan and from there to Saudi Arabia, either to study in *madrasas* or for guerilla training, while tens of thousands of Muslim volunteers were trained in Pakistani madrasas, which sprang up like mushrooms after rain. There was a preexisting Wahhabi apparatus in the region. As early as 1912, the Medina native Sayed Shari Muhammad had settled in the Fergana Valley in the heart of Central Asia. But the bulk of the work now depended on one of the movements that was related to Wahhabism and now fully convergent with it: the Deobandi, one of the principal sources for the Taliban.

Mullah Omar, the guru of the Taliban and Osama bin Laden's brother-in-law, had been trained in a Deobandi *madrasa*; the two confederates had met for the first time in 1989 in the Deobandi mosque of Banuri in Karachi. We will not repeat here the history of Saudi intervention in Afghanistan, but certain salient points are worth emphasizing: the essential role played by Prince Turki al-Faisal, the role of his protégé and subordinate Bin Laden, the countless trips by the prince to Kandahar and Kabul, the special relationship uniting the spiritual brothers, the Saudi Wahhabi and the Pashtun Deobandi. It was Riyadh's fundamental decision to put its Afghan eggs in the Taliban basket—and to withdraw its support from the other factions fighting over Afghanistan—that enabled the Taliban to take power.

For the seven years of horror lived through by the Afghan population—massacres, the extermination of knowledge, the promotion of illiteracy, the violent repression of women, the systematic effort of these Pol Pots in turbans to move the country backward, renaming it the "Islamic Emirate," not into the Middle Ages but into the Dark Ages—Saudi Arabia's responsibility is evident. Its responsibility for the atomization of an entire country is overwhelming. As low as Soviet aggression had brought Afghanistan, the reign of the Taliban fostered by the Saudis—they were the last to break diplomatic relations with the regime—aggravated, exacerbated, and destroyed everything, verifying the intrinsically destructive and nihilistic nature of Saudi Wahhabism, prepared to sacrifice everything for the triumph of its power and its ideology.

This enterprise of social, national, intellectual, and religious demolition was not directly carried out by the Saudis, except for a few thousand volunteer *jihadis* from the kingdom and the rich young bourgeois paying royally for a brief spell of *jihadi* tourism over the border between Pakistan and Afghanistan. Pakistan, which had been re-Islamized since the 1970s, with Saudi support, funds, clerics, and doctrines, was complicit in the crime. Before examining the catastrophic impact of Wahhabism on Pakistan and the disintegration that it caused, we will briefly take note of the depredations committed by Wahhabism in Central Asia, recently liberated from Soviet Communism.

From the early 1990s, we see the Islamic Movement of Uzbekistan (IMU) and the Islamic Renaissance Party (IRP) in Tajikistan, "the Islam of which largely derived from Saudi Wahhabism and from the interpretation given to Deobandism by the Taliban," unleashing civil wars. We observe the activity of the clandestine pan-Islamic movement Hezb ut-Tahrir al-Islami founded by Palestinians in Saudi Arabia and Jordan in 1953 and led by a sheik from Al-Azhar.

Ahmed Rashid relates typical careers: that of the young born-again Muslim who goes to Saudi Arabia to get a religious education. Back in his country, Uzbekistan in this case, richly endowed with dollars by some Wahhabi foundation, he builds a mosque and a *madrasa* where the strictest Islamic practices are enforced. Then, the recruits attracted by this enterprise set up in every neighborhood vigilante committees resembling the *mutawiyin* (the "street police") in Saudi

Arabia. They demand complete application of *sharia* and agitate for an Islamic revolution. Like the neophytes of the *Ikwhan* of the past, they understand nothing of Islam but slogans, to the intransigence of which they are all the more violently attached because they have replaced faith and spiritual sustenance. About the Muslim tradition of Central Asia, deeply rooted in Sufi pluralism, they know nothing. In Namangan, where this story takes place, there are 130 mosques. Their Korans and other books come from Saudi Arabia, as do the imams, who work in concert with the IRP, which for its part is associated with the Taliban and Bin Laden's organization. "From his base in Kabul [the leader of the IRP] sent a constant supply of funds, materiel, and volunteers provided by the Taliban, bin Laden, the Uzbek diaspora, charities in Saudi Arabia and the Gulf states, and Islamic parties in Pakistan."[11] The Saudi paymasters provided the huge quantity of $15 million worth of high-tech weapons: rifles with telescopic sights, transmission equipment, infrared night vision goggles.

We are familiar with the overall strategy of the Saudis described in these terms. "In Central Asia, Saudi Arabia had not made much effort in state to state relations, preferring to have charitable organizations and other Saudi Islamic groups promote Wahhabism by financing Islamist groups, mosques, and *madrasas*, and sponsoring travel to Mecca for the *hajj*. Missionaries, scholarships, Islamic literature, millions of copies of the Koran translated into the languages of the various countries were sent to Central Asia by Saudi charitable organizations," according to Rashid. He goes on: "But Saudi generosity had a price; the Saudis intended to turn Central Asia toward their Wahhabi extremism," whereas, "despite the considerable oil wealth of the region, Saudi Arabia had invested very little in it. Saudi Arabia systematically supported the most extreme Islamist groups in the region, from the 1980s on, and financed Hekmatyar's Hezb-i Islami in Afghanistan . . ."

The Muslim demographic giant of Pakistan, with its 120 to 130 million inhabitants, offers the most tragic example of the destruction wrought by Wahhabism in a society when it has the opportunity to put its doctrines into operation. Pakistan was driven toward disintegration. Saudi dominance, Riyadh's policy of assimilating foreign bodies and transforming them into Wahhabi entities, invariably destroys everything it touches.

Because it was created in opposition to a secular and republican India, the Muslim identity of the new nation was particularly cherished. The absence of a general purpose other than Muslim hatred of India prevented the establishment of a genuine national identity: the provinces—Sind, Punjab, Baluchistan, Northwest—were dominated by large landed proprietors, and their ethnic groups did not blend into a nation, neither the Pashtun of the North-West Frontier Province nor the *mohajir* who had come from India in 1947. Divided between Sunni and Shiites, Sufis, Barelvis, and Deobandis, the country had only one national institution, the armed forces, which in a coup soon seized power from the civilians to whom they had ceded it for a few years.

The endless intrigues and manipulations of the populist demagogue Zulfikar Ali Bhutto led to the secession of the eastern half of the country, which became Bangladesh in 1971, and the humiliation of the armed forces by the Indian army. The soldiers would not rest until they got their revenge. In search of legitimacy, Bhutto mutated from the socialist he ridiculously claimed to be into a devout Islamist. In 1973, Pakistan provided material support to the Arab armies at war with Israel.

In 1977, the military got its revenge; another coup overthrew Bhutto, who was imprisoned and finally hung by his successor General Zia ul-Haq, a devout Deobandi and an ardent admirer of Mawdudi. The dictator crushed the press and political parties, cancelled elections, imposed martial law, and manipulated the legal system, including the

Supreme Court, which he deprived of any power. In 1978, Zia announced to the Pakistani people that he would thenceforth follow the *Tehrik-e Nizam-e Mustafa*, the "Way of the Prophet": Islam prevailed over the Constitution and the laws. In 1979, the courts, applying *sharia* (Islamic law), took control over a large part of the legal system. Zia "Islamized" the banking system.

Zia's relationship with Saudi Arabia was simple: in the terse formulation of General Shahid Mahmud, "If it had been possible, Zia would have imported all the sands of Saudi Arabia to make Pakistan resemble it."[12]

We can assess the development of Pakistan by comparing the rate of growth of *madrasas* with the increase in illiteracy: from barely two hundred in the 1950s, *madrasas* have reached a current total of twenty thousand.[13] The literacy rate was calculated to be 36 percent in 1981, and it has now fallen to 26 percent—an extremely rare case of rapid decline in the contemporary world; the results of the experiment are conclusive. In rural areas, close to 90 percent of the population is illiterate, the rate for women reaching 98 percent.[14] When the *Maulana* Samiul Haq, rector of the extremist *madrasa* of Haqqania was asked why he had his five- and six-year-old pupils demonstrate against the United States, he replied: "It is never too early to do good." And he went on: "Young people must not think." Nor must they learn. The *madrasas* teach the theology of rage, they are factories turning out *jihadis*. They now have more students than the public education system, which has been nationalized but remains neglected. Pakistan spends eight dollars per capita annually for education, in clear, nothing. And from 60 to 90 percent of the financing of *madrasas* comes from abroad, primarily from Saudi Arabia.

That did not prevent the "Zia model" from spreading throughout the Muslim world: Saudi Arabia re-exported the prototype developed in the Pakistani laboratory. From Morocco to Indonesia, from the Philippines to Algeria, *madrasas* proliferated, and Muslim immigrant communities in Europe and North America were also provided for.

Zia's dictatorial regime was both obscurantist and military, ruled by the Pakistani army. Inside the army, from 1948 on, the Inter-Services Intelligence (ISI) gradually developed, growing from a simple military intelligence service into a state within the state, an organ of the army totally independent from the government. "As the first blossoms of democracy were fading, the clique of high-ranking officials and soldiers around General Iskander Mirza . . . began to develop the ISI as a tool of government." From then on, the ISI, armed with its 40,000 members, its huge Saudi financing, and the army's control over the government, was the puppet master of the politicians. The ISI exercised plenary powers, it was omnipotent. The state had entered into a state of decay because its sovereign powers had been usurped by one of its instruments. All Pakistani dictators and all civilian leaders have strengthened the powers of the ISI: General Ayub Khan, General Yahya Khan, Bhutto the father, Zia, Bhutto the daughter, Nawaz Sharif. We will see later how the ISI pulled the wool over the CIA's eyes, manipulated American policy for its benefit, and came out on top.

General Hamid Gul, probably the most fanatical of the ISI heads, himself an extremist Islamist, orchestrated the election of Benazir Bhutto, the entry of Pakistan into the Afghan conflict, and the Pakistani attack on Indian Kashmir. Among his successors were fundamentalist members of the Jamaat-e Islami and the Tabligh-i Jamaat. The ISI has long operated as a factory producing terrorists by the thousands, and it has set up countless front organizations to train terrorists from Algeria, Bosnia, Thailand, Burma, the Philippines, Arab nations, and Central Asia.[15]

Saudi Arabia's money had enabled it to buy a country. And that was done at the price of the devastation of that country. The financial assistance of the oil monarchies, about half of which came from Saudi Arabia, made Pakistan one of the principal beneficiaries of fraternal aid. The huge Islamic University Institute in Islamabad and the gigantic King Faisal mosque provided concrete evidence. In exchange, hundreds of thousands of skilled and semi-skilled Pakistanis slave away in Saudi Arabia in frightful conditions, in a kind of indentured slavery. Two battalions of Pakistani commandos are stationed in Saudi Arabia as a Praetorian guard for the royal family. The pilots of the Pakistani air force are the pilots of the Saudi air force. As a result, one Pakistani became secretary general of the Organization of the Islamic Conference and another governor of the Saudi central bank, the SAMA.[16]

After nearly thirty years of gradual "Saudi-ization," a kind of balance sheet can be drawn up: in Pakistan, two states coexist, two worlds governed by different principles and different goals. One, now in full retreat, favored by the founder of the country, Mohammed Ali Jinnah, hoped to make it into a modern Muslim state open to the world. The other, now flourishing, is an Islamic state that is dissolving the other one and seizing its prerogatives.

The triumph of the latter has led to the general deterioration of the society. Economic growth is minuscule, the rate of poverty has increased from 23 percent of the population in the 1980s to more than 40 percent today, even as Pakistan has received $58 billion in foreign aid—it is the third largest recipient in the world. An unstable country with thousands of murders annually in the streets of every large city, Pakistan obviously does not attract much foreign investment and depends for one quarter of its budget on international assistance. According to the United Nations criterion of "human development," it is among the lowest. It hardly fares better in the area of freedom.

The sinister role played by the ISI has led to a "Talibanization" of the country: nowhere in the world can there be found such a concentration of weapons and of men trained to use them. "Islamized soldiers and their officers, who make up an army within the army, often join forces with the unofficial militias of the religious parties and block all efforts to restrict the activities of the *madrasas* and their irrational students."[17] Attacking Shiites is a kind of team sport for these students, coupled with attacks on Christians. Ethnic disturbances have proliferated in Sind and Baluchistan. In the Pashtun North-West Frontier Province on the Afghan border, "tribal emirates" have sprung up, headed by warlords relying on drug money who harbor the Taliban and other friends of al-Qaeda.

Thirty years of Saudi-ization have atomized, liquefied Pakistan, a demographic, political, and religious bomb that is also a nuclear power. It was Saudi Arabia that financed Pakistan's development of an "Islamic bomb." "Saudi Arabia participates in the financing of programs for the purchase of nuclear and ballistic technologies from China, which has made Pakistan a state producing nuclear weapons and a proliferating state," according to a former official of the Defense Intelligence Agency (DIA). Riyadh, he went on to say, is probably "in the process of purchasing nuclear capacity from China through an intermediary country, Pakistan." The author, Thomas Woodrow, specified that the Saudi defense minister, Prince Sultan, "has inspected the uranium enrichment factory and the factory in Kahuta where [ballistic] missiles are produced" and reported his presence at both Pakistani nuclear tests and at the launching of the *Ghauri* missile, which has nuclear capability. Saudi Arabia paid China to transfer the technology to Pakistan. In this connection, Chinese technicians are at work in Pakistan. "If the influence of Riyadh on Pakistan includes the nuclear program, Saudi Arabia could quickly become a de facto nuclear power, because it would only need to have missiles and nuclear warheads shipped to it."[18] Saudi ambitions are not modest. Having largely succeeded in swallowing up a vast Muslim country that has become a combat training area for *jihadis*, it has made Pakistan into its certified mercenary and a shining example of Wahhabization.

CHAPTER 8

The Chain of Terror

S audi Arabia has for years been the target of diatribes from Osama bin Laden. He does not have words harsh enough to stigmatize the corruption, the luxury and debauchery, the abandonment of the principles of Islam, and the prostitution of the holy territory of Saudi Arabia by the presence of troops of the infidel "crusaders." The Saudi authorities, for their part, have called him all the names in the book, accused him of a thousand crimes, and in 1994 stripped him of Saudi nationality. No holds are barred; there is war without quarter between the Al-Sauds and the bearded prophet of al-Qaeda.

If there is a war, it is unfolding in the realm of the intangible. Bombs have indeed gone off in Saudi Arabia, but no one has attacked the royal family or its henchmen, its symbols, or its foundations. Television, radio, and the newspapers are intact. The countless royal palaces, ministries, and princely properties have never been touched. King, princes, princelings, and courtiers all peacefully go about their business. The soft targets supposedly represented by the palaces, villas, and manor houses in Marbella, Geneva, Paris, Aspen, Surrey, and London have not even had a stone thrown at them. For an evil genius able to destroy the Twin Towers, this is negligent. The manual of the good terrorist has not been followed.

A few attacks have taken place in Saudi Arabia, but they were exclusively against English and American targets. On

November 13, 1995, two bombs exploded in Riyadh, killing six, five of whom were Americans, and wounding sixty, more than half of whom were Americans. On June 25, 1996, a perfectly professional attack was carried out against the American military mission to the National Guard in Dhahran. The bomb, engineered to maximize the blast and heat effects, augmented with fuel tanks, and ignited by sophisticated electronics, killed nineteen Americans and wounded several hundred. The two attacks demonstrated the capacity of the terrorist enterprise to prepare a complex action of great scope under the nose of the authorities, and the existence of a well organized local support network and infrastructure.

There is an explanation, I was told by an Arab foreign minister, confirming a piece of information that had been rumored for some time in international intelligence circles: a deal had been made between Osama bin Laden and the royal family, represented at the time by the chief of the General Intelligence Directorate, who resigned twelve days before the September 11 attacks, after twenty-six years of service—a fine example of professional longevity and an excellent sense of timing for retirement. In return for a sum of $200 million, according to the minister, it was asked, and Bin Laden agreed, that nothing be done against Saudi Arabia, leaving in return complete freedom of action to the prodigal son to sow the whirlwind in the four corners of the world. The story is difficult to confirm. The source is unimpeachable. Several Western intelligence services confimed it. We must keep a question mark on it pending confirmation. We will illustrate this piece of intelligence by showing the probability of a non-aggression pact between the rivals and its consistent application by the contracting parties.

The tale illustrated with precision the difference between Osama bin Laden and the royal family, between the *jihadis* and the notables: on one side, fat and contented, the Saudi old guard; on the other, thin and angry, the ambitious young men. "Yon Cassius has a lean and hungry look," says

Shakespeare's Julius Caesar. Against those established in their kingdom, crouching on their heaps of gold, stand the others who hunger for Islamic glory, the blood of infidels, and holy war. The potbellied elders, forced to take into account certain geostrategic imperatives, stand against the bearded warriors who are unaware of them.

The reader will have noted the parallel with the monsters created a century ago by King Abdulaziz ibn Saud, the fanatical warriors of the *Ikhwan*: the relation is a direct one. Having brought forth and used his *jihadis* to conquer his kingdom, the war leader understood the need for a pause in conquests. He also knew that it is futile to attack someone who is immensely stronger than you: in 1930, the interests of the British Empire in the Middle East were a prey too difficult to swallow. His former accomplices of the *Ikhwan*, however, lacked those sensitivities, and were determined at any cost to follow their predatory instincts. The confrontation was violent. The same thing is true today, with one crucial difference: the plump princes have neither the charisma nor the combat experience of Ibn Saud. Their fat fingers can handle nothing but telephones and checkbooks. Their kingdom is fragile.

Consider the long-range dialogue between the adversaries: one is in favor of the regulation of terrorism and has for a long time been concerned with orchestrating around the world a *jihad* controlled by its Islamintern; the other, Osama bin Laden, favors the deregulation of terrorism, with no subjection to the constraints incumbent on a state. Important tactical differences may very well make them opponents at one moment or another. One operates in the shadow of caves, the other in air-conditioned offices. After the Iraqi occupation of Kuwait, the royal family, in a panic, appealed to the Americans. Bin Laden saw in it the dreamed of opportunity for a *jihad*, first to drive out Saddam, and then to conquer the Middle East. The "Desert Storm" operation, supported by Riyadh and violently opposed by almost the entire constellation around the Muslim Brotherhood, created a gulf. The ensuing years filled it in. The community uniting them is stronger than their divergences.

The Saudi royal family and Bin Laden have much of their DNA in common. Riyadh and the princes have been overtaken by the monster they created, but they are tied to him with a thousand threads that they cannot cut. Between the two, there is continuity, not discontinuity. Later on, we compare the content of sermons in Saudi mosques, of Saudi schoolbooks, and of statements from members of the royal family with Bin Laden's harangues: the language is the same, the ideas are the same, the ambition is the same. The army once set up by Prince Turkir, over the span of an entire generation, has gone to war against the United States and the West, and against the rest of the Muslim world that does not bow down before Wahhabism, even if the general in command is not the prince but the commoner bin Laden. This makes it possible to resolve a question that has frequently arisen in recent years: is Saudi Arabia with or against the terrorists? It is both at once at the same time. It conducts a perpetual balancing act between support for all kinds of *jihads* and *jihadis* and an attempt to contain them and to be neither affected nor sullied by the fallout. It burns the candle at both ends. The gap has been growing, and it is at the breaking point.

The Islamists' theology of hatred and terror holds to one essential position: the Other exists only as an enemy, an emanation of Satan, and therefore does not have the right to exist. We are the elect and therefore have all the rights; we are above ordinary law, because we are the bearers of our own law, which raises us above the infidels. There are no innocents: every infidel is guilty. Even civilian children are part of the enemy camp. Children are future enemies, women produce enemies, and old men are retired enemies. It is therefore legitimate to kill them, and it is recommended that they all be killed. The "elect" have to be conditioned to adopt these ideas. The Other has to be dehumanized, turned into a subhuman creature. The lesson is hammered home by

84

all of official and semi-official Saudi Arabia, its princes, ministers, civil servants, clerics, teachers, radio, television, and schoolbooks. The position is in the direct line of the history of Wahhabism. It is the basis and illustration of the continuity that links the royal family to Bin Laden's Islamist terrorists.

"A classified American intelligence service report based on a survey conducted in mid-October [2001 by the] Saudi intelligence service among a sample of educated Saudis between the ages of 25 and 41 concluded that 95 percent of them support the cause of [Osama] bin Laden," according to a report in *The New York Times*.[1] Prince Nawaf, Prince Turki's successor at the head of the secret service, confirmed the existence of the survey without breathing a word about the extent of the support for Bin Laden.[2] This happy unanimity points to a society that is rather united in its aspirations and views.

Where does this unanimity come from? One of the principal mechanisms in the power contract on which Saudi Arabia is based sheds some light on the question: Saud needs Wahhab to be legitimate, Wahhab needs Saud to maintain dominance. "To satisfy the obligations that arose from their agreement, and that removed the *ulamas* from political decision making, the regime granted the clerics a dominant voice in the sphere of education, including higher education. From this came deep fundamentalist influence on Saudi education, even in universities that were not particularly designated as 'Islamic,'" according to an expert on fundamentalism in the kingdom.[3]

A study in progress on Saudi curricular materials, both for domestic use and exported at great expense, is revealing. Teaching is based on the principles articulated by Muhammad ibn al-Wahhab in the eighteenth century. Elementary and secondary school students must be trained to "fight spiritually and physically for the sake of Allah,"[4] to promote loyalty to Islam, and to denounce any system and any theory in conflict with Islamic law as conceived by the Wahhabis. "The aim of education is to understand Islam in a complete and appropriate manner, to implement and spread the Muslim faith, to arm the students with Islamic values and teachings . . . [and to] provide them with the ideas, the awareness, and the ability to preach the message of Islam."[5]

Another prominent aim is to train students "in the spirit of Islamic combat." "To aspire with all one's strength to fight for the love of Allah is an absolute duty, an ancient tradition, and an existential necessity. This aspiration will remain alive until the Last Judgment"; it is inspired by "the systematic teaching of history, by the crucial lessons derived from that history, and by the explanation of the Islamic point of view." "To awaken the spirit of the struggle of Islam to resist our enemies, restore our rights and glories, and fulfill our duties in accordance with the Islamic message."[6]

Clearly, this is a militant education that takes young people in hand and indoctrinates them beginning in childhood. Only one point of view is legitimate, excluding all others. The resemblance to the totalitarian educational systems of the last century is patent: the Bolshevik, Nazi, and Maoist catechisms differed only in the particular "god" hammered into the children's heads. The totalitarianism is identical. The authorities prohibit entry into the kingdom and the use in teaching of any book whose content is not in accordance with Islam. The covert conditioning of teaching does not remain at the level of abstraction. From the age of fourteen, students are taught *jihad* for the sake of Allah, *al-Jihad fi sabil Allah*, the glory of the participant in *jihad*, the *mujahid*.

The eighth-grade textbook explains why Allah cursed the Jews and the Christians, who were "turned into monkeys and pigs." In the ninth grade, the course on *hadiths* (deeds and saying attributed to the Prophet) quotes this one: "The hour [of the Last Judgment] will not come until the Muslims attack the Jews and kill them. A Jew will then hide between a stone and a tree, and the stone and the tree will call the Muslim:

'Oh Muslim, oh slave of Allah, there is a Jew behind me, come and kill him!'" The text elaborates on the lesson:

1. "It is the wisdom of Allah that wants the fight between Muslims and Jews to continue until the Day of Judgment."
2. "The *hadith* announces the good news of the final victory, with the help of Allah, of the Muslims over the Jews."
3. "The Jews and the Christians are the enemies of the faithful. They are not favorably disposed toward Muslims and it is good to be careful in relations with them."[7]

Recently, in the course of a sermon at the Suleiman bin Muqiran mosque in Riyadh, Sheikh Majed Abd al-Rahman al-Firian asserted that "Muslims must train their children for *jihad* . . . educate their children in jihad and hatred of Jews and Christians and infidels; educate the children and revive the embers of *jihad* in their souls. This is what is needed today."[8] On the first anniversary of September 11, 2001, in an interview with the daily *As-Sharq al-Awsat*, the interior minister Prince Nayef bin Abdulaziz vigorously defended the educational system, although it had frequently been accused of fostering terrorism: "We are convinced of the excellence of our educational programs . . . and of their aims. We will not change our system because other people order us to do so."[9] His brother the defense minister, Sultan bin Abdulaziz, echoed him: "We will never change our educational system. . . . Our country has its policy, and above all the courses in religion that must never be changed. Every demand to change the curriculum formulated by a foreign country constitutes unacceptable interference, an invasion of sovereignty." And, flagrantly lying, the assistant education minister Khalid al-Awad insisted: "Saudi curricula are very good, and they do not encourage terrorism or hatred of members of other religions or other faiths."[10]

Having reached adulthood, young Saudis hear only a single voice emanating from the mosques, the 54,000 religious officials, and the media. The preachers at Friday prayers, the most important service in the week, speak without restraint. Traditionally, they believe that they are heard only by the Saudi public, or at most, by the Arab-speaking public. They thus have no hesitation in speaking frankly. Listening to and transcribing their sermons is thus extremely edifying.

In April 2002, Crown Prince Abdallah bin Abdulaziz visited President George W. Bush at his Crawford, Texas ranch. On April 19, one of the most eminent clerics in Saudi Arabia, Sheikh Abdulrahman al-Sudais, preached at the Great Mosque in Mecca, a central locus of Islam, of which he is the *imam*. He asserted in particular that the Jews are "the dregs of the human race . . . the rats of the planet . . . killers of prophets . . . pigs and monkeys," and prayed to God to "exterminate them." He asserted that Israel "wishes to demolish the Al-Aqsa mosque [in Jerusalem] to build on its ruins their so-called Temple." On September 28, 2001, the same firebrand had asserted that "it would be a calamity if the advocates of terrorism were to use religion as a disguise, because true Islam is innocent of all that." That precept was obviously reserved for an outside audience.[11]

Let us listen to Sheikh Mohsin al-Awajim, who was *imam* of the great mosque of King Saud University in Riyadh: Bin Laden is wrong, he said, to attack various clerics and political leaders, "without evidence," to conduct *jihads* in Muslim countries, and to attack innocents "around the world, of all religions and colors." Reassured by this human warmth, what follows takes us by surprise: "Given that, Bin Laden is seen as a man of honor, a man who has renounced the world, a brave man, and a man who believes in his principles and sacrifices himself for them. . . . If the entire world oppressed by America adores Bin Laden, is the Islamic nation not entitled to love one of its sons as a human being? The truth must be spoken: The Saudi people love every warrior in the *jihad*, every fighter, and every man of honor, whether in Afghanistan, Chechnya, Kashmir, or southern Sudan. . . . We are proud," he went on, "to be defined as those who strike terror into the hearts of the enemies of Allah and our enemies. . . . The Saudis firmly maintain that the Arabian peninsula is the haven of lions . . . [who] confront America in Afghanistan, in Chechnya [sic] and in Kashmir [sic] . . ." because the Saudis, "who are conducting *jihad* around the world, have set out without asking permission from the masters of the world. They have broken down barriers to go forth. They have gone in pursuit of death . . ."[12]

Reaching the heart of the subject, Al-Awajim elaborates: "The glory of the [Islamic] nation arose when the Prophet taught us the industry of death, when he taught us how to create death. Then life appeared to us as devoid of value. . . . When one of the sons of our [Islamic] nation is killed, he cries out: 'I have conquered,' and the Master of the Kaaba [Allah] swears that he has conquered. We conceive of that as the industry of death. We, Saudi society and other Islamic societies, have finally understood that that is the right path to confront the deadly strategic arms of our time. America may have intercontinental missiles and bombs, but our jihad fighters are our bombs, the ones America calls suicide bombers, and whom we call 'martyrs.'" And Bin Laden? He is the Che Guevara of Islam.[13] This deadly conception is everywhere in Saudi Arabia.

A *fatwa* issued on September 16 by Sheikh Hamoud bin Oqla al-Shuaibi, an eminent Wahhabi authority, provided the complete set of arguments of the admirers of terrorism.[14] "Whoever supports the infidel against Muslims will be considered an infidel," he asserted. The *fatwa* explained that:

1. The United States is a democracy, people voted, and they are therefore responsible as fighters or auxiliaries.
2. *Sharia* prohibits Muslims from being friends with the impious, and the Unites States is an impious state.

3. It is legitimate according to *sharia* to kill women and children if they are not separated from men.

Hence, the Taliban must be supported in every way because they are conducting *jihad* in the name of religion. America is guilty, Americans are the terrorists.

But neither they nor their co-religionists lose anything by waiting. Blithely mixing apples and oranges, Sheikh Abd al-Muhsin al-Qahdi preached from the pulpit of the Al-Salaam mosque in Al-Unayzah: "Today let us speak of one of the deformed religions, a faith that has strayed from the true path. . . . Christianity, that false faith. . . . Let us examine its history full of hatred, abomination, and wars against Islam and the Muslims," he began. His colleague, Sheikh Adnan Ahmad Siyami, added that the infidels, Christians and Jews, will end up "in the deepest pit of Hell." Commenting on the visit of Pope John Paul II to Syria, he went on: "The call [of the pope], may Allah punish him as he deserves, for people of different religions in Syria to live together in peace is nothing but an impertinent call for the unification of religions on the basis of the principles of religious harmony. . . . What motivates the pope is his dissatisfaction: not content with stealing the lands of Muslims, he also wants to steal their religion." The sermon concluded: "There can be neither agreement nor a point of contact between the people of Islam and the peoples of the Book, Jews and Christians."[15]

Besides, the pope had better hold tight. Sheikh Muhammad bin Abd al-Rahman, *imam* of the mosque of the King Fahd Defense Academy, promised him that "we [Muslims] will take control of the Vatican; we will occupy Rome and make Islam rule there. Yes, the Christians who have carved crosses on the chests of the Muslims of Kosovo, and before that in Bosnia, and before that in many other places in the world, will have to pay us the *jizya* [the poll tax that *dhimmis*, non-Muslims, must pay in Islamic states as second class citizens] in humiliation, or convert to Islam."[16]

One might call that a lunatic principle of commutative logic: If a Muslim does something bad, Islam is never stained by it, but if a Muslim does something good, it is automatically attributed to Islam. On the other hand, if a Christian (or a Jew) does anything at all, all the Christians or all the Jews, or Christianity or Judaism themselves are stained with guilt. This contagion making everyone responsible for and guilty of the deeds of others is at its deepest level an expression of the tribal, primitive, archaic nature of the Saudi worldview and Saudi religion: The individual does not exist, either as an autonomous subject or as a holder of rights, he is only one of an infinite number of examples of the same substance, the same essence. No one exists except as a fragment of the tribe. It is thus legitimate to kill the children of enemies, because they are part of an enemy tribe. No one is ever innocent, because he is contaminated by his nature as co-religionist of the enemy, or even by proximity to him. This is at the very heart of Wahhabism and Saudi Arabia. Rome will be conquered by the armies of Islam, according to the sermon preached in the Al-Nour mosque in Khobar by Sheikh Nassert Muhammad al-Nasser.[17]

The Shiites are worth no more than the others. On March 13, 1998, Sheikh Ali Abdurrahman al-Hudhaifi, *imam* of the Nabawi mosque in Medina, delivered a violent diatribe against the Shiites, directly in line with all Wahhabi tradition. Because he had the audacity to speak in the presence of the state visitor Ayatollah Hashemi Rafsanjani, former president of the Islamic Republic of Iran, who had come to sign a strategic alliance with the Riyadh rivals, the authorities were angry, prohibited dissemination of the *khutba*, and arrested the preacher. Soon freed, he was prohibited from preaching. In thirty pages of uninterrupted invective, this Savonarola of the oases, after insulting Christianity and Judaism, turned to Shiism: "What sensible and intelligent person can believe that God can be carried in a mother's womb? Can reason accept a God who eats and drinks, travels on a donkey, sleeps, and defecates? How could there be the slightest association or the slightest compromise between such a ridiculous religion and Islam?" Moving from one religion to another, the preacher took on Judaism: "How could there be the slightest compromise between Islam and Judaism, since Islam is unique, it is purity, light, brilliance, honesty, justice, tolerance, magnanimity, and high moral principles for men and *djinns*, while Judaism is the sum of materialism, narrowness, wickedness toward men, betrayal, servility and moral degradation, lawlessness, avarice, and greed?" Shiism is a "religion built on lies." The Shiites "insult and curse" true Muslims, they "insult the holy Prophet." They "destroy Islam." Shiism is "the fruit of the association of Abu Luluah Majuzi [a Zoroastrian] and Abdullah bin Sabah Yahudi [a Jew]," he went on, repeating a Wahhabi myth that has become commonplace. They are *kafirs*, infidels, and so on ad nauseam. The *Haramayn-Asharafayn*, the kingdom of the two holy cities, Saudi Arabia, is threatened by infidel and imperialist plots, but it is "the fortress of the Muslims," and the *jihad* will triumph, or so concludes the rhetorical flight.[18]

This brief survey of Wahhabis in the pulpit would not be complete without a member of the family of Wahhab himself, the hereditary dignitaries of the established religion. The Grand Mufti of Saudi Arabia, Sheikh Abdelaziz Aal al-Sheikh, delivered a sermon at the Nimra mosque in Arafa: "What have those who attack Islam and its people given to humanity? What do they have to be proud of? They have given it a false and contemptible civilization, they have inflicted all sorts of harm against human freedom and human rights, on the pretext of protecting them. They have created discrimination on the basis of skin color, sex, language, and race. They have created the technology that produces weapons of mass destruction in order to destroy the human race. They have given us lies and falsehood."[19]

Sheikh Wajdi Hamza al-Ghazawi was thus right to conclude, in a sermon preached at the Al-Manshwai mosque in

Mecca, that: "The kind of terror that Islamic religious law permits consists in terrifying the cowardly, the hypocrites, the secularists, and the rebels, by punishing them according to the religious law of Allah. The meaning of the term 'terror' used by the media is *jihad* for the sake of Allah. Jihad is the zenith of Islam . . . the *jihad* that defends Muslims and the lands of Islam . . . or the *jihad* that extends the reach of religion, is the pinnacle of terror, as far as the enemies of Allah are concerned. The *mujahedin* who go in search of the death of martyrdom or victory and return with their spoils are terrorists only for the enemies of Allah . . . *Jihad*, oh believers, is an integral part of our religion. The word 'terror' is used to insult that noble and blessed foundation."[20]

It is not the content of these constant appeals to hatred and murder that troubles the Saudi authorities, but the fact that they sometimes come to the attention of the media of the rest of the world. What can be done in such circumstances? Assert that "Islam is a religion of peace," that Saudi Arabia is Islamic, and therefore—an irrefutable syllogism—that the kingdom is peaceful, tolerant, and so forth. And in the face of clerics who in their thousands every Friday hammer home the same poisoned propaganda? On November 14, 2001, Crown Prince Abdallah held a conference of the religious dignitaries of the kingdom to set forth policy, among other things, on Saudi-American relations. Accompanied by his half-brother Sultan, minister of defense, the Grand Mufti Aal al-Sheikh, the minister of Islamic affairs, and others, he ordered the clerics to soften their incendiary remarks, explaining: "Enemy ears are listening to us." As the president of the High Council of Justice, Sheikh Saleh bin Muhammad al-Khedian formulated it: "We must do better . . . and watch what comes out of our mouths [and say only] what serves our country and our Islamic nation."

Councils of moderation were dispensed only sparingly, as evidenced by the statements of Crown Prince Abdallah at the same conference: "I must remind you of the unjust attacks that foreign media have launched against the Saudi kingdom. I mean the foreign newspapers, and you know who is behind them. These newspapers, behind home lies hidden you know who, criticize your religion, criticize what is dearest to you, your faith and your Holy Scriptures . . ."[21]

CHAPTER 9

"Islamists of All Countries, Unite"

From the forges and workshops of militant Wahhabism flow ideology, teaching, and multiple forms of propaganda. All of this must be given articulate form, which is the role of teachers and preachers, utilizing mosques, schools, media, schoolbooks, and literature of all kinds. This is followed by export, which needs means of transmission and organizers.

We have already encountered some of these organizations, at the time of their formation and their first flowering. It is time to consider them more closely, to sample some of the international operations of the Saudi-Wahhabi complex that, while not constituting a thoroughgoing investigation of the international circuits of terrorism, will shed light on the role that Saudi Arabia plays in this galaxy.

Inter-Arab relationships are steeped in violence. Since their independence, generally achieved at the end of the Second World War, the Arab countries have struggled against and fought each other unceasingly, with warfare between neighbors, and indirect warfare for those that did not share borders. Because overt political life is reduced to a bare minimum in most of these countries—elections are fixed, parties are caricatures, parliaments, when they exist, are rubber stamps for the authorities, freedom of expression, the press, and association are non-existent or minimal—whoever wants to carry out any change cannot freely discuss it without risk in a public forum in which a variety of interests and opinions is recognized as legitimate, desirable, and fruitful: only one opinion must prevail, only one may be expressed. Whoever wants to change things can change neither policies, nor men, nor institutions; only violence remains. What holds for the "secular" dictatorships also holds for the monarchies. In the Arab Middle East, violence is not the continuation of politics by other means, and politics *is* violence. What prevails domestically also prevails internationally; Arab ministers of foreign affairs, whose role is purely to spin words to distract the gallery, are not the ones who make policy. That is done by the secret services. The countries of the region meet and confront one another through their secret services and the myriad front organizations that they have created. They confront each other in camouflage and by proxy. The names of these countless organizations—Brigade of Martyr X, Y Liberation Front, league, party, group, association—kaleidoscopic coalitions of emanations of secret services, occupy center stage. Because maneuvers behind the scenes always play such a significant role in the unending chess game with many players of Middle Eastern politics, no political statement is to be taken at face value. It is advisable to ask what ruse is hidden behind the ruse.[1]

It is in this context that we can understand the exportation of Wahhabism.

In the course of the year 2000 alone, according to the Saudi government daily *Ain-Al-Yaqeen*, the *Al-Haramayn* Islamic Foundation "opened eleven hundred mosques, schools, and Islamic centers," printed 13 million Islamic books, and employed 3,000 recruiters. The International Islamic Relief Organization (IIRO) built or completed 3,800 mosques, spent $45 million for Islamic education, and employed six thousand teachers and recruiters. The World Assembly of Muslim Youth (WAMY) provided $26 million in aid to students and for the establishment of mosques.[2]

These three organizations have been subject to international indictments and investigations in order to determine their role in the funding and logistics of terrorism, including but not limited to al-Qaeda. On the initiative of the U.S. Treasury Department—with Saudi Arabia tagging along although dragging its feet—the assets of the Bosnian and Somali branches of *Al-Haramayn*, a "private charitable and educational foundation," were frozen on March 11, 2002; it was suspected of diverting some of its funds to support terrorist activities. The foundation is not in the remotest sense private: the most important front organization in Saudi Arabia, it is under the direct control of the ministry of religious affairs, which provides it with enormous sums from the government to promote Islamic extremism around the world. The foundation operates in ninety countries; it has its own offices in fifty and operates out of Saudi embassies in forty. Since the police actions against two of its offices, the foundation has opened three new ones: the Saudi regime holds nothing against it. On June 3, 2002, the Bosnian police discovered a pile of evidence suggesting direct terrorist activities conducted from the foundation's offices.[3] According to admissions made to the American authorities by the al-Qaeda representative in Southeast Asia, Omar al-Faruq, "*Al-Haramayn* was the funding mechanism [for al-Qaeda] for all of Indonesia."[4]

In Bosnia again, in October 2001, NATO forces searched the offices of the Saudi High Commission for Relief to Bosnia-Herzegovina, founded by Prince Salman bin Abdulaziz and supported by King Fahd. In the offices of this charitable organization were found "before and after" photographs of the World Trade Center, the American embassies in Kenya and Tanzania destroyed by al-Qaeda bombs, and the American Navy vessel the USS *Cole*. There were also blueprints of official buildings in Washington; material for accurate forgeries of State Department badges; files on the use of crop-dusting planes; and anti-Semitic and anti-American documents intended for children.[5]

Then there was the case of Waed Hamza Jalaidan, a Saudi subject from a prominent family, and reportedly a co-founder of al-Qaeda. His friendship with Bin Laden and his notorious extremist views did not interfere with his career as a high Saudi official. Head of the finance division of the World Muslim League (WML), it was under his leadership that the Rabitat Trust was suspected of funding al-Qaeda and other terrorist groups. The Rabitat Trust had been set up in 1988 under the patronage of the Pakistani dictator Zia ul-Haq, the man who oversaw the Saudi-ization of Pakistan. On September 6, 2002, the U.S. Treasury Department announced that Jalaidan was suspected of funding terrorism and he was placed under arrest. Two days later, the interior minister publicly denied that his government was involved and suggested that Jalaidan was innocent. His career path was nonetheless that of a high-ranking Saudi official: for a time in Afghanistan, he headed the Saudi Red Crescent and the WML branch. After leaving Afghanistan in 1992, Jalaidan moved to Bosnia to supervise the Saudi High Commission for Relief to Bosnia-Herzegovina. He was placed at the head of the WML endowments. Among the members of the board of directors of the Rabitat Trust were the secretary general of the WML, the secretary general of the IIRO whom we have already encountered in the galaxy of terror, the president of the Saudi Arabia Chamber of Commerce, several members of the Pakistani government, the representative of the Saudi *Rabitat Alam al-Islami*, and the Saudi Prince Talal bin Abdulaziz.

As the analyst Alexei Alexiev has suggested, "Saudi charitable organizations are no more private than Soviet 'peace' movements were in the past. In a totalitarian dictatorship such as Saudi Arabia, 'private charitable organizations' exist only as tools for the execution of the policy of the government."[6] Members of the royal family and the entourage of the princes, royal officials, and Wahhabi clerics hold positions in all governing bodies of these organizations. The porosity and osmosis are total between these worldwide charitable organizations and the Wahhabi government and hierarchy.

With more than $4 billion of international assistance disbursed annually since 1975, according to official Saudi sources, more than half of which seems to have been devoted to "Islamic" activities, the Saudi budget for subversive activities exceeds by far the Soviet budget that had been devoted to this kind of activity.

The great majority of the approximately fifty Islamic organizations that, since September 11, 2001, have been searched, banned, closed down, and whose assets have been frozen, were either led or funded by Saudi Arabia: the SAAR Foundation—which received the huge sum of $1.7 billion for the year 1998 alone—was created by one of the richest Saudi families; the World Muslim League; the WAMY, the American division of which was headed by a brother of Bin Laden's; the Safia Trust; the Success Foundation; the Benevolence International Foundation; and many more.[7]

The usual Saudi protestations, along the lines of "we cannot control what our citizens do," sound all the more hollow because the government in 1993 banned the collection of money within the kingdom for "charitable" Muslim causes without authorization from the interior ministry; the decision had at the time the explicit purpose of reducing the flow of funds intended for Islamist causes linked to terrorism.[8] Personally implicated, Prince Salman Abdulaziz asserted in November 2002, in a tone half outraged, half distressed by the spitefulness of people: "If recipients used the assistance they received to commit bad acts, we have no responsibility for that."

In any event, Princes Muhammad al-Faisal al-Saud, Turki al-Faisal al-Saud, and Sultan bin Abdulaziz have been accused of murder and complicity in three thousand assassinations in a complaint filed by families of victims of September 11, along with several members of the Bin Laden family and enterprises of the group, and various organizations and Saudi banks. (It should be noted that the lawsuits against the Saudi Kingdom; the princes; Al Baraka, Saleh Abdullah Kamel; Tariq, Omar, and Bakr Bin Laden; and some of the organizations and banks were dismissed by the U.S. district court in January 2005.)[9]

The report *Terrorism Financing: Roots and Trends of Saudi Terrorism financing*, presented to the United Nations on December 19, 2002, at the request of the president of the Security Council, by the French investigator Jean-Charles Brisard, is damning. It establishes that in one decade, Saudi Arabia transferred one half billion dollars to al-Qaeda. "One can only wonder about the real ability and the desire of the kingdom to exercise control over the use of religious alms within and outside the kingdom," he writes, going on to say that groups that are classified as terrorists by the United States and the European Union continue to benefit from Saudi largesse, in formal violation of the commitments made and renewed by the rulers of the kingdom. Brisard's study establishes that the organized collection of *zakat* (alms) is controlled by the department of the *Zakat* and income tax of the Saudi ministry of finance and national economy.[10] In a royal decree of 1994, King Fahd created a Supreme Council of Islamic Affairs charged first with getting around the deep reluctance of many *ulamas* favorable, if not to the letter, at least to the spirit of Bin Laden and his accomplices, and second, with "centralizing, supervising, and controlling the requests for assistance coming from Islamic groups"—a kind of clearing house headed by his brother Prince Sultan.[11]

"Saudi cooperation in the war against the funding of terrorism is largely insufficient, not to say inconsistent," according to Brisard. In 1999, the minister and adviser to King Fahd, Abdullah al-Turki, became business partners with Muhammad Zouaydi, who, at the time, was the head of al-Qaeda finances in Europe. Zouaydi was prosecuted in Spain three years later, for participation in terrorist conspiracy. Al-Turki is now secretary general of the World Muslim League.[12]

On November 25, 2002, the American press revealed that a task force of the National Security Council (NSC) had just given President Bush a plan of action intended to compel Saudi Arabia to go after the financiers of terrorism within three months, or else the United States would unilaterally take its own steps to prosecute them. Along with the plan, developed interdepartmentally in Washington, there was a list—still classified at this writing—of the twelve principal financiers of international terrorism, seven of whom are Saudis. Those names appear in this book.[13] According to the ABC television network, those names had been discreetly turned over to the Saudi authorities nine months earlier.[14] Richard Shelby, chairman of the Senate Intelligence Committee, commented: "I am afraid that a large number of the members of the royal family or those close to the royal family have helped or supported the terrorists, voluntarily or not." The next day, the Menl press agency wrote: "The United States has discreetly concluded that Saudi Arabia has not stopped funding al-Qaeda. Government and congressional sources report that the kingdom has done nothing. . . . The CIA has traced the path of millions of dollars from Saudi Arabia to al-Qaeda during the past year." In Congress, a well-informed source reported: "There is not the shadow of a doubt about the facts. The CIA has informed the principal congressional committees: Saudi Arabia has violated its commitment to stop funding al-Qaeda. Disagreements now concern what should be done."[15]

In mid-December, the Council on Foreign Relations, the New York policy think tank, published the harsh report of its independent task force on the funding of terrorism.[16] It proposed that the American administration put pressure on Saudi Arabia, even at the risk of a sharp reaction likely to destabilize the Saudi government. "For years, individuals and charitable organizations based in Saudi Arabia have represented the principal source of funds for al-Qaeda and, for years, the Saudi authorities have turned a blind eye." The head of the task force, Maurice R. Greenberg, CEO of the huge AIG insurance group, was emphatic: "The administration ought to be much more vigorous" toward Saudi Arabia. It should "leave no respite" to the Saudi government; "remaining seated in our corner doing nothing is not an option."

As though to confirm the rising anger, *Newsweek* set off a small bomb: the tidy sum of $130,000 had been transferred in early 2000 from the bank account of Princess Haifa al-Faisal, wife of the Saudi ambassador to the United States, Prince Bandar—in fact the "minister of American affairs" of Saudi Arabia—to the account of Omar al-Bayoumi, a Saudi "student" in San Diego. The student, who had long worked in the Saudi defense ministry, later met two of the September 11 hijackers at the airport and helped them to settle and get acclimatized. It seems that Al-Bayoumi was a Saudi military intelligence agent. The man was in contact with an employee of the Islamic affairs section of the embassy. That section, as in all Saudi embassies, resembles the old *rezidentura* of the KGB in a Soviet embassy. The money provided by the helpful princess had then moved, in mysterious ways, into the pockets of the future hijackers. The contradictory, embarrassed, lying, and flatly ridiculous explanations offered by the ambassador and his chorus of sycophants merely aggravated the case for the Saudis: it was by chance, by accident, unknown to those involved, the effect of generous charity that had been abused, that the transfer had taken place.[17]

Let us not forget: with the boldness that only absolute power confers, the princes have never stopped claiming, insinuating, and asserting not only the total innocence of Saudi Arabia for the attacks of September 11 and terror in general, but they have also not stopped accusing Israel and its intelligence service, the Mossad, of having been the "real" authors of the attacks. On October 22, 2001, Prince Sultan, the minister of defense, told the Kuwaiti daily *As-Siyassah* that another "power" had to be involved, because the United States was not "an easy or feasible target." And he went on: "The great question then arises: who is hiding behind this terrorism? And who carried out this complex and carefully planned terrorist operation? Osama bin Laden and his companions claim that they accomplished this well prepared action. But we ask for our part: are Bin Laden and his associates the only ones behind it, or is there another power possessing advanced technical expertise that acted with them?"[18]

Lest anyone believe that this was a gaffe made by a prince, his brother Prince Nayef bin Abdulaziz, the interior minister, joined in. To the question: "Are there al-Qaeda 'sleeper' cells in the kingdom?" he answered: "That is an exaggeration. In the kingdom of Saudi Arabia as elsewhere, there are certain attitudes adopted by certain people"— which sheds a good deal of light on the question. Then he went to the heart of the matter: "The relations between the Saudi and American governments are solid despite the Zionist controlled media that have manipulated the events of September 11 to turn American opinion against the Arabs and against Islam. We have major questions, we wonder who perpetrated the events of September 11 and who benefited from them. Whom did the events of September 11 benefit? I think they [the Zionists] are the ones behind these events." Vigorously condemning terrorism ("we have to protect young people from it"), the prince went on to say that he "strongly suspects that these terrorist organizations are in contact with some foreign intelligence service working under the direction of the Israeli secret services against Arabs and Muslims . . ." He also remarked that it was "impossible that nineteen young men, fifteen of whom were Saudis, had carried out the September 11 operation . . . [and that] these men were either agents, or ignorant, because their action was against Islam and against Muslims."[19]

When a *Newsweek* reporter asked a third princeling, the minister of foreign affairs Saud al-Faisal, what the Americans would think when they heard Prince Nayef raving about a "Zionist plot," Saud merely repeated, with some embarrassment, his brother's foolishness while minimizing it as much as he could: it's hard to get away when your hand still is in the cookie-jar.[20] When the journalist asked him at the end of the interview to justify "the bogus stories in your press claiming that all the Jews want to use Muslim blood to make matzos," his royal highness firmly stated: "We want to make that completely stop." *Newsweek*: "Shouldn't someone start by reducing the venom?" The prince: "We have started."

The beginning was hardly obvious. On March 10, 2002, the government daily *Al-Riyadh* published a column by "Dr. Umayna al-Jalahma" of King Faisal University. According to the article by this woman professor, Jews use the blood of Christian and Muslim adolescents to make matzos. She described in great detail the method used to obtain blood, a traditional practice of the Jews at Passover. What a beginning!

If there is one example of pathological hatred on the part of the Saudi-Wahhabi complex, it is, as we have seen on numerous occasions, the hatred of Jews. The impertinence of these second-class individuals, these *dhimmis* who used to be scorned for their weakness, now guilty of having defeated—a supreme humiliation—the glorious Arab armies, and the unbearable pride they have taken in building their own state and defending it has raised the level of hatred to fever pitch. Since 1967, the funding of Arafat's Palestinian terrorism has been a constant of Saudi policy. The violently anti-Semitic speech delivered at the United Nations in November 1974 by the Palestinian leader—not two years after the massacre of Israeli athletes at the Olympic Games in Munich—had everything to do with the new Saudi power, that protected him as it had welcomed the war criminal Haj Amin al-Husseini, organizer of the Muslim legions of the Waffen SS, as did the "Zionism-racism" resolution adopted by the UN General Assembly.

There is thus one constant: the funding of terror against Israel by Saudi Arabia. There is complete osmosis between the funding of Palestinian terrorism and the funding of Islamic terrorism in general. Yasin al-Qadi, a "specially designated global terrorist," identified by the U.S. Treasury Department as a financier of al-Qaeda, transmitted exactly $820,000 to an Islamic "charitable" organization in Chicago, which turned the sum over to a Hamas weapons dealer. The organization, the Quranic Literary Institute, was headed, according to the FBI, by "an avowed Hamas agent," arrested and convicted for arms trafficking for Hamas in Israel.[21]

Documents seized in the offices of the Palestinian Authority by the Israeli army are damning. The report that reproduces, translates, and comments on them indicates:

1. "During the operation 'Defensive Shield,' Saudi and Palestinian documents were seized indicating systematic and continuous transfers of large sums of money to the Palestinians to 'support the *Intifada*.' Among the various institutions, the Saudi Committee for the Support of the al-Quds *Intifada*, headed by the Saudi interior minister [Nayef], is the most prominent.

2. "The documents seized demonstrate that Saudi support was not only of a religious [and] humanitarian nature, as Saudi spokesmen in the United States claim. The documents clearly reveal that Saudi Arabia, among other things, has systematically and continuously transferred large sums of money to the families of suicide bombers and to Hamas (which is on the U.S. list of terrorist organizations). According to the seized documents, the Saudi Committee for the Support of the *Intifada* was fully aware of the intended recipients of the funds, the families of terrorists who carried out fatal attacks against Israeli cities in which hundreds of Israelis were killed and wounded . . .

3. "The transfer of Saudi funds to Palestinians has three implications.

    a. It encourages terrorist attacks, including suicide bombings. The family of a dead terrorist receives a donation from Iraq and one from Saudi Arabia . . . which we estimate at six years worth of wages. . . . All that considerably increases the motivation for terrorist attacks, including suicide bombings.

    b. It strengthens the terrorist apparatus of Hamas . . . the endowments from Saudi Arabia and the Gulf States constitute the largest portion of its budget . . .

    c. It increases the status of Hamas in the Palestinian population."[22]

The royal family at least acts in a coherent manner: it has not varied since the founding dynasty; it changes only under the pressure of circumstances, when the survival of the dynasty is at stake.

CHAPTER 10

The Export of Terrorism

Understanding of the scope of the direct and indirect involvement of the highest authorities of the kingdom in the international networks of terror would be incomplete without an examination of the Saudi-Pakistani complex. We have seen the way in which Saudi Arabia asserted control over Pakistan, or, if you like, the Wahhabi acid bath into which Saudi influence plunged Pakistan. This new examination will allow us to shed light on certain aspects of American policy, that of the CIA in particular, toward the Taliban, their sponsors the Pakistani Inter-Services Intelligence (ISI), and the benefactors of both, the Saudi kingdom.

In contrast to the dismal attitude of Jimmy Carter, who had been "surprised" by the Soviet invasion of Afghanistan, so greatly had his confidence in Leonid Brezhnev been abused—like Chamberlain's in Hitler, with even less excuse—Ronald Reagan came to power with a solid understanding of the Soviet phenomenon. This is what enabled him and his advisers to grasp not only the vulnerabilities of the "Evil Empire," but also to exploit them coherently and systematically. The idea of "imperial overstretch" is a striking formulation summarizing the nature of the problem that the Soviet Union had created for itself: the empire was reaching the outer limits of its capacities. Economically as well as militarily, technologically, mentally, morally, and politically, the USSR was living well beyond its means. It was stretching its resources to the breaking point, and the pressure had to be increased until that point arrived. Afghanistan was one of the principal fronts in this war of tension. Victory in the cold war came through these final battles.

Against the advice of his wisest military advisers, notably Marshal Nikolai Ogarkov, who was all too aware of the technological backwardness of the country, Brezhnev, obsessed with quantity, territory, and control at any price, ordered the invasion of an Afghanistan that was already subservient to Soviet power. Reagan and his team, including the underground warrior William J. Casey, his Director of Central Intelligence, decided to arm and support the Afghan resistance and to help the Soviet bear to get tied down in the forbidding Afghan terrain. To accomplish this, the Americans had weapons—including the famous Stinger anti-aircraft missile, which deprived Soviet forces of air superiority by downing their helicopters and killing their pilots. They had financial resources, but wanted to increase them. They needed a strategic base to organize, relieve, and support the resistance. Only Pakistan met these criteria. The interest shown by the Saudis in the anticommunist struggle against "atheistic materialism," the oil aims behind the Russian drive toward warm-water ports, and the broad scope of relations between Saudi Arabia and Pakistan made the alliance almost a matter of course. Opportunity created the thieves.

In alliances, every partner brings to the table not only its capacities, but also its intentions, its vision, and its interests: there are no innocent alliances between states. Despite the shared opposition to the Soviet advance, the course of events was to reveal the magnitude of the divergences and lead to a parting of the ways. As Roosevelt, appropriately entering into an alliance with the monstrous Stalin to defeat the monstrous Hitler but, carried away by his enthusiasm, allowing him needlessly to pocket half of Europe as payment, Washington, carried away with characteristic American enthusiasm and pragmatism, wanted to "get the job done" at any price, and agreed to close its eyes to the evils of its allies of the moment. Eyes were closed all the more easily because the geostrategic nature of the cold war in western and southern Asia lent itself to that course: India was allied with the USSR, while China and Pakistan were allies of the United States; Saudi Arabia, the gas station, was an ally, even though it had just inflicted violent shocks on Western economies. In the face of revolutionary Iran, American geopolitics in the Middle East was in tatters: the remaining ally was all the more precious. There are often good reasons for making mistakes and acting badly. The road to Hell, we have long been told, is paved with good intentions.

Pakistan was at home in the Afghan theater and its environs. Suddenly, the North-West Frontier Province had become the central point in the cold war, from which emanated the hot war in Afghanistan. The masters of Pakistan, the ISI, received huge Saudi and American payments, and it was up to them to distribute them. We have already seen how the ISI excessively favored the most extremist of the Afghan fundamentalists. Worse was to come. The ISI completely controlled the huge infrastructure of guerilla training financed by the CIA and created around it an impermeable *cordon sanitaire* to prevent the CIA from getting inside.[1] Whoever is surprised by the cowardice of the American intelligence service should read the memoir by the former CIA officer Robert Baer, *See No Evil: The True Story of a Ground Soldier in the CIA's War on Terrorism*.[2]

If we are to believe the head of the Afghan bureau of the ISI, General Mohammad Yousaf, the Director General of the ISI through the crucial years from 1980 to 1987, General Akhtar Abdur Rahman, "faced many problems with the Americans and the CIA." Akhtar adamantly refused to allow the Americans to train the *mujahedeen* themselves or even to have direct access to them. "Akhtar never allowed Americans to become directly involved in the *Jihad*," but on the contrary insisted on "keeping Americans out" of the entire training and supply system. The ISI was the sole "provider" of training for the *jihad* in Pakistan and Afghanistan. "[N]o American or Chinese instructor was ever involved in giving training on any kind of weapon or equipment to the *mujahedeen*. . . . This was a deliberate, carefully considered policy that we steadfastly refused to change despite mounting pressure from the CIA, and later from the U.S. Defense Department, to allow them to take over." The ISI, armed with unconditional support from the Pakistani government, could even impose unilateral restrictions on visits by CIA and other U.S. officials to *mujahedeen* training camps although the U.S. government was financing them through the CIA. When the pressure grew too great, the ISI orchestrated deceptive visits to satisfy the American ally.[3]

What was the reason for this secretiveness? Islamabad was training not only Afghan *jihadis* and legions of Arab extremists, filtered, conditioned, and trained by Pakistani and Afghan Deobandi and Wahhabi extremists, but also thousands of *jihadis* who had come from Indian Kashmir and were prepared for the merciless war that Pakistan was conducting there against India. For Afghanistan, it is estimated that 70 percent of the aid intended for the Afghan resistance went in fact to the ultra-Islamist parties, in particular the Hezb-e-Islami of Gulbuddin Hekmatyar, the ISI's favorite hatchet man, who was virulently anti-American. The ISI was also able to purchase the good will of Saudi Arabia. "Islamabad calculated . . . that the Saudis would be the most effective advocates for American military assistance . . . The ISI also needed its Saudi counterparts to endorse Gulbuddin Hekmatyar as the most genuine and successful *mujahedeen* leader so that most of the U.S.-funded support could go to his Hezb-e-Islami despite its virulent anti-American policies."[4]

The Islamist Pakistani dictator Zia-ul-Haq, who had accelerated the frenetic Islamization of Pakistan initiated by his predecessor Ali Bhutto, died in a 1988 airplane accident (often attributed to the Soviet secret services) along with the American ambassador and the head of the ISI. Bhutto's daughter Benazir, a feminist pinup for the Western press, succeeded Zia. She was largely a puppet of the ISI and the Islamist camp. Feminism was appropriate only for rich feudal heiresses educated at Oxford and dabbling in "Socialist" politics. She forged a long-term strategic alliance with Iran, Syria, China, and North Korea: ballistic missiles and military nuclear capability on one side, and extreme Islamism supported by Saudi Arabia on the other. Islamism, from this perspective, was the only ideology capable of avoiding the breakup of Pakistan into centrifugal ethnic components. "Consequently, the ISI's support for and sponsorship of sisterly Islamist terrorist movements throughout the Arab world became a cornerstone of Pakistan's national security policies," according to Yossef Bodansky.[5]

This strategic reorientation came into full force under the direction of the new head of the ISI, General Hamid Gul. A fanatically extremist Islamist, Gul was known for establishing far-reaching relations with Iran, Sudan, and Iraq. As an example, we might mention the summit conference of leading members of this "International" held in Khartoum in December 1993 under the auspices of the Armed Islamic Movement and the Arab and Muslim People's Conference, two front organizations designed to bring together terrorists of all countries. In the Pakistani delegation were two close collaborators of Benazir Bhutto, General Mirza Aslam Beg, former army chief of staff, and General Hamid Gul. The ISI offered its partners a whole panoply of training programs, lasting from four months to two years. From them there radiated thousands of officers and soldiers of the international *jihad*, including the Arab *jihadis* of Bin Laden, who fought little in Afghanistan, except after the departure of the Soviet troops: it was in the Afghan civil wars that they won renown, and in the unbridled Islamism they showed when they returned home. The

Algerian "Afghans" were the shock troops of the GIA in the Algerian civil war.

The ISI "invented" the Taliban. Saudi Arabia was delighted, but certain aspects of them troubled the Saudi leadership. In early 1995, Prince Turki al-Faisal came to Benazir Bhutto with a tempting proposal: in return for very generous financial assistance and massive support with the Americans, the ISI would agree to contain the "Afghans" of Saudi nationality, those angry young men sent off to the Afghan *jihad* by Saudi leaders reassured to see their youthful and brutal energy dissipated several thousands of kilometers distant from Riyadh. Saudi Arabia would use all its influence to persuade Washington to lift sanctions against Pakistan and to secure for it substantial economic and technical assistance. Turki even promised to put the Saudi public relations machine in Washington at the service of Pakistan. Benazir Bhutto made all the requested promises, and reaped the rewards during an exceptionally fruitful trip to Washington in April 1995.[6] As might have been expected, the ISI did little or nothing to moderate the fervor of its extremist protégés.

When the various currents of the terrorist "International" came to an agreement to expand the use of Karachi as a financing center, Osama bin Laden was put in charge. Prince Turki, who seems at first not to have known of the role given to Bin Laden, "assured Islamabad that . . . Riyadh would tolerate the use of Saudi financial institutions and international companies for . . . 'humanitarian' operations, even in the United States." On the other hand, "When Riyadh was later informed of Bin Laden's role in the Karachi center, Prince Turki ignored the information and continued to allow the use of Saudi financial institutions [for the funding of terrorism]." Bodansky concludes: "By now Riyadh was so concerned with the revival of Islamist terrorism and subversion in Saudi Arabia that it was ready to do almost anything to ensure that these Islamists operated outside Saudi Arabia."[7]

The Al-Saud dynasty and Bin Laden are in reality the two faces of a decidedly troubling kingdom. We have described the complex dance that simultaneously opposes and brings together the Saudi royal family and its former protégé Osama bin Laden. Reasons of state and reasons of *jihad* match and contradict each other. In Saudi Arabia, nothing is ever black or white, everything is under a gray veil; what is important are the nuances and the tones of gray. The Saudi *modus operandi* has never varied. Just as King Abdulaziz ibn Saud told anyone who would hear him that he had nothing to do with the *Ikhwan* that he had created almost from scratch, so concentric circles and buffers of multiple interfaces separate the royal family from the terrorist enterprises that it ultimately finances and supports. It does not need to control them at the tactical and operational level: *de minimis non curat praetor*, said the Romans; rulers do not need to worry about minor questions. That makes it possible to issue denials when they are caught red-handed. The Saudis, royal and terrorist, are spread over a diversified spectrum marked by a basic continuity, the Wahhabi credo, and by a variety of positions on the spectrum.

In this context, the tortuous history of the antagonistic relations between the royal creator and the *jihadi* creature provides a wonderful illustration of the organic but complicated relations that the royal family maintains with terrorism.

On the occasions when he returned home, the young Bin Laden, who had been a *jihadi* fighter for several years in Afghanistan, used the privileged contacts of his family with the Saudi royal family and established a relationship with Prince Salman and Prince Turki, leaders of the support network for the Afghan *mujahedeen* during the war with the Soviets. He was given the mission of organizing elements of the special forces of the Saudi National Guard to fight against the "republican" regime in Yemen. The Al-Sauds had always had the policy of dividing Yemen in order to rule in Arabia. The adage "Arabia will be happy only if Yemen is unhappy" was attributed to King Ibn Saud. To reward his enthusiastic efforts, King Fahd in person offered Bin Laden lucrative contracts for his companies, including the expansion of the Prophet's Mosque in Medina. Bin Laden politely refused, asking rather for an increase in aid to the Afghan *jihad*, which did wonders for his reputation. In any event, his father's company was given the contract that had been offered him by the king.[8] Through the 1980s and specifically during the first Afghan war, the relationship between Turki and Bin Laden deepened. "Like his father, Osama became a conduit for the quiet flow of Saudi funds to deniable causes . . . [He] personally handled the politically sensitive funding of the Islamist groups considered hostile to the house of al-Saud and other conservative regimes in Arabia. The cynically pragmatic Riyadh government was happy to see these Islamists operating in distant Afghanistan and thus away from their homeland. Paying for their keep in distant Afghanistan was a cheap price for stability."[9]

In 1989, returning from victory in Afghanistan, Bin Laden was welcomed as a hero and celebrated by Saudi society. An icon for the masses, and a justification for the elite, he became a celebrity. The official edition of his audiocassettes, on the theme of the eternal victory of the *jihad*, was issued in 250,000 copies. "Riyadh capitalized on the Islamist message to enhance its own posture. Riyadh's pleasure with Osama was manifested financially as the Bin Laden businesses received numerous government and private contracts." When Saddam Hussein invaded Kuwait in August 1990, Bin Laden hurried to see Prince Sultan to present his plan for defending Saudi Arabia with a *jihad*, which he also presented to Prince Turki. The princes were in a panic: even if he had to battle fiercely with his court *ulamas* to have them accept the decision, King Fahd called on the American *infidels* to protect the territory of "the two holy cities." Strictly observant Wahhabis were nauseated, starting with Bin Laden. A loyal but critical subject, Bin Laden let his discontent be known. The royal family behaved as it always had: in discreet conversations they threatened the lucrative contracts and expropriation of his companies, and they widened the threat to his family and the entire Bin Laden group; they threatened to cut the special ties between the royal family and the Bin Laden family, and to bankrupt the company.

"At the same time, however, Saudi intelligence continued to maintain contacts with Osama bin Laden to make sure he did not cross over to the anti-Saudi subversive movement and to ask favors from him, mainly to reach out to segments in the vast network of 'Afghans' and like-minded Islamists all over the world on their behalf."[10]

Prince Sultan, for his part, never broke off contact, which made it possible for Saudi funds to continue to flow to the *jihadis* from around the world who gravitated around Bin Laden: a paradoxical situation as long as you disregard the tribal and personal nature of political relationships in Saudi Arabia. The kingdom did strip Bin Laden of his nationality in April 1994, and "expropriated" his Saudi assets, while the rest of the family "denied" the black sheep. This was all a façade: nationality means nothing, family everything in the tribal context. The family continued to see, visit, and finance Osama.[11] On the one hand, pressure was put on the Sudanese authorities for them to expel Bin Laden and send him to Afghanistan; on the other, threatening letters were sent to the personal fax machines of Princes Turki, Nayef, and others, with highly secret numbers. This is a normal means of negotiation in Arab politics, feint and counter-feint, threat and counter-threat, parry and counter-parry. When the ISI, wanting to be sure of the exact status of Bin Laden in the eyes of the Saudi authorities, had him placed under relaxed house arrest in Kandahar, watched by a Taliban group under their control, and asked Riyadh—in light of the public proclamations denouncing Bin Laden—whether they wanted him extradited, an official and formal response arrived a few days later, which was presented in connection with his duties by the Saudi ambassador: "Mr. Bin Laden has committed no crime in Saudi Arabia. The kingdom has never asked for his arrest." Riyadh never changed its attitude.

Bin Laden returned the favor. His "declaration of war" on the United States, a twelve-page charter for his group's action, emphasized that the enemy was America, that a *jihad* against Saudi Arabia was only a minor element in the global *jihad* against the United States that had absolute priority. Gently, Bin Laden explained: "It is crucial for us [Muslims] to be patient and to cooperate in righteousness and piety and to raise [our] awareness to the fact that the highest priority, after faith, is to repel the incursive enemy. . . . [I]t is crucial to overlook many of the issues of bickering [among Muslims] in order to unite our ranks so that we can repel the greater *kafir* [infidel]."[12] It would be difficult to speak more clearly: armistice and cooperation. The position was strengthened on May 17, 1998, when the World Islamic Front for Jihad against Jews and Crusaders, Bin Laden's organization properly speaking, issued a basic declaration. "The Arab/Muslim rulers, including the House of al-Saud, were now defined as victims, to one extent or another, of U.S. oppression and presence. In the Islamist view, once the United States and Westernization were evicted from the Hub of Islam [the Arab world], even those rulers would adopt Muslim ways and rejoin the Muslim Nation," that is, Bin Laden and his associates. Prince Turki could get back on the road and restore ties.[13]

In early summer 1998, Turki and the Saudi minister for the *hajj* and religious property arrived in Kandahar with new offers: protect Arabia by restraining Saudi Islamists in exchange for lavish Saudi support. Shortly afterward, two members of two great Saudi families knocked on the door of Bin Laden's compound in Kandahar with a large sum of money and a request that he not conduct operations in Saudi Arabia. It was clearly explained to him that the small fortune they were carrying came in part from the royal family.[14] Agreement was reached in July. "In mid-September 1998

Riyadh was actively formulating a new anti-American strategy that would enable it to satisfy the Islamists without arousing Washington's ire. Those in the House of al-Saud have no illusion, however, that if forced to choose between pacifying Bin Laden or the Clinton administration, they would pacify, placate, and appease Bin Laden."[15]

Meanwhile, Crown Prince Abdallah bin Abdulaziz was solidifying his position, as King Fahd was sinking further into his intermittent coma. "Prince Abdallah is a devout Islamist and a staunch supporter of the *ulama's* political power. He is also a staunch supporter of pan-Arab and pan-Islamic causes, including worldwide *jihads*, and moreover is anti-Western and mistrustful of the United States."[16] God protect me from my friends.

CHAPTER II

Washington on the Auction Block

"If the reputation, then, builds that the Saudis take care of friends when they leave office, you'd be surprised how much better friends you have who are just coming into office." Thus spoke Prince Bandar bin Sultan, grandson of Abdulaziz Ibn Saud, and son of the current defense minister, ambassador of Saudi Arabia to the United States, or rather, as he is known, Saudi minister of American affairs, as the *Washington Post* reported on February 11, 2002.

A foreign ambassador must obviously have an extraordinary degree of impudence to boast so openly about how he "takes care" of officials of the nation in which he is a guest. To show such gall, one must be certain of one's impunity and convinced of one's omnipotence. But he said more. He worried about the "clash of civilizations" and, heart on his sleeve, insisted: "If we start to speak ill of the religion of others, there is no more common sense."[1] The ambassador spends so much time in his large compound in Potomac, a fashionable Washington suburb, or in his compound in an upscale neighborhood of Aspen, or in his country house in Surrey, England, that he clearly has no time to go to Saudi Arabia with his eyes and ears open. He does not read the Saudi press. He never goes to a mosque and never listens to the vindictive *khutba*. He listens neither to his *Grand Mufti* nor to any other high religious dignitary. He is no doubt too busy with manipulating the Americans.

Saudi Arabia enjoys a status of extraordinary impunity in Washington, or at least it has until now. It has held over the United States the perpetual threat of blackmail through oil since its success with the oil embargoes of 1973 and 1979. It interferes in American political life. It buys politicians, government officials, journalists, academics, diplomats, colonels, generals, and intelligence officers. It buys "experts" at bargain prices, and countless propagandists and lobbyists. When it sees fit, it demands that television programs be censored. It has flooded the circles of power with its petrodollars. It demands that American companies accept its political conditions in order to be able to do business, even in violation of the U.S. Constitution. When Americans are assassinated by terrorists in Saudi Arabia, the authorities block investigations, put spokes in the wheels of FBI agents, and lie through their teeth. When a few hundred thousand American soldiers were on its territory to save the dynasty's skin, they were denied the right to conduct Christian or Jewish religious services. American troops stationed on Saudi soil are prohibited from celebrating Christmas: Christmas trees are destroyed on entering the kingdom. While the Saudis do as they like in the United States, on Saudi territory the Americans' hands are tied. The Saudis blithely violate American laws, while Americans, like all other foreigners, are subject to the brutal and irrational whims of the *mutawayin*, the religious police.

Does his almost royal highness the heir apparent Prince Abdallah dislike American policy in the Middle East? "Starting today, you [the Americans] come from Uruguay, as they say," that is, from nowhere. "From now on, we will protect our national interest, without regard for American interests in the region"[2] (as if Saudi Arabia had been chiefly motivated by selfless love of America!) When he visited President George W. Bush in Crawford in April 2002,

Abdallah benefited from a story by *New York Times* reporter Patrick Tyler who reported Abdallah's barely veiled threats of triggering a new oil embargo.

In order for this endless series of insults, affronts, and attacks not to provoke the Americans, hardly inclined toward humility or the forgiveness of injuries, and very conscious of their power, either an explosion of anger or harsh reprisals, an inhibiting factor has to play a role: the Saudi lobby. There is a good deal of talk, especially outside the United States, about the Jewish lobby and its influence. I remember with amusement the question a French television journalist asked me, whispering and slightly uneasy: "And the power . . . of the Jews . . . in Washington?" not realizing that the American Jewish community is riven by deep divides so that it joins political battles in disarray, whether they involve the policies of Ariel Sharon or social issues. There may be Jewish lobbies, plural please. On the other hand, the Saudi lobby does not emanate from a popular base in the United States itself, but from the embassy of the Kingdom of Saudi Arabia: it operates in a unified and centralized manner, with virtually unlimited financial resources.

Of course, oil has played a central role in this history since 1945. Almost from the very beginning, Aramco identified itself with Saudi Arabia. The Aramco lobby (a better expression than the oil lobby: not all companies have the same interests or the same politics) pressed President Truman in 1948 not to recognize the state of Israel "for fear of offending the Arab countries, particularly Saudi Arabia."[3] In 1952, when Saudi forces attacked the territory of the sultanate of Oman, Aramco mobilized in favor of Saudi Arabia and its oil and territorial demands. In 1973, the oil companies sent a delegation to the Secretary of State to ask that the United States support King Faisal, and frequently entered into public debate on the theme of "Saudi-American friendship." One of Aramco's parent companies, SoCal, had no hesitations: "[W]e need to take some positive action whereby we can demonstrate to SAG [Saudi Arabian government] that we are not unmindful of their interests and problems."[4] The chairman of Standard Oil, Otto Miller, sent a letter to the company's 260,000 stockholders and 40,000 employees urging the United States to "work more closely with the Arab governments to build up and enhance our relations with the Arab people."[5] Where was the legendary arrogance of the oilmen? The arrogance of the multinationals?

When Saudi Arabia, unable to implement on its own the oil embargo that it had decreed, demanded that Aramco take care of it, the company then set up against the United States an embargo decreed by a foreign power to which it gave full allegiance. "American imperialism" made a pitiful showing.

An American court had earlier harshly criticized the company, decrying the "film of oil which blurs the vision of Aramco."[6]

Aramco did not merely have opinions. The company made sure to disseminate them, to insert them into American politics and the public mind, functioning like a ministry for friendship with Saudi Arabia, or an American Department of Saudi Interests. "Since 1967," according to one analyst, "Aramco has been sponsoring, facilitating, and subsidizing a broad network of political and 'educational' activities in the United States designed both to create an illusory image of support for the Arab position in the Arab-Israeli dispute and to weaken public, congressional, and governmental support for Israel. Aramco has disbursed more than $5 million through 1984 to scores of lobbyists, academicians, educational institutions, and even groups intimately connected with the PLO. In some instances, Aramco helped create organizations from scratch, while in other cases, Aramco entered into tactical alliances with such radical countries as Libya and Iraq in order to sustain the active political operations of various groups."[7] Special funding went to a program for "the promotion of Islam, Arab culture, and international understanding [in order to] assist programs to disseminate balanced, objective and accurate information about the situation in the Middle East which led to the displacement of the Palestinians from their homeland." The donations committee of Aramco, made up of company insiders and the Saudi oil minister Yamani, contributed to what a State Department official called "the unofficial academic wing of the PLO," the Institute for Palestine Studies, and its quarterly journal, *The Journal of Palestine Studies*. The committee also funded an organization called Americans for Justice in the Middle East, which worked directly with the PLO and faithfully reproduced the worst excesses of its propaganda. The committee provided more than 40 percent of the funding for the Middle East Institute (MEI) in Washington, whose mission was to translate into intellectual terms Saudi and Arab political positions on the conflict. Americans for the Middle East, American Near East Refugee Aid, and other organizations benefited from the self-interested largesse of Aramco. Americans for Middle East Understanding, established in 1969, "evolved into a major organization within the Arab lobby." It also received funds from Prince Khaled bin Sultan and from the World Muslim League. Aramco money also supported the pro-Palestinian propaganda of the National Council of Churches.[8] A National Council of Arab-American Relations was established using the same resources.

"When somebody like the king would call me in and express his dismay or inability to do what he thought we ought to do, we had to respond to this request in some way or at least show that we were interested in their aspirations . . . we simply couldn't fail to cooperate on a reasonable request," according to the former president of Aramco, Frank Jungers.[9]

In this symbiosis between Saudi Arabia and Aramco, the oil company was the hostage and the tool, and the dynasty controlled the game. Just how far the housebroken Aramco was prepared to lower itself was revealed when the consortium agreed to extend to its own employees the prohibition against Jews working in the kingdom's oil fields, a clear violation of the U.S. Constitution.

One of the mechanisms for the extension of this pro-Saudi servility was the application of the Arab boycott against Israel. The weapon of the economic boycott is, if not commonly used, not unheard of on the international stage. What is out of the ordinary is the extension of a boycott: any country or any company trading in one way or another with a particular country would itself be boycotted. What this meant was that, since the Arab countries had decreed an economic boycott of Israel, any company trading with Israel would be boycotted. And, under the direction of Saudi Arabia, which had the appropriate means of blackmail, the "secondary" boycott was extended to a third level: no company hoping to avoid the boycott could sign a contract with a boycotted company. The interference with the mechanisms of the market was intolerable, the illegality blatant and unbearable. Under threat, many American companies began to apply the provisions of the boycott without even being asked. The construction firm Bechtel, in charge of huge contracts in Saudi Arabia, prohibited its subcontractors and suppliers from having any contracts with Israel or with any boycotted company. A certain number of major banks, such as Chase, Morgan Guaranty, Bank of America, and Citibank, began issuing letters of credit including documentation proving that the company concerned had no relationship with Israel. The Saudi minister of planning, Hisham Nazer, pulled no punches: "[I]t is up to U.S. firms with vital interests here [in the Middle East] to safeguard the right to work and earn. Others are willing and ready to take their place."[10]

The logic of the economy directed and controlled by the state and religion overcame the logic of the market. The Wahhabi economy imposed itself on American capitalism. It arbitrarily restricted the freedom of choice of market participants in order to foster purely political and religious principles. It was a veritable return to the Dark Ages.

When American public opinion grew alarmed and bills began to be introduced in Congress, Prince Saud al-Faisal announced "that Saudi Arabia would not countenance any anti-boycott legislation, and warn[ed] of adverse effects on American trade, economy, and energy."[11] Blackmail had become a choice tool of international politics. But companies that had contracts with Saudi Arabia were absolutely convinced: "We can't afford to make the Arabs mad at this time."[12] It seems that the time and the circumstances are never right to "make the Arabs mad."

Saudi Arabia buys things in Washington. Since the oil crisis, it has bought more than $100 billion worth of modern armaments from the United States which, more often than not, it cannot put in service, pilot, use, or repair, whether what is involved are air war management devices such as Boeing AWACS planes, F-15 and F-16 fighters, Abrams M-1 tanks, Bradley armored personnel carriers, ships, or radar systems. One cannot plunge and keep an entire society into archaic Islamism with impunity. Two thirds of the doctorates awarded by Saudi universities are given in Islamic studies. Annual military expenditure per capita is three thousand dollars, which places the kingdom statistically far in advance of any other country, without giving it real defensive capability. "An air of unreality bordering upon lunacy hangs over the whole of this martial extravaganza," according to J.B. Kelly, with the Saudi military budget almost as large as that of Great Britain. "Moreover, the Saudis cannot operate most of the advanced weapons and highly complex defense equipment and installations . . . let alone maintain them properly."[13]

The unprecedented magnitude of weapons purchases obviously fostered pro-Saudi attitudes in the military-industrial complex and support for Saudi interests. Saudi purchases have three principal aims: to create the illusion that Saudi Arabia is capable of defending itself; to recycle petrodollars; and to create a dependent relationship between the U.S. military industry and the kingdom, similar to those in the oil business or in banking, flush with billions of dollars in deposits from Saudi institutions and individuals. The lucrative commissions paid to Saudi intermediaries in arms deals include substantial return favors.

The Defense Intelligence Office for the Middle East in the Pentagon functions as a revolving door for officers leaving uniform, as does the Middle East section of the International Security Assistance Agency of the Defense Department, and the U.S. Army Corps of Engineers. The Corps' Mediterranean headquarters was moved from Italy to Riyadh and renamed the Middle East Division in light of the huge size of its contracts with Saudi Arabia: over the years, it was the prime contractor for the construction of three enormous bases, including King Khalid Military City valued at $6 billion, a military academy, two bases for the Saudi navy, air bases, and barracks. When signed, the contracts were worth a total of $14 billion, a figure that should be multiplied by three or four for current value. Good will and friends are bought through contracts.

An example is provided by Colonel Robert Lilac, who moved directly from the National Security Council to the service of Prince Bandar bin Sultan, the ambassador to the U.S. Marine General Anthony Zinni, who headed American forces in the Middle East, has personal ties with the royal family that are so close that he participates in their falcon hunts. "Our general," say the princes.[14] At lower levels can be found, for example, a human resources director for the Defense Intelligence Agency who served in Saudi Arabia and was subsequently hired by a large Saudi company. The huge consulting firm BDM, whose military department is one of its flagships, has an annual contract of $50 million for the training of the Saudi National Guard. Other major military consulting firms involved in training and supervision, such as Vinnel and Avco, are not far behind.

Desert hospitality is a traditional virtue of Saudi Arabia. The generosity demonstrated by an emir, however meritorious it may be, the sumptuous banks, the opulent gifts, the dispensing of lavish charity, manifest his power and his wealth, create prestige, and reinforce hierarchy. They establish a relationship of benefactor and dependent. In the Saudi manner of acting, a major purchase—whether it be war planes, a petrochemical factory ready for operation, or a construction project—is never limited: it creates dependency and "good will."

The CIA is no exception to the rule. Among the causes of the colossal series of blunders that made the September 11 attacks possible, intelligence failures are blindingly clear. The CIA has long been banned by itself from conducting intelligence within Saudi Arabia! The kingdom is exempt from the common rule: until the month of April 2002, no National Intelligence Estimate (NIE) had been devoted to Saudi Arabia in years. The NIE is the document that summarizes current knowledge and analysis and assesses the prospects for the development of a country or a situation. It was not until that recent date that a twenty-five page document was prepared and submitted to the National Security Council and to the State Department.

How can the intelligence agency put its head so deep and so firmly in the sand? The CIA is an organization that operates "on demand," not "supply-side": the Director of Central Intelligence indicates his intelligence priorities to his analysts and stations through "operational directives." If a country is not among those priorities, it disappears from the map of the world. According to Robert Baer: "The raw reporting on Iran was simply buried, all to keep it out of the hands of Congress and the press. Incidentally, the same thing happened with Saudi Arabia. The CIA was not allowed to produce an NIE on the growing fundamentalist threat there. Had it leaked, it would have offended the Saudi royal family."[15]

The position of CIA station chief in Riyadh is eminently political. It does not involve collecting intelligence about Saudi Arabia, but being friendly with Prince Turki, from 1975 to 2001, or his successor Prince Nawwaf. One former station chief, Raymond H. Close, who spent seven years in the post, retired early and set up a consulting firm, Manara Ltd., to do business with Saudi Arabia. It is hardly surprising to see him frequently appearing in the press taking Saudi positions. This echo chamber recently explained that "Crown Prince Abdallah clearly stressed the fact that he would not agree to use the oil weapon as in 1973 and 1974. But it is, however, certain . . ." The entire article published by this "impartial" analyst in the *International Herald Tribune* told the story of the oil embargo and the overwhelming responsibility and even guilt of the Americans: King Faisal, it was claimed, had been forced to declare an embargo.[16] Another former station chief, who became extremely friendly with Saudi Arabia, is Frank Anderson, whose expertise seems to point only in the direction desired by the Crown Prince on questions of Middle Eastern politics. Until 1995, he headed the Near East Division of the CIA's Directorate of Operations, then became vice president of Foreign Reports, Inc., a firm specializing in the political analysis of the oil markets.

CHAPTER 12

Self-Interested Friendships

Winning the support of former spies and dignitaries of the oil lobby is a valuable element in the strategy of conquest—peaceful in appearance—of Washington. But it is not enough. Hence it is in the quiet world of American diplomacy that the heights of special friendship have been reached.

As developing fluid reveals the lineaments of a photograph, my Pentagon briefing, "Taking Saudi out of Arabia," provoked a hue and cry among former American ambassadors to Saudi Arabia. Tenors or sopranos, they spoke with one voice, or nearly so. They had no words harsh enough to stigmatize the sacrilege and showed unlimited empathy for the kingdom that had been so unjustly maligned. Walter Cutler, who had served twice as ambassador to Riyadh, explained: "No, this is not the time to reevaluate our relations. . . . [The Saudis] are very, very careful not to appear dependent on us, for very understandable domestic reasons." Cutler is head of the Meridian International Center, an international exchange organization that organizes high-level diplomatic contacts, a kind of annex to the State Department. Its regular budget, Cutler told *The Washington Post* in February 2002, is very generously supplemented by Saudi subsidies. The former deputy chief of mission Ned Walker, president of the Middle East Institute, stated: "We cannot condemn an entire people for the actions of a few of its citizens. Saudi Arabia is far from the worst in comparison to the rest of the world," a comforting thought after September 11. One seventh of the budget of the MEI officially comes from official Saudi donations. A listener to a radio program asked him to speak about the dictatorial nature of Saudi Arabia. The answer is worth its weight in servility: "I was just talking about this with an important Saudi prince the other day. The members of the inner circle of the royal family understand it. He told me that he wouldn't hesitate to bet that within ten years there would be free elections in Saudi Arabia. This is a weighty statement, coming from a member of the ruling family." The crucial words are no doubt these: "I was just talking about this with an important Saudi prince the other day."

The former ambassadors have a wealth of understanding for the slightest whims of the powerful in Saudi Arabia. Richard Murphy, who spent nearly three years in Riyadh, noted the "anguished feelings" of Crown Prince Abdallah in the face of the "humanitarian crisis" confronting the Palestinians, which no doubt explains the collection of $50 million on a Saudi telethon to finance suicide bombings in Israel, the massacre of whose citizens elicits less anguish in the heart of the distinguished diplomat. When the Saudi ambassador to Great Britain took the liberty of insulting President George W. Bush, Murphy found all sorts of justifications for him. Murphy even gave fulsome explanations to the Saudi funding of suicide bombings against Israeli civilians. Ned Walker, for his part, advised humble silence before the crown prince: "Whoever thinks that Abdallah is not capable of going to extremes is seriously mistaken. He has forced his cabinet ministers to give in." A reporter commented: "Close your eyes and listen: it's a Saudi passport-holder talking." Continuing our survey of ambassadors, Wyche Fowler (1996–2001) justified clothing restrictions—full *abaya* covering head and body—imposed on female members of the American armed forces in Saudi Arabia. This was the least of his offenses. Consider the case of Pat Roush, an American woman who asked for his help: her two daughters were kidnapped by their Saudi father sixteen years ago and forcibly taken to Saudi Arabia. They are now both in their twenties, American citizens, and threatened with arranged marriages by their father. Fowler's predecessor had tried to find a solution, but Fowler put an end to that. Testifying before a congressional committee, Roush stated: "He threw me out like a rude girl who had the nerve to talk to him. He spent six years in Saudi Arabia. He worked hard to get the job, and he got a lot of money out of it. Now he poses as a great man, an expert, the president of the Middle East Institute. He is responsible for what happened to my family. He is a criminal."[1]

American ambassadors to Saudi Arabia never speak Arabic. This has been the case since the dismissal of the late Ambassador Hume Horan. As number two in the embassy from 1972 to 1977, he had developed an impressive network of contacts and friendships in Saudi society. When he became ambassador, this eminent linguist with fluent Arabic was instructed by the State Department to deliver a severe reprimand to King Fahd to express American displeasure: American intelligence had just discovered a clandestine purchasing program by Saudi Arabia of Chinese CSS2 missiles with a range of 1,800 kilometers. The contract was in excess of one billion dollars. Horan knew that King Fahd would not be pleased. He therefore asked Washington to confirm the instructions and to be aware of the consequences. He was told to go ahead, which he did. Hardly had he returned from his delicate mission when another cable arrived from Washington, revoking the previous instructions. Prince Bandar had convinced the Reagan administration not to present an official protest over the affair of the missiles. Washington then sent the veteran diplomat Philip Habib, who took Horan with him to see the king. This is how *The Washington Post* described the scene: "Fahd was obviously furious with the ambassador . . . and demanded from Habib, in [Horan's] presence, that he be replaced. When Habib raised the question of the missiles, the king told him imperiously that he had told Horan 'not to stick his nose into it.' And he complained to Habib about Horan's Iranian origins." Horan was dismissed and replaced at lightning speed by the fawning Cutler, who did not speak a word of Arabic. "We rolled over. This was the end of the slightest influence of the ambassador of the United States in Riyadh," Horan correctly complained.[2]

One curious example was that of U.S. Saudi Ambassador James Akins, who was appointed in 1973 and dismissed two years later by Secretary of State Henry Kissinger because of his public condemnation of proposed U.S. foreign policy toward Saudi Arabia.[3]

The list is endless. One common characteristic emerges: "[T]he most successful way in which the former envoys have retained their access to the Arab elite has been to propagate the Arab point of view before the American public and policymakers. . . . [T]he success of their new careers depends on the maintenance of their Arabist views. . . . With the knowledge that their future incomes could well depend on engendering the liking of Arab governments, American officials might very well factor decisions accordingly while in government."[4] Former ambassador and former South Carolina governor John West became infatuated with Saudi Arabia. He went so far in the imitation of his benefactors that his colleague in Cairo, Herman Eilts violated diplomatic niceties, asserting that West has operated as a "public relations firm for the Saudis." Remarks he had made to his staff in Riyadh had been reported. When the Egyptian president criticized the Saudis for not supporting the Camp David agreement, West asked, "Why can't Sadat keep his big mouth shut?" And at the time of the second oil shock, he was intent on widely publicizing his views: "The Arabs are very sensitive, the Saudis particularly. . . . Every time they see a statement critical of their oil prices or policies, they take it to heart."[5]

We seem to be dreaming, but the dream is quite real: the head of the Saudi intelligence services, Prince Turki, contributed an undisclosed amount to the West Foundation.[6] The Saudis are indeed very sensitive.

If diplomats seem not to have resisted Saudi generosity, this is also because the American government gave them free rein. The self-interest of political circles themselves is an explanatory factor. During a visit to Saudi Arabia, former president Jimmy Carter demonstrated exuberant friendship toward his royal hosts: "I'm particularly proud in a personal way of my relationship with the Saudi leaders. This has been a very gratifying thing to me both while I was President and the last two years since I left the White House." He noted that King Khalid, Crown Prince [now King] Fahd, Prince Abdallah, and Prince Sultan "have gone out of their way to be helpful in times of crisis and challenge and to provide me advice, counsel, and support . . ." He went on: "I've especially come to comprehend and to appreciate the high significance of family life in the worlds of the people of Saudi Arabia and the great respect that's paid to the elderly, and also the ties that bind those of close kinship together, the extraordinary hospitality, the desire for accommodation, the need to preserve and protect the community of Islam." He also understood the "need for unanimity" felt by the Saudis "to prevent a division and separation in the Arab world." Finally, he advised American businessmen that if they wanted to "form alliances that are mutually profitable in the world of Saudi Arabia, there needs to be a special effort to understand" the Saudis and the Arab world. It is true that Jimmy Carter never met a tyrant in whom he could not find deep humanity and authentic sincerity.

The investigative reporter Steven Emerson comments sarcastically: "Six months [later] a wealthy businessman picked up the . . . tab for a benefit held . . . in New York City to raise funds for Carter's Presidential Library in Atlanta. The businessman was the prominent Saudi sales agent, Adnan

Khashoggi."[7] We might add that the Carter Center for Peace Research at Emory University in Atlanta received a $20 million donation from King Fahd.

If the example comes from so high up, why shouldn't smaller fry feed at the same trough? Bad examples abound. In 1991, the governor of Arkansas asked Saudi Arabia to contribute to the financing of a new Middle East studies center at Arkansas State University. There was no response for a year. In November 1992, King Fahd personally called the newly-fanged president-elect of the United States, Bill Clinton, to announce the good news: $20 million would go to finance the center. Nurture, water, and soften up: the same king had given a million dollars to Nancy Reagan to finance her campaign against drugs; a similar sum was contributed to Barbara Bush's campaign against illiteracy. One half million dollars was transferred from the royal treasury to Philips Andover Academy to endow George Herbert Walker Bush Scholarships.[8] Friendships have to be kept up.

But these are compromising friendships. When Prince al-Walid bin Talal, grandson of Ibn Saud, with a fortune exceeding $20 billion according to *Forbes*, visited New York, he gave Mayor Rudolph Giuliani a check for $10 million for reconstruction, a check that the mayor promptly returned because it was accompanied by a letter exhorting the United States to "reexamine its policy in the Middle East and to adopt a more balanced attitude toward the Palestinian cause." Gifts that come wrapped in conditions and demands, exhortations and propaganda, are not welcome. The prince is a major shareholder in Citigroup, AOL Time Warner, Motorola, Apple, and Kodak. At the same time, he sent a half million dollars to the Council on Islamic-American Relations, an organization whose founder is a supporter of Hamas, and the New York branch of which accused Israel and Mossad of the September 11, 2001 attacks.

The prince's acquisition of a minority participation of $590 million in Citigroup, one of the largest banks in the world, was arranged by a large private investment company, the Carlyle Group. The forty-nine partners in Carlyle, a company with annual revenues of $16 billion, are mostly "big names" in politics, who are exploiting their past positions for current business. They own 94.5 percent of the shares. The chairman, until recently, was Frank Carlucci, former defense secretary and former deputy director of the CIA. Among the partners are George H.W. Bush's former budget director, Richard Darman, and as special adviser, James Baker, who was his secretary of state. Also among them is the former British prime minister John Major, and many other similar figures. "They are big, and they are discreet," according to one journalist.[9] The business of Carlyle consists of raising private funds, without going through the stock market or banks, and placing them in profitable enterprises. Carlyle has approximately five hundred fifty clients, pension funds, banks, etc., interests in seventy-four companies employing a total of seventy thousand people, including important defense contractors in the United States, such as United Defense. The estimated net worth of Carlyle exceeds three billion dollars. "When Carlyle goes to raise funds in the Middle East, they take George Bush (senior) with them" to speak to Arab leaders and investors.

Carlyle works directly as an adviser to the Saudi government in the framework of the Economic Offset Program through the intermediary of Carlyle Arabia. This program ensures that American arms manufacturers return a part of their contract prices to Saudi companies as a form of compensation.[10]

Certain aspects are particularly noteworthy. "Among its most enthusiastic investors," according to the London weekly *The Observer*, are "Prince Bandar [bin Sultan], ambassador to Washington, and his father Prince Sultan [bin Abdulaziz], the kingdom's defense minister."[11] Remaining in the entourage of the Saudi royal family, we also find among

Carlyle investors the Bin Laden family and the Saudi Binladen Group (SBG), the family business that has invested two million dollars in the Carlyle Partners II Fund since 1995. According to *The Wall Street Journal*, "a foreign financier tied to the Bin Laden family explains that the family's investments in Carlyle are much larger. According to him, the two million dollars was only an initial stake."[12] Frank Carlucci, head of Carlyle, is co-chairman of the board of trustees of the Center for Middle East Policy of the Rand Corporation. The fury he showed toward the author in August 2002 now becomes more comprehensible.

In the atmosphere following September 11 that was not very favorable to the Saudis, the excessively political friendships of Carlyle became embarrassing. "Carlyle is a typical example of a foreign policy that too often reflects commercial interests at the expense of the public interest of the country," according to a Washington analyst.[13] This is why Carlyle announced shortly after the attacks that it was breaking all ties with the Bin Laden Group. Is this also a possible reason why the company announced in November 2002 the replacement of Carlucci by the former chairman of IBM, Louis Gerstner?[14]

The presence of former president George H.W. Bush in the Carlyle Group—he receives $100,000 for each speech he delivers—is troubling. For all that, the presence of a flock of former associates, cabinet secretaries, and deputy secretaries of the former president is equally troubling. We should not forget that it was in response to the urgent appeals of King Fahd in 1991 that Bush senior abruptly halted the advance of American forces toward Baghdad, thus saving Saddam Hussein's skin. We should also recall this president calling on the Iraqis to rise up but unforgivably allowing Saddam Hussein to crush the Shiite rebellion in the south without lifting a finger. Saudi influence paralleled that of James Baker, the national security adviser Brent Scowcroft, and others, to prevent any American intervention. The Saudis claimed that a Shiite victory would have opened the way in Iraq to a repetition of the Iranian revolution, a patent absurdity in view of the defeat and demoralization of the Iranian army in the Iran-Iraq war and the presence of a victorious coalition. It was rather fear of the impact that a Shiite victory in Iraq would have in the eastern Shiite provinces of Saudi Arabia that troubled the royal family. The insurrection was crushed in blood, and three hundred thousand people paid with their lives for this cynical game. Saddam Hussein survived his crushing defeat, ready to plunge into new adventures. The Middle East observed an American president more willing to listen to the oil-rich sirens of the Saudi princes than to protect the victims of his own fecklessness.

What Bush, Baker, Scowcroft, and the others were protecting went well beyond the financial interests of their friends, the oilmen, arms dealers, and bankers, and beyond preserving the privileges of the corrupt princes of the Saudi dynasty; their tacit agreement protected the geopolitical status quo inherited from 1945 and 1956. It protected the "Eisenhower doctrine," which places the Americans at the service of Arab tyrannies, and gives more than its due to a dynasty whose interests, practices, and ideas are poles apart from what the United States represents.

The former president is not only part of the old snobbish New England establishment, but he also holds, so to speak, a "membership card in the Saudi party." Relationships are not confined to the political and financial spheres. When it was proved that the pocket money of Princess Haifa al-Faisal, wife of Ambassador Bandar bin Sultan, had mysteriously flowed from her bank account to that of the hijackers, and the American press began to look for lice in the heads of their royal highnesses, it was the matriarch Barbara Bush, wife of the former president, who made a consoling telephone call to the princess, saddened by this nastiness (another call came to her from Alma Powell, wife of the former secretary of state).[15]

On the basis of oil, geostrategic concerns, and corruption, a regional structure has grown up in the course of more than a half century. The elements of this structure correspond to realities: the oil needs of the world market, the United Sates and the Western countries, the protection of the sources of oil, preventing others from destroying or benefiting from them, blocking Soviet expansion in the Middle East, the control of Arab nationalism with its dangerous impulses. The huge sums of money swirling between Riyadh and Washington created, as we have seen, special friendships. Year by year, decade by decade, friendships and interests interlocked, blended together, supported each other. Institutions were created, political lines established, ideas became habits.

No one better embodies today the dogma of this geopolitical oil religion than its principal guardian in Washington, General Brent Scowcroft. His is a brilliant résumé: a graduate of West Point, where he also taught, air attaché to a military mission, military assistant to President Richard Nixon, Scowcroft has often been called on to sit on presidential commissions. National security adviser to Presidents Gerald Ford and George H.W. Bush, between-times assistant chairman of Kissinger Associates, the consulting and lobbying company of the former secretary of state, the general is one of those powerful Washington figures who, in the course of long careers (he is in his mid-seventies) learn how to use all the devices of American government machinery, civilian and military, executive and legislative. After the Bush presidency, Scowcroft set up his own consulting company, The Scowcroft Group, and a sister organization, the Forum on International Policy (FIP). Among the services that it offers, the group can "provide access to government bodies."

Scowcroft's politics? Drink toasts with the butcher of Tiananmen Square less than six months after the massacre, "in order to avoid isolating China." "Lay down a path that brings us together." We should never oppose tyrants. When President Ronald Reagan spoke of the "Evil Empire,"

Scowcroft found the "rhetoric excessive" because it "frightened our allies and made American leadership of the West more difficult to maintain." As for Saddam Hussein, Scowcroft headlined his August 15, 2002, *Wall Street Journal* article "Do Not Attack Saddam, That Would Weaken Our War on Terror."

And Saudi Arabia? In a long interview in October 2001, Scowcroft explained that Saudi Arabia, to be sure "is not a perfect regime," that "the Saudis are worried," because "Osama bin Laden is probably a more dangerous threat to Saudi Arabia . . . than to the United States"—a few weeks after the September 11 attacks! He conceded that the Saudis are "apparently" corrupt. Apparently? The Saudis, he went on, are "deeply concerned" at "the collapse of negotiations between Israelis and Palestinians . . . from their perspective, they see us as standing aside and letting that happen."[16] That says it all: Scowcroft does not judge events from the American "perspective" but from the Saudi "perspective."

Is there collusion between Washington and Riyadh? "There is no great conspiracy at work." And the fifteen Saudi hijackers? And fundamentalism? And the funding of terrorism by charitable organizations? "Yes, something like that is going on in Saudi Arabia," he grudgingly admits. But, "I see no reason to distance ourselves from the existing regime. Is it our kind of system? No. But it's their kind of system." And, fortunately, "they are in the process of gradually changing. Are they changing in a way that suits us? I don't think that that should concern us, especially not at this time." He goes on: "We have no problem with Wahhabism." And the refusal of the Saudi authorities to cooperate with the FBI in investigating the deadly attacks against Americans? "That is a different problem. It's partially true, and it makes me somewhat uncomfortable."

Scowcroft's conclusion: "I do not think that we should be intolerant because people do things a little differently." The Saudi government is playing a double game, isn't it, Mr.

Scowcroft? "It is playing a double game because it is in a very difficult position. . . . They are anxious: in case of need, can they count on us? *The problem is not Saudi Arabia, it's the United States.*" It's hard to believe our eyes. Here is a former very high-ranking official who was deeply wedded to the Saudi point of view. And the horrors make the poor man "uncomfortable."

Scowcroft is the honorary chairman of the Saudi lobby in Washington. He is not the "chairman" of an established institution, but the key figure who indicates the direction followed by the lobby. As for organizations, the Saudi government has leased, purchased, and mobilized an army of lawyers, lobbyists, and propagandists, whose mission is to promote, defend, and illustrate Saudi Arabia, influence the executive and Congress, the media and opinion leaders, and economic and social organizations, by projecting an illusory and lying image of Saudi reality and the politics of the kingdom, and to buy votes, consciences, articles, and television programs.

The case of Frederick G. Dutton, known as "Fred of Arabia," has been thoroughly examined. In 1975, as required by the Foreign Agent Registration Act, he registered as an agent of Saudi Arabia. His known revenues from the Saudi government amount to millions of dollars. What did he do? He invited for lunch or dinner the media elite, leading Washington political figures, high government officials, and Congressmen and Senators. He provided the Saudis with "legal advice and political counsel," and taught them how to manipulate the levers of American political life. Then-Governor Ronald Reagan once called him, in another context, a "lying son of a bitch." Dutton has provided his services for thirty years. The Washington lobbyist in the Brooks Brothers suit has orchestrated the public relations activities of the kingdom."[17]

Saudi investments are diversified. To strengthen threatened ties with the White House, in late 2002 the kingdom secured the services of the influential Texas law firm of Tom

Loeffler, former Republican congressman, one of President Bush's chief fund-raisers: he headed fund-raising operations for Bush's first Texas gubernatorial campaign, and was co-chairman of the fund-raising committee for the 2000 presidential campaign.[18]

In the course of the six months ending September 30, 2002, the public relations firm Qorvis Communications was paid the extraordinary sum of $14.6 million for its services intended to "increase American awareness of the commitment of the kingdom to the war on terror and to peace in the Middle East." Qorvis "placed" interviews with the foreign affairs adviser to Crown Prince Abdallah, Adel al-Jubeir, who appeared frequently on television. A presentable and polished Saudi, he defends the indefensible with unshakable aplomb. When the crown prince came to the United States, it was Qorvis that orchestrated his media strategy. It also organized a trip by congressional staffers to Saudi Arabia.[19]

At the request of the Saudi embassy, and with funds supplied by it, Qorvis engaged in a campaign of disinformation and, according to the chairman of the House Committee on Government Reform, Dan Burton, the Saudi government worked through Qorvis to "undermine the action of the committee and the efforts it has made to return American citizens to their country." The Saudis, wrote Burton in a stinging letter to Ambassador Bandar, "have issued many deceptive statements concerning cases of kidnapping and the efforts of the committee."[20] Confronted with the fear and anger provoked both by kidnappings and Saudi muzzling of the media and dirty tricks, the lobbyists had the nerve to demand diplomatic immunity to avoid testifying and turning over to the committee the documents that it had requested. Shortly afterward, three of the founders of Qorvis resigned, "essentially because of increasing evidence of ties between eminent Saudis and the financing of the al-Qaeda terrorist network."[21]

Qorvis is a subsidiary of Patton, Boggs, LLP. The huge Washington law firm, which employs more than 110 lawyers, is a lobbyist for 225 companies and organizations and operates as a registered foreign agent for foreign countries. Patton, Boggs is the chief agent for the kingdom of Saudi Arabia. The kingdom has others, including the influential law firm Akin, Gump, Strauss, Hauer & Feld. The Strauss of the firm was also a member, with Brent Scowcroft, of the board of directors of the Forum for International Policy. Akin, Gump has represented wealthy Saudis, some of whom have been scrutinized by American authorities for possible involvement in financing Bin Laden or al-Qaeda. The firm also represents the Holy Land Foundation for Relief and Development, an Islamic charitable organization in the United States. In July 2004, the U.S. Justice Department handed down a 42-count indictment against the foundation and its top leaders in a conspiracy to provide aid to a terrorist organization and the families of suicide terrorists.

The following story is worth hearing. It should have been shown on television. The reasons for which viewers were deprived of seeing it shed light both on the nature of the Saudi regime and on the hidden and manipulative influence it has been able to acquire abroad.

A Saudi princess eloped with a commoner in order to escape from the marriage arranged by her father, one of the great princes of the royal house, Muhammad bin Abdulaziz. "Adultery!" stormed the father, whose "honor" had been stained. He demanded from the king that his daughter be condemned to death. Permission granted. She was executed with a bullet to the back of the head. Her lover was then decapitated by saber.

The story might have ended there, but an English acquaintance of the tragic lovers wrote a script and sent it to a producer. Associated Television Corporation (ATC) in England and WGBH, the Boston affiliate of PBS, produced a "docudrama" which took the essential elements and situated them in "Arabia" (with no Saudi). It is what followed that goes beyond fiction.

When broadcast of the docudrama was announced, on April 11, 1980, Foreign Minister Saud al-Faisal summoned the British *chargé d'affaires* to Riyadh and demanded that the program not be shown, He threatened that the kingdom would impose an oil and trade embargo. In London, the Foreign Office meekly apologized: "We profoundly regret any offence which the program may have caused in Saudi Arabia." The foreign secretary, Lord Carrington offered apologies for "the . . . offence . . . this particular television film had caused to the Royal Family in Saudi Arabia, and other Saudis and Muslims everywhere." The trade secretary exploded in rage against the television producers and their "ego trip . . . knowing as they did that it would cause the gravest offence to the country in question to which we are doing our very best to increase our exports." Saudi Arabia had no doubt: it was a Zionist plot.

A certain number of American companies were advised to boycott English companies. Would *Death of a Princess* be seen in Italy? Not on your life. The government blocked the broadcast. In Germany, the story was the same. And in France, "the cradle of human rights"? No, the docudrama was never broadcast.

In the United States, the Saudi ambassador, never short of low-class blackmail, spoke of "possible repercussions" on oil supplies and defense agreements.

The influential Republican Senator Charles Percy told President Jimmy Carter that "there would be support in Congress should the President make a determination that the showing of the program would not be in the national interest," freedom of speech be damned. Admiral Thomas Moorer, who had resettled to Texaco after retiring from the military, when asked by an interviewer whether the United States should give in to Saudi pressure to kill the show, responded bluntly: "See you down on the gas line! . . . You can't stand on principle in the face of blowing up the free world." The second clause was perfunctory. "You can't stand on principle" was the operative principle, not in front of so much graft.

With the reverse heroism that is both a professional and a personal defect, Acting Secretary of State Warren Christopher, who later held the post under President Bill Clinton, passed on to PBS a relatively mild letter he had received from the Saudi ambassador. But the day before, the ambassador had been more emphatic: "The timing of the showing of the film in the present period makes it clear that it is part of the continuing and recent stepped up effort to undermine the internationally significant relationship between the United States and Saudi Arabia." The same expression, as though it came from a phrase book, is used every time a newspaper sneezes about the kingdom. To satisfy the desires of a foreign power, the State Department was caught in the act of trying to influence the programming of an American television network. *Death of a Princess* was broadcast on April 11, 1980.[22]

The lesson should be retained: Saudi Arabia tries to impose its mores, its way of acting, its practices on the entire world. It stops at nothing as long as it meets no resistance. It has no respect for the laws of others and respects only the force given to it by its money, its influence, and its terrorists. It buys shamelessly on all sides everyone who is willing to sell himself. Like the former Soviet Union, it projects its methods extraterritorially and rejects any reciprocity. Saudi Arabia is an outlaw country.

Not that illegality is a new idea for the Al-Sauds and their Wahhabi associates. Their entire history is imbued with it.

The Rags of the Emir

The saying goes that all kingdoms and dyn ties originate in highway robbery. In the c of Saudi Arabia, we are still close to highway. This kingdom, a newborn in the eyes of history an empire engendered by the union of a visionary preacl and a clan of bandits, an Arab version of the Gran(Compagnies that plundered the France of the Hundred Ye War. Toward the middle of the eighteenth century, t founder of a religious sect, Muhammad ibn Abd al-Wahh who had become a religious judge or *qadhi*, met the am tious head of a clan of obscure origin named Muhamm ibn Saud, tribal chief of Bedouin Arabs in the heart of Na in the center of the Arabian peninsula, from the Mousal clan of the Rwala tribe of the Anaiza tribal confederatio The sword of one joined with the sectarian Islam of the oth to create the bond of alliance, Saud and Wahhabi, Wahha and Saud, that still rules Saudi Arabia.

The stage on which their alliance was established was th of the poor and isolated life of oases lost in the san(Although Islam had originated in Arabia, it had soon move outward to reach cities of ancient culture, Damascus an Baghdad, and countries with long histories such as Egypt an the kingdoms on the borders of India. By the eighth century Islam had escaped from its creators, the camel drivers o Arabia. Since it had migrated outside Arabia, the Bedouin had remained apart from the great movements of the world

whether Arab, Ottoman, or Islamic. In ten centuries, or close to it, not much had changed in the heart of the peninsula. Out of touch with the great trade routes, the peninsular Arabs were also removed from intellectual movements except for the Hijazis and the merchants and pirates of the Gulf. Of the many high points of the world of Islam, Umayyad Damascus, the Baghdad of the Abbassids, the Cairo of the Fatimids, the wonders of Samarkand, Tashkent, and Bukhara, Andalusia, and the India of the Moguls, Arabia knew nothing, shared nothing. It remained stubbornly rooted in the seventh century, isolated and isolationist, except that it sometimes unwillingly suffered incursions from some and expeditions by others. But there was no great wealth to be seized, and the numbers that came were few, especially for the pilgrimage to Mecca, the *hajj*. The holy city is located in the western province of Hejaz near the Red Sea. Central and desert Najd played no role in it. Its Bedouins early on either became extreme Islamic sectarians, Kharijites or Ibadites, or reverted to being pagans as before Muhammad's Prophethood. A contemporary observer describes the desert nomad—with the admiration of a romantic Westerner inclined to a return to primitive nature for the "noble savage"—as having a "soul [that is] bare and primitive. . . . His sensations blunted, his intellect fallow and incurious, the Bedouin is primal, instinctual, contemptuous of nuance."[1]

In order to understand their mentality, let us call upon the Tunisian Abu Zayd Ibn Khaldun, born in Tunis in 1332, died in Cairo in 1406, the founder of modern history and sociology. His masterwork, *The Muqaddimah* (An Introduction to History) makes it possible to learn about and understand the Bedouins and their empire. The Bedouins (or "Arabs" as Ibn Khaldun calls them) are "the most savage human beings that exist. Compared with sedentary people, they are on a level with wild, untamable animals and dumb beasts of prey. Such people are the Arabs . . . [who] make deeper excursions into the desert and are more rooted in desert life [than others]."[2]

"[The Arabs have a] poor life, hard conditions, and bad habitats. . . . [T]heir subsistence depends on camels and camel breeding and pasturage. The camels are the cause of [their] savage life in the desert . . ."[3]

"The Arab tribes are in a state of almost perpetual war against each other," according to a nineteenth-century historian.[4] How could they survive and defend themselves? "Their defense and protection are successful only if they are a closely-knit group of common descent. This strengthens their stamina and makes them feared, since everybody's affection for his family and his group is more important [than anything else]," explains Ibn Khaldun.[5] Very real blood ties, or an invented common descent that everyone accepts, encompass not only the extended family, but the clan, the tribe, and even the confederation of tribes. Included within it are clients and allies. Close connection, group solidarity, *asabiyya* in Arabic, are the foundations of social life. The tribes have no state, they are only networks of relatives and clients.

Relations among men are thus based on ties of blood and dependency. Lineage is of primary importance: everything comes from it, it is the starting point for everything. "[T]heir pedigrees can be trusted not to have been mixed up and corrupted. They have been preserved pure in unbroken lines," according to Ibn Khaldun.[6] The matter is so important that a half century ago the Saudi royal family requested that researchers from Aramco, the oil company that was American at the time, provide them with a family genealogy. With a good bit of legerdemain, astute deceit, and some vigorous contempt for the facts, the oil "historians" came out with a compilation that "established" a fanciful but prestigious pedigree for the Al-Sauds.[7] The founder of the "dynasty" became, it was said with some grandiloquence, the "emir" of the oasis of Al-Diriya around 1710: the little settlement contained a total of seventy clay houses. This was evidently the price for the "purity of lineage," a fetish common to archaic societies: isolation, backwardness, ignorance.

Ibn Khaldun explains that, thanks to the solidarity that unites them, savage nations are "better able to achieve superiority and to take away the things that are in the hands of other nations."[8] This is an important definition: in the desert, there is no wealth; in the oasis, dates and a few meager crops. The rest of the territory offers no resources. The Bedouin has contempt for the peasant whose labor seems unworthy to him, and for the city-dweller, in his eyes softened and made effeminate by luxury. "All the customary activities of the Arabs lead to travel and movement. This is the antithesis and negation of stationariness, which produces civilization," according to Ibn Khaldun, who continues with a startling summary: "For instance, the Arabs need stones to set them up as supports for their cooking pots. So, they take them from buildings which they tear down to get the stones, and use them for that purpose. Wood, too, is needed by them for props for their tents and for use as tent poles for their dwellings. So, they tear down roofs to get the wood for that purpose. The very nature of their existence is the negation of building, which is the basis of civilization. This is the case with them quite generally."[9]

Now as then, the diagnosis retains its validity as a description of the Bedouin kingdoms, whether the size of a pocket handkerchief, an oasis, or two million square kilometers, whether their principal resource is dates or oil. They seize what they have from other nations; that is the essential fact. The members of a savage nation, the historian says, "have the strength to fight other nations, and they are among human beings what beasts of prey are among dumb animals."[10]

The Bedouins go on the attack. In order to do so, they need a religion binding them together and instilling in them the necessary fanaticism, because, independent and rebellious against any authority, they can be disciplined only by religion: "[B]ecause of their savagery, the Arabs are the least willing of nations to subordinate themselves to each other, as they are rude, proud, ambitious, and eager to be the leader. . . . But when there is religion among them through prophecy or sainthood, then they have some restraining influence in themselves. . . . It is, then, easy for them to subordinate themselves and to unite."[11]

Thereby overcoming their centrifugal tendencies, the Bedouin tribes, exalted by a new religious inspiration, unite in the love of booty and the contempt for death—or the desire to die—while their enemies cling to life and do not dare resist them. This is how Bedouin conquest occurs.

Toward the middle of the eighteenth century, Muhammad ibn Abd al-Wahhab gradually developed a reputation as a destructive zealot, and sought out a warrior partner. He specialized in the profanation, pillage, and destruction of the tombs of the companions of the Prophet. Another of his claims to fame was his restoration of the stoning of women for adultery or "fornication," thereby terrorizing the area with his exploits.[12] Having incurred the hostility of the most important tribal chief in the region, Ibn Abd al-Wahhab took refuge in Al-Diriya in 1744. There he encountered the minor local emir, Muhammad ibn Saud. They met, understood each other, and made a deal: Wahhab would sanctify Saud and Saud would spread Wahhab. Plunder and *jihad* were united before God. *Gazya*, origin of the word "razzia," became sacred. To seal this virtuous and useful alliance, one gave his daughter to the other. In the following two and a half centuries, the two families would continue to prefer intermarriage with each other. In 1772, the family pair seized the oasis town of Riyadh, and by 1785 had imposed its law on all of Najd, preparing to attack more wealthy prizes.

What was this religion that was able to transform the Bedouin into a conqueror, the Wahhabism forged in the alliance between the *umara* (*emirs*) and the *ulama* (clerics)?

What is immediately striking in the doctrine promulgated by Ibn Abd al-Wahhab is the endless list of actions, gestures, and thoughts that are prohibited, condemned, forbidden, reprehensible, dangerous. Nothing is too trivial to escape from the vigilance of this ferocious censor: mustache, laughter, music, the pilgrimage to Mecca (if it is not directed solely to the *Kaaba*, the sacred black stone), the celebration of the Prophet's birthday, the tombs of Muslim saints and of the Prophet's companions, ornaments in mosques, and Shiism. Everything is prohibited except what is explicitly prescribed or recommended, literally, by the Koran.

These are slogans, not ideas, of a religion that has been reduced to the simplistic rote of the simpleton, thanks to which—or because of which—there are no questions, never anything but answers. Everything that existed in the year 700 must remain the same. Wahhabism is first of all a historical stratum, a frozen moment in time defined as the ideal and unsurpassable golden age.

The other, the foreigner, change, these are the sources of all evil. Two hundred fifty years later, the founder of Saudi Arabia properly speaking, Abdulaziz ibn Saud said that "the Arab people was suspicious [of Westerners] in the past because misfortune always came to it from abroad."[13]

The other must therefore be excluded and all change must be prevented. To this end, Ibn Abd al-Wahhab invented a mythical past: of everything that had happened in the world of Islam since the third century of the Hegira, that is after the year 932, nothing could be saved or kept; everything was branded with the mark of infamy, everything was null and void. The founder of Wahhabism wanted to restore the mythical world of the year 700. What had taken place in the great cosmopolitan urban centers—the integration of Hellenism into Islam, carrying with it Greek science, Persian culture, and its own art of governing, the contribution of Judaism, the Chinese influences transmitted by the Mongols, the wisdom of India—all had to disappear at the price of a gigantic purge.

Everything that came from "innovation" was a "heresy." The two concepts are expressed by the same word: *bida*. Legal or jurisprudential innovation, religious innovation, innovation in relation to the slightest comma of the text of the Koran, all were prohibited. This solipsistic doctrine was a retreat to positions established in advance, from which no movement would ever have to be made. Is laughter one of mankind's distinguishing characteristics? It was banned, according to the historian Rihani.

The great work of Ibn Abd al-Wahhab, *Kitab al Tawhid* (The Book of Monotheism) is a tedious, though revealing, read. It violently attacks "those who paint" (chapter 61), and a certain number of first names considered idolatrous in themselves (chapter 50). One chapter (58) is entitled "The Prohibition against Cursing the Wind." Chapter 2 analyzes the Koran to determine vigorously "the textual evidence that there are seven earths as there are seven heavens." Chapter 3 uses various *hadiths* (remarks attributed to the Prophet) to prohibit curing through magic "except in cases of jealousy or scorpion sting." The work in short is a mixture of trivialities, scraps of religiosity, and selective and rather specious readings of the Muslim scriptures. With a pitiful intellectual level, the doctrine is narrow, provincial, insular, isolationist. In form, it is a series of exegeses, of which there are thousands of examples in Muslim literature, in which the writer demonstrates what he wants to prove by carefully selecting verses and *suras* of the Koran and spicing them up with appropriate quotations drawn from the huge volume of *hadiths*. The exegesis is dry and scholastic and the casuistry twisted: the author trims and prunes everything that stands out, and implicitly, everything that might stand out.

The purpose of the work is to explain, justify, and magnify what the author calls *tawhid* ("the oneness of God"); he goes beyond the Muslim profession of faith, "there is no God but God and Muhammad is his Prophet." Nothing is or truly exists outside this God. The assertion of the existence, the importance, or the effectiveness of any other factor is characterized as *shirk* (polytheism) the supreme sin.

There can be no doubt that Al-Wahhab was connected with the narrowest currents of the Muslim tradition, the Hanbali school, one of the four principal schools of Muslim law, and with its successor, the thirteenth century Syrian theologian Ibn Taymiyya. One of the distinctive characteristics of this movement is the fanatical negation of the slightest degree of human free will: everything has always been decided beforehand by God. "'The first thing that God created was the pen. He ordered it to write the exact measure of all things until the Day of Judgment.' Oh my son, I have personally heard the Prophet of God say: 'Whoever dies not believing in that is not one of mine.'" It is a "duty" to "believe in fate," Ibn Abd al-Wahhab goes on, "the fates have all already been written."[14]

The doctrine is a religion of unhealthy harshness, sterile as the desert, like the desert devoid of mineral, vegetable, animal, or human pluralism. Nothing exists but the One. Divinity is dilated by the desert sun to the point that it swallows everything. "Wahhabism regulated even minor details of human behavior," according to one historian. "For example, it advised people how they should laugh, sneeze, yawn, joke, embrace, and shake hands when meeting a friend . . ."[15] It is a creed which, beneath the trappings of religion, is besieged by Satan the tempter, present everywhere, infiltrating the most hidden corner of the behavior of the believer. This is why he must submit to constant rituals, the only remedies against the tempting microbes that pollute the entire world. He must rely on the rite and the imam.

This theology, to give it a flattering name, is a thought that moves around a narrow circle, like a goat attached to the same stake for a millennium. Cut off from contact with the main currents of civilization, evolving in the closed world of the Najd desert, it is a doctrine that opened no doors or windows onto a world that it has ignored.

These are the Wahhabis: their eyes are turned inward in their skulls rather than outward onto the external world. They see only their own inner landscape. The world does not exist, except in the form of Hell.

Confined to its oasis, a sect of this kind is rather inoffensive, except for its local victims. It is its expansion that creates anxiety and destruction. The Wahhabis considered all the Muslims of their time who did not share their doctrine as polytheists who were even worse than the Arabs of the pagan era before the Prophet. Even worse, whoever heard their call and did not join them was an infidel.

The division, typical of any sect, between an inside ("us") blessed by God and an outside ("them") consigned to Evil was in place, with no nuance.

The inside of the Wahhabi sect is the *dar al-Islam* alone, "the house of Islam"; everything outside it is *dar al-Harb*, the "territory of war." "Fanaticism simultaneously united and disciplined the Wahhabis . . ."[16] Muhammad ibn Abd al-Wahhab was thus simultaneously the founder of a sect, an *alim* (the singular of *ulama*), a teacher, a *qadhi*, a military organizer, and in charge of a part of both internal and external affairs. He corresponded with other *ulamas*, took care of propaganda, and preached loyalty to the *emir*, discipline, and fanaticism. He was the supplier of bellicose zealots devoted to the *emir*, a sort of Trotsky to the *emir's* Lenin.

Coming from a long sectarian tradition, too backward and ignorant to go beyond simplistic egalitarian ideas, the Bedouins, in the appropriate circumstances, were inclined to join enthusiastically and to adopt its elementary slogans: the sect gave them an identity, a purpose, something to raise them above their miserable daily existence. They were the ones whom Muhammad ibn Abd al-Wahhab recruited and indoctrinated, and whom Muhammad ibn Saud could then launch against the other tribes of Najd, and then the rest of Arabia. In addition, adhesion to Wahhabism involved obvious material rewards. Before, the *rezzou* had merely been a bravely executed raid; now, it became the seizure and transfer of the goods of the "polytheists" to the hands of "true Muslims."

In summary, flattering portraits of the Bedouin, idealized as the Middle Eastern embodiment of the "noble savage," have been drawn by Westerners seeking vitality, who find in the desert and its creatures an antidote to their "bourgeois" malaise. The "Bedouin" thus becomes an image of rediscovered animal vitality, purity, and simplicity, which could be idealized by those who would not share in Adolf Hitler's idolization of Neitzsche's "beautiful blonde brute." As the astute English analyst of the Arab world, David Pryce-Jones points out, in Western travel writing, "the Arabs of Arabia . . . seem to live in a branch of fiction rather than in the real world. Far from engendering a free and noble life, Bedouin tribal life was rigid and formalistic, because, in the first place, of the very harsh conditions imposed by climate and geography, and because of a no less rigid adhesion to the codes of honor and shame inherited [from the past]. For sedentary Arabs everywhere, the backward and uncultivated Bedouins were a threat, thieves and assassins living in tents, far from the mosque, lacking in the slightest tradition of religion or knowledge."[17]

It began then with a traditional chieftainship, like dozens of others in the Arabian desert. This family of pirates scouring the seas of sand practiced, like the others, an economy of plunder. Its ambitions, and the alliance with Abd al-Wahhab, began to raise it above the others. Their symbiosis created a system that "may be defined as a politico-religious confederacy, which legalizes the indiscriminate plunder and thralldom of all peoples beyond its own pale . . ." according to a nineteenth-century historian of the Persian Gulf.[18] That assiduous apologist for the Saudi dynasty, the English Nazi fanatic Harry St. John Philby himself recognized that the driving force behind it was "constant expansion and aggression at the expense of those who did not share the great idea."[19] In 1787, lacking a sense of proportion and reality, Abd al-

Wahhab proclaimed himself head of the *Umma*, the world-wide Muslim community, and declared *jihad* against the Ottomans.

The Bedouin hordes of the Al-Sauds then swooped down on oases and caravans, spilling beyond the traditional territories of Najd. They seized the eastern province of Al-Hasa on the Persian Gulf, largely populated by Shiites, considered beyond the pale by Wahhabism. They launched marauding expeditions to the north against Ottoman Iraq and Syria, to the southeast against Oman, to the west against Hejaz. In 1802, they took the Shiite holy city Karbala, now in Iraq. This was the site of the mosque of Husain, the grandson of the Prophet. Centuries of pious donations had produced a considerable accumulation of treasure.

This is from a contemporary account: "12,000 Wahhabis suddenly attacked [the mosque of] Imam Husain; after seizing more spoils than they had ever seized after the greatest victories, they put everything to fire and the sword. . . . Old people, women, and children—everybody died at the barbarians' sword. Besides, it is said that whenever they saw a pregnant woman, they disemboweled her and left the fetus on the mother's bleeding corpse. Their cruelty could not be satisfied, they did not cease their murders, and blood flowed like water. As a result of the bloody catastrophe, more than 4,000 people perished. The Wahhabis carried off their plunder on the back of more than 4,000 camels."[20]

They were not much better in Sunni Mecca and the other towns of Hejaz than in Shiite Karbala. Taif was taken, the inhabitants killed down to the last one, infants included. They also destroyed thousands of books. In Mecca, which they entered in April 1803, Saud "the Great" ordered the destruction of all the domes that had been erected over the graves of the family of the Prophet. They razed the mausoleums built in honor of the revered figures of Islam and all buildings whose architectural features did not meet their precepts. Saud took the opportunity to seize the treasures of jewelry from the mosque of the Prophet. "Even the tomb of the Prophet himself was broken open in 1810 on the orders of the Saudi imam and its jewels and relics sold or distributed among the Wahhabi soldiery."[21]

In the south, the Wahhabis seized the Hadramaut in Yemen in 1810. The pirates of Oman, vassals of the Saudis, assembled a fleet of several thousand small vessels to dominate the Persian Gulf and to attack the ships of the British East India Company, the largest multinational company in the world. The company, concerned with maintaining good relations with the conqueror, sent him presents, the first inkling of the British imperial support that a century later enabled Abdulaziz ibn Saud to establish present day "Saudi" Arabia.

Responding to the megalomania demonstrated by the Wahhabi religious leader, the political leader, Saud, exclaimed in 1800: "What is to the west of the Euphrates is mine, and I leave to the [Ottoman] pasha what is to the east."[22] The fact was that Bonaparte's invasion of Egypt and the English presence that thwarted it had placed the Ottoman Empire on the defensive. Istanbul's control over the peripheral regions of the empire, the most costly to hold and providing a meager return, became looser. For the moment, the sultan was too occupied to pay attention to the caravan routes of Arabia, even if their new master interfered with the pilgrimage of Muslim inhabitants of the empire. In 1808, Saud Abdulaziz, who had been launching raids against Iraq and Syria for several years and had laid siege to the Gulf port of Basra, sent a letter to the sheikhs[23] of Damascus and Aleppo, far to the north, and of other towns, to demand that they adopt the Wahhabi doctrine, that they submit to his authority, and that they pay tribute to him. His troops plundered the region around Aleppo and penetrated into Palestine. A force of several thousand Wahhabi fighters almost reached Damascus. From then on, the new empire controlled, directly or indirectly, the entire Arabian peninsula.

The end of the threat that Napoleon posed to the Sublime Porte restored the Ottoman sultan's freedom of maneuver. He asked the ambitious potentate of Egypt, Muhammad Ali to bring the insolent Bedouin to heel and to retake the *Haramayn*, the two holy cities of Islam. After a few false starts and several failures, the son of the despot of Cairo, Ibrahim Pasha, calmly set to work. In 1812, four thousand ears cut from Wahhabi fighters were sent in brine to Istanbul. In 1813, the port of Jeddah was taken, then Mecca was recaptured. By the time of his death, Saud had lost all of Hejaz, Oman, and the port of Bahrain. A year later, Asir was lost, in 1816 Medina, and finally, in 1818, Al-Diriya, the mud hut capital of the first Saudi empire, which was completely razed and its population dispersed. Eighteen members of the Al-Saud family perished in the war. When he was captured, the Wahhabi *imam* Abdallah was put in chains and sent to Istanbul, where he was executed and his corpse thrown to the dogs. Ibrahim Pasha also used a refined form of torture on Sulaiman ibn Abdallah, a grandson of the founder of Wahhabism: before having him executed he forced him to listen—blasphemy!—to a tune played on a *rabab*, a single-stringed Egyptian violin. The sect hated any kind of music. A sense of gallows humor is not necessarily lacking in wars among Arabs and Muslims.

Egyptian garrisons were stationed in the oases and the towns. The first empire of the Sauds had come to an end.

It was external pressure on the Ottoman Empire that had opened up room for maneuver for the minor actors stirring in the Arabian peninsula, the Al-Sauds like the others. The end of the Napoleonic threat, as we have seen, restored the sultan's freedom, including the freedom to punish the insolent. Similarly, it was an external event—the collapse of the empire of Muhammad Ali the Egyptian—which, from 1840 on, freed the remains of the Al-Saud family from a domination that they could not challenge: the strategic depth of an Egypt that was more populated, more advanced, and richer, was incomparable. The Egyptian troops had to evacuate the peninsula and return home. Three years later, Faisal al-Turki, head of another branch of the Al-Saud family, until then in exile in Egypt, made Riyadh the capital of a second Saudi state, of which he was *emir*, *imam*, commander in chief, chief judge, and chief executive, and behaved more cautiously than his predecessors attacking neither the sultan nor the pasha.[24] As often happened in Bedouin tribes, the death of the chief, Faisal, unleashed an endless battle for the succession which turned into a deadly feud. The kaleidoscope of a succession of *emirs* and the ways in which their uncles, nephews, cousins, and other relatives cheerfully slaughtered each other to seize some feeble power, is both long and tiring. Let us merely point out that fratricidal vendettas undermined the stability of the second Saudi state. Further north, in the Shammar region, the power of the Al-Rashid *emirs* of Hail was rising as that of the Al-Sauds declined, despite the support they received from the British crown in 1873. For the British authorities, the region was defined by its place on the route to India. This is why, both in the Persian Gulf and in the peninsula, they relied on and moved on the chess board the pawns of empire that the Al-Sauds were, just as the Ottomans moved their own pawns.

The expansion, the period in power, and the fall of nomad chieftainships all followed the same dynamic: "Wars, raids, pillage, and constant expansion constituted the political foundations of the Wahhabi state," to the extent that expansion guaranteed large revenues for the Bedouin "nobility"; it was with this currency and this currency alone, success, booty, that the Al-Sauds could ensure the loyalty of other Bedouin groups and underwrite the costs of their own maintenance, since the entire "budget" went either to buy loyalty or to support the "court."

In the early twentieth century, we find the Al-Saud family having taken refuge with a client of the British, the *emir* of Kuwait, where it played the role of poor relative. It had two strokes of luck: first, the British were seeking to weaken the pro-Ottoman forces of the Shammar region and the Al-Sauds came to hand as a rallying point for the inhabitants of Najd who were unhappy with the reign of the Al-Rashids. And then there arose in the family a chief of stature who would show throughout his life political astuteness of the highest order.

CHAPTER 14

Arabs Made in Britain

B orn in 1880, Abdul Aziz Abd al-Rahman ibn Faisal al-Saud grew up in an exile family, driven from central Arabia by the rival clan of the Al-Rashids. By 1887, the second Saudi state had ceased to exist. In 1893, the family settled in Kuwait under the protection of the local sheikh, Muhammad al-Sabah.

Ten years later, the young Ibn Saud restored a Saudi emirate. Thirty years later, in 1932, he became king of a new country, Saudi Arabia. Prominent Western admirers of Ibn Saud—a large number of whom turn out to have been Nazi sympathizers, including Harry St. John Philby of England and Jacques Benoist-Méchin of France—have produced, with the help of many clichés, a flattering portrait of him, as though he were a demiurge who had created one of the wonders of the world. Here is a classic example of these idolatrous portraits, penned by the English specialist on the Arab world, Gertrude Bell:

> He is a man of splendid physique, standing well over six feet, and carrying himself with the air of one accustomed to command. Though he is more massively built than the typical nomad sheik, he has the characteristics of the well-bred Arab, the strongly marked aquiline profile, full-fleshed nostrils, prominent lips and long, narrow chin, accentuated by a pointed beard. His hands are fine, with slender fingers, a trait almost universal among the tribes of pure Arab blood,

and, in spite of his great height and breadth of shoulder, he conveys the impression, common enough in the desert, of an indefinable lassitude, not individual but racial, the secular weariness of an ancient and self-contained people, which has made heavy drafts on its vital forces, and borrowed little from beyond its own forbidding frontiers. His deliberate movements, his slow, sweet smile, and the contemplative glance of his heavy-lidded eyes, though they add to his dignity and charm, do not accord with the western conception of a vigorous personality. Nevertheless, report credits him with powers of physical endurance rare even in hard-bitten Arabia. Among men bred in the camel saddle he is said to have few rivals as a tireless rider, as a leader of irregular forces he is of proved daring, and he combines with his qualities as a soldier that grasp of statecraft which is yet more highly prized by the tribesmen. . . . Politician, ruler, and raider, Ibn Saud illustrates a historic type.[1]

We recognize the noble savage, draped in all the clichés imaginable, with the vast desert vistas, the solitary courage of the bold Bedouin chief, the visionary giant, and so on.

It was the time rather than the man that in fact made history. Let us situate his rise in its historical context.

Until the First World War, the Middle East was in a state of stable equilibrium. The empire in Istanbul ensured the rule of its *pax ottomanica*. Having lost most of its European provinces, the Maghreb to France, Egypt to Great Britain, and the Caucasus to Russia, the sultan firmly held on to the Arab provinces, playing adroitly on the rivalries among European powers to maintain his position. The disastrous miscalculation by the Young Turks who had seized power shortly before the outbreak of the Great War plunged the empire into a crisis that could have been avoided: the balance of powers had been upset. The British Empire, until then determined to ensure Ottoman survival in order to counter Russian ambitions and the aims of other powers, reversed course.[2]

Gradually, as the war continued, vassals that had been loyal to Istanbul for centuries, took their freedom. The British, Ottomans, Germans, Russians, and French all pounced on these allegiances for sale or lease in a ceaseless free for all. The fevered imaginations of adventurers, scoundrels, and visionaries—it was often difficult to distinguish one from another—gave themselves free rein.

It was in this context that the battles for the control of Arabia took place. Ibn Saud demonstrated a good deal of political shrewdness, an acute sense of maneuver, and unfailing ambition and greed. His talent was to take advantage of every opportunity to serve his ambitions. In this sense, he was indeed an empire builder. But he would have built nothing at all if he had not astutely placed himself under the protection of the British Empire: Saudi Arabia came into the world thanks to Their Britannic Majesties Victoria, Edward VII, and George V.

British administrators governed the Persian Gulf while allowing the local *emirs* to reign over the camel drivers, pearl divers, fishermen, semi-pirates, and quarter-smugglers. The British "political resident" in the Gulf was the political and military arm of the Indian Empire, in the hierarchical ladder of the Indian Civil Service. It was the security of the land and sea approaches to India that was of primary importance. In 1902, Ibn Saud's first contacts with the British had not been fruitful. Sir Percy Cox, the Gulf Resident, did not even deign to answer a letter from the young chief. The British services evaluated him in these terms: "In combat he was a brave but poor strategist; indeed, he was never once victorious in conventional face-to-face confrontations. His coups were surprise attacks . . ." In desert campaigns, however, he "had the nerve and courage to stand his ground and to keep his forces fighting."[3] As the young tribal leader based in Kuwait was reconstituting the kernel of a fighting force and the nucleus of an emirate, "the British administration in India observed Ibn Saud's activities with growing benevolence."[4] Attacking for personal reasons the local allies of the Ottomans, he was helping British interests and became a useful tool in this peninsula riven by tribal rivalries, a mosaic of petty sultanates and chieftainships. We should note that the Foreign Office in London, preoccupied by great European policy, was barely concerned with Arabia. It was only with the Great War that the balance finally shifted.

As time passed and his military capacities grew, an agreement was reached: Ibn Saud gave up for the time his clan's old claims on Muscat and Oman, but "received" from the British what did not belong to him, the province of Hasa (Hajjar), with the Royal Navy protecting its coast. In exchange, Ibn Saud recognized and accepted a British protectorate over his emirate. He promised not to engage in warfare against anyone without British consent. The British were given the right to exploit the mineral resources of the peninsula and agreed to provide him with subsidies and arms.

The religious factor distinguished Ibn Saud from other tribal chiefs in Arabia. In the wars between Muslims, he was able to mobilize for his benefit the energies that sprang from Wahhabism to restore not only the emirate but the Saudi empire.

According to the historian J. B. Kelly, the "means by which he intended to attain [his] goal was the same as that employed by his ancestors to achieve their conquests—the arousal of the latent fanaticism of the Bedouin tribes, its harnessing to their predatory and warlike instincts, and the launching of the resultant engine of destruction upon his neighbors."[5]

As early as 1910, Ibn Saud was dispatching *mutawiyah*, Wahhabi preachers, to the nomads of the desert. They inflamed the zeal of the Bedouins by preaching *jihad*. The descendant of Abd al-Wahhab, a kindred spirit of Ibn Saud, Abdallah ibn Muhammad ibn Abd al-Latif, *qadhi* of Riyadh, from the Al al-Sheikh family, and other Wahhabi dignitaries fostered indoctrination and fanaticism, loyalty to the *emir*, the refusal of any contact with Europeans and with inhabitants of the country themselves who were in contact with those infidels, and loyalty to the group.

The preaching bore fruit. By 1912, Ibn Saud was in a position to settle his recruits in military-agricultural colonies located in the oases of Najd. The first, Artawiya, was 250 kilometers north of Riyadh. The second, Ghatghat, was to the west. The colonies, called *hijra*, an explicit reference to the Hegira of the Prophet—his flight from Mecca to Medina—spread rapidly in the following years. From several dozen, they increased to more than two hundred in Najd, none of which was more than a day's march from another. Ibn Saud appointed the *qadhis*, generally from the Al al-Sheikh family, and provided them with "political instructors," kinds of political-religious commissars, *mutawiyah*. Ibn Saud had thus assembled a military force of tens of thousands of fighters, estimated at sixty to seventy thousand.

The "colonists" called each other *akh*, "brother," and thereby formed the "brotherhood," the *Ikhwan*. Islamic neophytes, these recently converted Bedouins wanted to distinguish themselves from others by their outward appearance, as new adherents to a faith often express their radicalism through clothing and conduct. Wearing white turbans, close-cropped mustaches, long beards dyed with henna, short and dirty robes, to ostentatiously exhibit their contempt for comfort, the "brothers" practiced egalitarianism and the rejection of any activity likely to "contaminate" their new-found faith. Filled with the pride of the "elect," they demonstrated punctilious intolerance of the slightest "innovation." It was reported that at the sight of an Arab from Iraq, they covered their eyes to avoid being soiled.

On their banners they inscribed the *shahada*, the Muslim declaration of faith. Lacking in any feeling of pity or compassion, they exhibited unequalled ferocity, putting every male prisoner to the sword. "On more occasions than one their bloodlust led them to slaughter women and children . . . a [gross] violation of the code of the desert tribes."[6]

"More and more Bedouins embraced the ideals of the *Ikhwan*, drawn as much by the vision of war and plunder in the name of Islam, as by money, houses, gifts of land, and aid for agriculture provided by the Riyadh authorities." The *Ikhwan* was to become the terror of Arabia. Hadn't Ibn Saud's grandfather, Faisal, told an English visitor that "[t]here were two types of desert warfare: religious war and political war. Political warfare involved compromise. But 'when the question is one of religion... we kill everybody.'"[7] Every one of the "brothers" was filled with the same fanaticism holding human life of no value, considering death in *jihad* an entry ticket to Paradise, and any opponent as subhuman, a "polytheist," an "unbeliever," an "infidel." "They simply killed anyone who refused their call to join the movement." In 1920, Ibn Saud declared: "I am the *Ikhwan*, no one else."

Taking advantage of the First World War, he consolidated his alliance with the British, hugely increasing the subsidies that he received from the British Empire, without raising a finger against the Ottomans. On the contrary, although he was a "friend" of the British, he supplied—in return for payment—the Turkish garrisons, and left to other Arabs the trouble of fighting the Ottoman army. The British never succeeded in having him move against the Turks. The only thing that was important to him was to launch raids against his tribal enemies, while refusing to disavow his allegiance to the sultan. He made the bidding go higher.

The British needed allies in the region: finally, a treaty of alliance was signed in July 1916, which made the Saudi realm a protectorate endowed with internal autonomy. In return for the fabulous sum of five million pounds sterling, Ibn Saud promised to have no relations with any third party and not to intervene in the Persian Gulf. At the same time, he maintained direct contact with the Ottoman government and with the commander in chief of the Turkish armies in the region.

Ibn Saud decided to lean to the British side and put an end to his double game in late 1916. He became "Sir Abdul Aziz Bin Saud," Knight Commander of the Most Eminent Order of the Indian Empire.[8]

The double game had succeeded beyond his wildest hopes. Without ever raising a hand against an Ottoman soldier, Ibn Saud had succeeded in developing his army, his stock of weapons, and his resources thanks to the British Empire. With the collapse of the Central Powers and the capitulation of the Ottomans in 1918, he was ready. He launched the *Ikhwan* on the attack: the emirate of Hail, fief of the hereditary enemies the Al-Rashids, the Shammar region, and Asir on the Red Sea, were conquered in 1920; in the winter of 1921, he laid siege to Kuwait, which had to be lifted when the Royal Navy intervened. Deadly raids were launched against southern Iraq.

Worried about stability, the Colonial Secretary Winston Churchill held a conference in Cairo in 1921, where his brain-trust, "the forty thieves" as he playfully called them, reorganized British possessions in the region. On this occasion, the Crown recognized Ibn Saud as "sultan of Najd and its dependencies." "[Despite his] conduct the British government and its officials, throughout the 1930s and the period of the Second World War and beyond, continued to treat him with an exaggerated deference which was warranted neither by his actual importance nor by his supposed attachment to their interests."[9]

London demanded that the southern border of Iraq and the border with Jordan be respected, while the *Ikhwan* was unleashed precisely against those regions, seizing and pillaging oases and reaching the borders of Syria. Three to four thousand *Ikhwan* fighters came within twenty kilometers of Amman. The tanks of the Arab legion, commanded by the British, and the planes of the Royal Air Force drove them back. Difficult negotiations set the old partners in the double game, Sir Percy Cox and Ibn Saud, against each other. Cox concluded the negotiations by drawing a line on a map: the border would be there, nowhere else. Ibn Saud still depended on British subsidies, and he gave in. It was not long before infiltrations began again.

In the immediate, Ibn Saud had in mind a more important target, the rich province of Hejaz, site of the holy cities of Mecca and Medina. He launched a call to his *Ikhwan* troops for a *jihad* for the conquest of the province. Through murderous raids in which villages were razed, Ibn Saud won victory. In December 1924, he entered Mecca, from which had fled Sharif Husain of the Hashemite family, descendants of the Prophet, who had administered it since 1073. The Sharif abdicated, complaining bitterly: "The British behaved as if they tried to ensure Ibn Saud's victory." It would be hard to contradict him, since London had cut off support for him in March 1924.[10] For Ibn Saud, twenty-three years of campaigning to capture Mecca had borne fruit: he became "King of Hejaz."

The iconoclastic fury of the *Ikhwan* was given free rein. The scenes that had marked the first conquest of Hejaz by the Wahhabis in the early nineteenth century were repeated. The Bedouins of Ibn Saud destroyed the monument that marked the site of the Prophet's birth, razed the houses of his first wife Khadija and Abu Bakr, the first *caliph*. When they occupied Taif, they started breaking mirrors, and, providing evidence of the perspicacity of Ibn Khaldun, used door and window frames as firewood. Ibn Saud in person gave the order to destroy the ornaments in mosques.

The solemn promises made to the Muslim world—after the conquest, the four schools of Muslim law would be allowed to coexist—went up in smoke. Only the Hanbali school, to which the Wahhabis were devoted, was authorized. "For years to come there was to be tension and ill-feeling between Hejaz and Najd, the Hejazis looking upon the Najdis as little better than barbarous Bedouin, while the Najdis viewed the Hejazis with contempt as *munafiqun*— hypocrites and libertines."[11] The *ashraf*, the Hejazi nobility, were persecuted, expropriated, and humiliated. The *Ikhwan* "would teach the world about the emptiness in their hearts, which reproduced the void of their social existence," according to one historian.[12]

The freshly minted king lost no time in imposing a totalitarian order. Almost everything became a crime: participating in a meeting whose purpose was to disseminate "harmful" ideas, spreading "false information" and "dangerous rumors"; even charitable meetings were subject to prior approval by the authorities.[13] Ibn Saud set up the League for Public Morality (the complete title is the Ministry for the Promotion of Virtue and the Prevention of Vice), a kind of Gestapo of daily life, of busybodies of obligatory "virtue," ignorant oafs intoxicated with their authority and imposing a never-ending inquisition on the population. This means of control imposed on the Hejazi guinea pigs was later extended to the entire country. The head of the *mutawiyin* was given cabinet rank. Control over the society was complete: the *ulamas* controlled the summit, the dregs of society the bottom.

In a book published in Boston in 1928, the historian Amin Rihani described the new Arabia: "If one laughs freely in one's house, someone will soon knock at the door. 'Why are you laughing in this ribald manner?' No one in that quarter ever dares to miss . . . one of the five daily prayers. . . . No pity has the piety of the *ulama*; no mercy in their ascetic justice."[14]

In 1926, Ibn Saud called an international Muslim congress and secured ratification of his possession of the Holy Places. Recalcitrant delegates, from the Indian subcontinent in particular, were expelled.

Having come to power and conquered the greater part of the Arabian peninsula, Ibn Saud nonetheless stumbled over an obstacle: the very men who had made him king, the *Ikhwan*, now intended, inside the kingdom, to establish their rigid utopia, to exterminate the Shiites, and to kill the Egyptian pilgrims who were not sufficiently Wahhabi in their eyes, and abroad, to continue and extend their *jihad* to the entire region. He repeated in vain "the *Ikhwan* are my children"; he found himself in a situation comparable to that of Adolf Hitler in 1934: having come to power thanks to the SA,[15] who had mobilized revolutionary passions, he wanted to stabilize his power and put an end to the National Socialist "revolution." "Having planted and fostered fanaticism in these simple folk, encouraging them to fear no earthly power and to welcome death as the gateway to paradise. . . . Abdul Aziz had sought to have the best of both worlds, to secure twentieth-century power with seventh-century means, and the contradiction had caught up with him."[16]

Hitler orchestrated the Night of the Long Knives in which he massacred the SA leaders. Ibn Saud and the *Ikhwan* had their own civil war. After a series of bloody raids against Iraq, which provoked the wrath of the British imperial power that Ibn Saud was neither willing nor able to confront directly, conflict broke out between the "brothers" who had become enemies. The "Brothers" of Najd were enraged at being blocked from further putting Hejaz to fire and the sword. Aside from rifles, they rejected the instruments of the devil that had come from the West. "You have . . . prevented me from raiding the [other] Bedouins, so we are neither Moslems fighting the unbelievers, nor are we Arabs and Bedouins raiding each other. . . . You have kept us away from both our religious and our worldly concerns," wrote one. "Since [Ibn Saud] has ruled, no one has raided an enemy and no one has stolen so much as a chicken! Nothing to do but stay at home like women," complained others.[17]

The indictment was harsh; Ibn Saud was accused of a variety of offenses:

- allowing his son Saud to visit Egypt;
- sending his son Faisal to London to negotiate with the infidels;
- importing the telegraph, the telephone, and cars;
- allowing the tribes of Transjordan and Iraq to graze their flocks in the Muslims' lands;
- prohibiting trade with Kuwait; and
- tolerating the "schismatics" (the Shiites) instead of either converting them to Islam or massacring them.[18]

In 1928, one of the *Ikhwan* proclaimed himself "*imam* of *Wahabbiyya*," a claim that withdrew religious legitimacy from Ibn Saud.

As British diplomatic cables indicated, they considered him the only real force in the peninsula. A new Anglo-Saudi treaty of "friendship and good intentions" was signed in Jeddah in May 1927, recognizing the "complete and absolute independence" of Ibn Saud's possessions. But they warned him that they would crush the *Ikhwan* if the raids did not stop.

The stakes were clear: Ibn Saud wanted to solidify "Wahhabism in one country," whereas the rebel Bedouins were preaching "permanent revolution," an odd echo in the depths of the Arabian desert of the battle for power raging in Moscow between Stalin and Trotsky.

The fanatics, having become an obstacle, were cut down in the hundreds by British machine guns and RAF aircraft at the battle of Sabillah. Artawiya, Ghatghat and other *hijra* (*Ikhwan* settlements) were wiped off the map. In September 1932, Ibn Saud unified his two kingdoms of Najd and Hejaz and became the king of a new country, on which he generously bestowed his family name: Saudi Arabia, the only country in the world to bear the name of a living person and a ruling dynasty.

Would Ibn Saud grow more moderate? He tried in vain to seize the emirate of Qatar and the sultanate of Oman. Violence, war, and conquest were decided on by him and him alone. He wanted to regulate violence not eliminate it. Three quarters of a century later, the same divergence was to separate the heads of the royal family from their former protégé, Osama bin Laden.

CHAPTER 15

1939: Hitler and Ibn Saud

King Ibn Saud, the royal family, the court, the courtiers, the hangers-on, the profiteers, and the crooks had until then lived on precarious revenue sources: large-scale theft from the inhabitants of the peninsula; taxes levied each year from pilgrims on the *hajj*; and British subsidies. Those subsidies had come to an end. Pillage of other "Saudis" could not go beyond certain limits. The great depression that wrecked the world economy considerably reduced the number of pilgrims. Bankruptcy loomed. It came in 1931, when the king had to declare a moratorium on his debts.

Failing divine intervention, salvation came from a strange trio of Westerners.

Harry St. John Philby, "the British Arabophile, explorer, entrepreneur, Wahhabi convert, historian, and confidant of Ibn Saud . . . [had an] abiding hostility to Great Britain. . . . He was an admirer of Hitler. . . . In later life he became an avowed if muddled communist, given to uncritical commendation of the beneficent influence exercised by the Soviet Union in the world . . ." He became rich in the service of Ibn Saud. An unrepentant sycophant, he constantly produced mythological versions of the history of the monarch. A sacred history, an official history of the party, a mixture of propaganda and cheap romanticism, which was easily accepted by the outside world, because "[i]t was, and it still is, virtually impossible for any independent Western scholar to visit Saudi Arabia. The Saudi government does not welcome foreign inquiries after knowledge . . ."[1] Ibn Saud made Philby one of his chief confidants.

The second character in the oil adventure was a manufacturer of toilets and bathroom fixtures from Chicago, Charles Crane, who used his inherited fortune to intervene in international political affairs, with unfailing amateurism which allowed him to confirm his large collection of prejudices. He was already known in the region for his sympathy with the Arabs since he had advised President Woodrow Wilson, in the run-up to the 1919 Versailles Peace Conference, on the postwar settlement in Palestine, as a leader of the "King-Crane Commission." President Wilson had earlier sent him on a mission to Bolshevik Russia, where he had developed an affection for the Russian people and in particular for the Bolshevik leaders, whom he praised for their love of democracy, their progressive policies, and their anti-imperialist international positions. Crane was the very archetype of the "useful idiot" that Lenin appreciated so much. On his return from his trip to the Middle East, he had become an activist in the "Arab cause." Linked with the Mellon family of bankers and oilmen, he returned frequently over the course of the decade, developing a private intelligence network along the way.

King Ibn Saud, meeting with an American for the first time, welcomed Crane. The "useful idiot" demonstrated his extraordinary capacity to be taken in. These are his own words: "The king turned out to be everything I could have wished for. He is a magnificent specimen of humanity, six feet three or four inches tall, powerful in every respect, but full of charm. While his duties allow no compromise, he is most generous to his former enemies." The hundreds of thousands of victims of the incessant wars that he had fomented were certainly unaware of that. "Toward me," Crane goes on, "he was most kind, open, friendly, frank, and informative. He tried with great care to answer my questions in the clearest and most thorough manner."[2]

Directly communicating his impressions to President Franklin Delano Roosevelt, the naïve but self-important visitor wrote: "Ibn Saud is the most important man to appear in Arabia since the time of Muhammad. Strictly orthodox, he conducts his business, his life, and his government in the way that Muhammad would have or as nearly as possible. He now holds supreme power in the peninsula."[3] It was Philby who had introduced Crane to the king of Arabia, and Crane who sent an American geological engineer to survey the regions bordering the Persian Gulf in the east of the kingdom. Karl S. Twitchell arrived in Jeddah in April 1932. One year later a lucrative contract was signed between Standard Oil of California and the impecunious king. Five years later, oil began to flow. The first royalty check received by Ibn Saud was for more than $1.5 million. He saw the money "as belonging to him personally, not to the state, a concept that had no meaning for him."[4]

In 1939, Casoc, a subsidiary of Standard Oil of California, and Texaco signed a supplementary concession contract: it granted them an exclusive right to prospect for and, if found, to pump oil in vast territories. It was this complex that was to give rise in 1944 to the Arabian-American Oil Company, Aramco, one of the giants of the global economy and the largest oil company in the world. The concession did not last until the contractual term of 1999, because the Saudis illegally took control of the company. It nevertheless provided fabulous financial revenues for the oil companies, and for Saudi Arabia huge investments establishing its oil and gas infrastructure. The installations, technologies, qualifications, technical, administrative, and managerial training, the adjunct personnel, the international distribution network, the financial know-how, were all imported and contributed by the Americans, red-faced Texans and rough-hewn Californians.

A city was built for them at Dhahran: Aramcoland in Petro-listan.

All of this took place after the Second World War. The First had been conducted on foot, or almost. The Second was a war of movement, on land, in the air, and at sea, the war of the internal combustion engine. The conflict transformed the status of oil from a commercial product into a strategic commodity. It gave the Middle East its geopolitical weight and Arabia its importance. As archaic as it was, the kingdom of Ibn Saud began its migration from the periphery of the world toward its central regions.

Major events force both participants and spectators to move away from vagueness and adopt clear positions: one cannot stand still in the midst of a battlefield. For Ibn Saud, the Second World War provided the opportunity for a shift: from being a client of the British, he turned into a protégé of the Americans, after passing through a prolonged flirtation with the distant Adolf Hitler. In every case, the double game had the purpose of pushing the bidding higher.

Until 1939, British influence predominated in Saudi Arabia. Protector of the Persian Gulf, mandatory power in Mesopotamia and the Palestine-Transjordan region, occupying power in Egypt, colonial power in Yemen and Aden, its army and the Royal Navy were joined with its economic power. In the king's entourage, there was no shortage of British agents of influence, spies, and friends whose support had been bought. The British controlled access by sea and hence the food supplies of the country.[5]

The challenger, in the second as in the first world conflict, was Germany. Emperor Wilhelm II had presented himself as protector of the East; Hitler declared himself the friend of the Arabs. One had wanted to provoke against the British and French a pan-Islamic movement led by his ally the sultan; the other a revolt of the Arabs to cut off the route to India and seize the oil. Hitler and Ibn Saud found an area of agreement: their friendship was initiated by a shared hatred of the

Jews. Ibn Saud asked Hitler for weapons and promised diplomatic relations.

Contacts had begun early, in 1937 in Baghdad, where Ibn Saud's political secretary, the Syrian Yussuf Yassin, had made contact with German industrialists. The king's personal physician, Midhat al-Ardh, also Syrian, traveled to Berlin, and in November of the same year met the leadership of the *Aussenpolitisches Amt* (APA) of the NSDAP, the "ministry of foreign affairs" of the Nazi Party, whose head was the party's chief ideologue, Alfred Rosenberg, author of the bible of racial hatred, the unreadable *Myth of the Twentieth Century*. Agreement was slow to be reached. Berlin was still wary of antagonizing London and had to take into account the imperial ambitions in the Middle East of its Italian ally. The Saudis insisted.

The Libyan Khalid al-Hud al-Qarqani, who was close to the king, continued Saudi pressure in Berlin, using the APA as an intermediary. The king needed rifles and ammunition and asked the Germans to sell them to him, or rather that a credit line be opened for him to buy them, as well as for the construction of a small weapons and ammunition factory. Since the promises made on that occasion had not yet been fulfilled, he sent his vice-minister of foreign affairs, Fuad Hamza, a Druze from Palestine, who spent a month in Berlin in the summer of 1938 and persuaded his German interlocutors. He explained to them his master's dependence on Britain and the hopes that he placed in Nazi Germany. The supreme command (OKW) of the Wehrmacht gave its agreement to the delivery of arms to Ibn Saud. They were intended for the Palestinian rebels of the Grand Mufti of Jerusalem, the pro-Nazi Hajj Amin al-Husseini, Hitler's "Aryan Arab," to fight against the British and the Jews.

Saudi perseverance finally bore fruit. In January 1939, the Third Reich decided to establish diplomatic relations with Saudi Arabia. Although it is now a matter of routine, this was at the time of great importance. There were only three ambassadors posted in Jeddah, those of the United Kingdom, France, and Italy, and the *chargés d'affaires* of other countries whose inhabitants visited the holy places of the peninsula. Germany was the first country to establish diplomatic relations without having any consular interest with regard to the *hajj*. Recognition by the Reich extended the palette and the scope of the double game. The principal agent of the Reich's diplomatic-cum-intelligence services in the Middle East, Fritz Grobba, immediately went to Jeddah, where he was honored with two meetings with the king himself. "The Saudis expected from Germany moral, technical, and material support, in the form of arms deliveries. For Ibn Saud, it was essential that the Germans support the Arabs on the Palestinian question."[6] According to Grobba, the king proposed a treaty of friendship and a trade agreement, as well as German support for Saudi territorial claims in the peninsula. In return, he offered his neutrality in the coming war. Ibn Saud had demonstrated benevolent reserve toward Mussolini's Italy when it invaded Ethiopia, and he had been one of the first to recognize its annexation by Rome. The king is full of hatred for the British, Grobba reported.

To accelerate the movement, Al-Qarqani again went to Berlin in May 1939. He went to see the power centers: the Abwehr of Admiral Canaris (military intelligence, which was developing solid networks in the Middle East), the APA for Nazi foreign relations, the foreign ministry with Ribbentrop. Each of them agreed to support the Arab cause. On June 17 came the supreme honor: King Ibn Saud's envoy had the signal honor of meeting the Führer at the Berghof in the Obersalzberg.

"The Führer gave a long harangue expressing his sympathy for the Arabs, derived from his childhood reading, and declared that he was prepared to give the Saudis 'active support.'" Al-Qarqani transmitted to him a personal letter from the king. The matter was in the bag. On July 17, they signed a credit for six million reichsmarks, four thousand rifles, and two thousand cartridges for each one.

Despite the arrival of a convoy of ten German trucks in Jeddah in August, the declaration of war, followed by the Franco-British naval blockade, put an end to the honeymoon. The Reich was never in a position in which geography enabled it to join up with its new friend.

In February 1940, the American ambassador to Egypt presented his credentials to the king in Jeddah. "Abdulaziz ibn Saud was clearly adept at being all things to all men," commented one historian.

Oil, everything comes down to oil.

In the summer of 1941, the U.S. State Department asked President Roosevelt to grant Saudi Arabia the financial and material assistance provided in the Lend-Lease law, intended for allies of the United States engaged in the war effort against the Axis. Roosevelt scribbled a note to his Federal Loan Administrator: "Will you tell the British I hope they can take care of the King of Saudi Arabia. This is a little far afield for us!"[7] Secretary of State Cordell Hull expressed skepticism. The Saudi government, in his view, was trying to "secure unreasonable advances" by multiplying "threats and pressures" on American oil companies. Already![8]

In 1943, the fear of an energy shortage worried American leaders. Gulf oil instantly acquired strategic value, as did the landowners who had underground rights. The Lend-Lease spigots opened with a flick of the wrist. Saudi Arabia was to receive $33 million in two years, "because, in their eagerness to make up for lost time, the Americans were paying lavishly." But the country was not eligible to receive American aid. The law specified that every recipient had to be an active belligerent against the Axis, which Saudi Arabia was not. The formation of the Arabian-American Oil company, Aramco, in January 1944, was the recompense for this violation of the spirit and the letter of the law: the American oilmen were not only established on the ground, they were ruling the roost.[9]

The United States had in the recent past seen the Middle East as falling within the sphere of influence of the European powers. Here as elsewhere, the war changed the circumstances. Internal debates in the American government and the influence of the oil companies led to a reevaluation. President Roosevelt sent a high-level representative to Jeddah, General Patrick Hurley; the same year, Ibn Saud sent two of his most cherished sons, both future kings, Faisal and Khalid, to visit the president and to hold discussions with Congress and the executive.

A report by American geologists summed up the results of a survey mission. The center of gravity for oil extraction in the world was going to shift rapidly from the Gulf of Mexico to the Middle East. The region of the Tigris, the Euphrates, and the Persian Gulf held the largest reserves in the world, and this oil was less costly to pump and refine. The wells often produced as much as three hundred times their American equivalents.

On February 14, 1945, on board the USS *Quincy*, President Roosevelt met His Royal Highness Abdulaziz ibn Saud to seal the new alliance, obviously anointed with oil.

American aid increased to $57 million. In exchange, Ibn Saud exerted pressure, demanding as the price for his alliance that the United States prevent the establishment of a Jewish state in the Middle East. President Roosevelt had tried to evade the issue, and even to persuade the king to help transfer the victims of Nazism to Palestine. He resolved the matter with an oral promise, followed six weeks later by an official letter stipulating that the United States would do nothing hostile to the Arabs, that no change would take place without consulting both the Jews and the Arabs. The Arabs had no responsibility for the fate of the Jews of Europe and thus should not be punished for it, Ibn Saud asserted.[10] The argument was specious, as the efforts of Arab leaders had provoked the blockage by the British of all official immigration to Palestine. Privately, President Roosevelt, who had just given some "verbal assurances" to satisfy his interlocutor, told a group of assistants, among whom was David Niles who later repeated it to President Harry S. Truman, that "he could do anything that needed to be done with Ibn Saud with a few million dollars."[11]

To the great fury of Churchill, who was aware that he had been outmaneuvered by President Roosevelt, the United States, encountering no opposition, had just replaced the British in Arabia. The British prime minister had to make do with a meeting with Ibn Saud. The City had just lost world oil dominance. The balance of forces in the Middle East was now the following: Anglo-Iranian (the future British Petroleum) controlled reserves of nearly 28 billion barrels, the Royal Dutch-Shell group 2.75 billion barrels, Gulf Oil 5 billion, Standard Oil of California with Standard Oil of New Jersey 2.75 billion, Standard Oil of California with Texaco 20 billion, and the Compagnie Française des Pétroles 2.75 billion; in all, 61 billion barrels. With the increase in Saudi production, the situation was going to change. Aramco had produced half a million barrels in 1938; it increased that to 21.3 million in 1945, to nearly 200 million in 1950, to more than 350 million in 1955, and to nearly 1.3 billion barrels in 1970.[12]

The U.S. Navy now got its oil supplies from Saudi Arabia. In the region, only Turkey received larger subsidies than the kingdom. And Ibn Saud was not only the potentate of Arabia, he was growing rich.

Under pressure from the "insatiable royal wastrel," the Saudi finance minister took out an irresponsible quantity of loans. Everything that foreign bankers agreed to lend was welcome, which drove the country to the brink of bankruptcy a dozen years later. When anyone spoke of finances to the king, "'That's my financial system,' he would say triumphantly, pointing at the bags of bullion surrounding him. 'I ask for the money and it appears. What more do I need to know than that?'"[13]

Strange relations developed between Aramco and Saudi Arabia, incestuous relations, a symbiosis between host and parasite, in a way that made it impossible to tell which was host and which parasite. The Saudis provided the land. The Americans brought the rest: not only technology, but also the transformation of crude into fuel and derivative products, the demand, the market, and the distribution network.

"Virtually from the day in 1933 when the first of Aramco's parent companies, Standard Oil of California, obtained a sixty-year concession for the Eastern Province, the company has served the house of Saud as guide, confidant, tutor, counsellor, emissary, advocate, steward, and factotum. Indeed, it is doubtful whether in the entire history of Western enterprise in the East . . . a great commercial corporation has so placed itself at the service of a foreign state as Aramco has done in Saudi Arabia," writes the historian J. B. Kelly.[14] The conduct of Aramco was marked by "a policy of complacent liberality" toward the kingdom, he goes on, "of concession in preference to bargaining, in the face of successive and various government demands."

On the American side, the motives were several: geopolitical, commercial, oil supplies. In the geopolitical realm, Washington, following President Roosevelt's views, was persuaded that empires had had their day and that it was opportune to accelerate the fall of the colonial powers, primarily the British and French. For the Middle East, this doctrine required the recognition of Arab nationalism in order to maintain some influence in the region. The independence of Arab countries thus became an American strategic objective. The reduction of the British geopolitical sphere of influence favored the American oil companies.[15] The entanglement was such that when Saudi Arabia launched a small military expedition against the emirate of Abu Dhabi to seize the oasis of Buraimi and the probable oil deposits in the surrounding region, it got Aramco to propagate the Saudi party line, had it endorsed by the State Department, and even by

President Dwight D. Eisenhower. "People," he told the astonished British prime minister Anthony Eden, "people in general . . . rather think that the whole of the Arabian peninsula belongs, or ought to belong, to King Saud." Aramco's propaganda had saturated Washington.

When "Engine Charlie" Wilson proclaimed that "what's good for General Motors is good for the United States," he was acting as a good head of an automobile company, but did not for all that determine American foreign policy. Aramco, on the other hand, worked on the matter with zeal. And Aramco, with its battalions of lawyers, its legions of scribes, its armies of the eager and the self-interested, depicted Saudi Arabia as a kind of Old West, its inhabitants as Puritan pioneers, Wahhabism being renamed "Unitarianism" (in reference to the benign Protestant denomination), and the whole kingdom as inhabited by an instinctive affinity with American values and virtues, including liberty. It is indeed appropriate to speak of the company's "industrious fabulists."

Financially, a complex arrangement made the share of profits paid by Aramco to the kingdom be considered by the U.S. Treasury as taxes that the company therefore did not have to pay in the United States, depriving the federal government of huge revenues. On the other hand, sums paid to the kingdom by Aramco made it possible for the American government to give it no direct aid, which in turn made it possible to prevent Congress from sticking its nose into Saudi affairs. There was something in it for everyone.

CHAPTER 16

State Anti-Semitism and Global Expansionism

A historian may sometimes have the good fortune to find a document that sheds exceptional light on events, men, and their intentions. Published in Beirut in 1970, the four-volume work of an official in the Saudi foreign ministry, Khair al-Din al-Zirikli. *The Arabian Peninsula in the Era of King Abd al-Aziz* (in Arabic, *Shibh al-Jazira fi Adh al-Malik Abd al-Aziz*), is one of those documents. It contains a secret document coming from King Abdulaziz ibn Saud: the instructions given in 1947 to Crown Prince Saud, who succeeded his father in 1953, before an important trip to the United States.

Persuade President Harry S. Truman of the importance of Saudi-American relations and of American involvement in the Middle East, and point out in exaggerated detail the divergences between Saudi Arabia and Great Britain the better to hook the American fish, were the opening sentences of the document. It sharply criticized Great Britain: "Britain deviated from its traditional friendly policy towards Saudi Arabia, gave up its balanced course between Saudi Arabia and its enemies, and encouraged the latter . . ." The document was in a sense a charter for a reversal of alliances. More was now to be gotten from the Americans than from the British, and Saudi eggs were put in the American basket.

The seventh clause described Saudi Arabia's attitude to the Soviet Union, considered an "indirect threat" to the kingdom because of the "firm relations" between communism and Zionism and because of the Orthodox Church's "Russian propaganda." "We oppose Zionism and communism and hold that the Orthodox Church should not be permitted to become a tool of Russian propaganda in the Arab countries."

The eighth clause dealt directly with Zionism:

We, the Arabs, are Muslims first of all. The Jews have been the enemies of our religion since the birth of Islam. At the same time, Islam does not share the principle of racism. . . . We are not racists. We do not oppose the Jews just because they are Jews. However, we oppose the tyrannical policy preached by some Zionist Jews. The reasons for our opposition to that policy are numerous. Zionism is based on a tyrannical principle. Zionism claims hypocritically that it is based on the liberation of oppressed Jews. How can one get rid of oppression by oppressing others, or eliminate injustice by committing a greater injustice? Zionism contradicts the Arab countries' current political interests. It threatens them from the military and strategic viewpoint.

The moralistic remarks at the beginning of the document were talking points, arguments that were soon replaced by those based on the calculation of interests. The ninth clause goes on:

The first problem we see is the need to liberate US policy from the influence of local Jewish elements and Zionist propaganda. The second issue is the need to distinguish between the problem of oppressed refugees and political Zionism, since: (a) Palestine cannot absorb all the Jewish refugees and therefore their problems will remain unresolved; (b) no country may be compelled to receive refugees without its consent; (c) it is unjust that the US refuses to receive refugees and at the same time insists on imposing them on Palestine; (d) the problem of 100,000 refugees is not a humanitarian problem, but a disguise used to justify the creation of a Jewish majority in Palestine; and (e) it is unjust and illegal that the US government allows its Jewish citizens to pursue a dual policy, as if they were citizens of two distinct states. They should be loyal to the US alone and should not be US citizens and Zionists simultaneously.[1]

It is ironic to see the Saudi despot giving citizenship lessons to the United States, in the process recycling the usual anti-Semitic myths, all the while playing on the two fields of material interests and pseudo-morality. We should also note the unusual tribute to the self-determination of peoples, a principle that had never previously crossed the king's mind. Beyond the circumstantial arguments, some truths were actually at stake. Had Ibn Saud not stated in 1937 "that he was sure that the Zionists' final goal was to seize not only Palestine, but all the land up to Medina, and to spread their control in the east as far as the Gulf coast"?[2]

Apart from the anger that gripped the Islamic potentate at the sight of those *dhimmis*, the ever-despised and submissive "protected people," suddenly wanting a state of their own and even daring to fight back, what was the logic behind his position? A long Muslim tradition encouraged him: in his view, the Jews were "a race cursed by God, as written in the Holy Book [the Koran] and doomed to final destruction and eternal damnation. . . . Our hatred of the Jews goes back to their condemnation by God for having persecuted and rejected Isa [Jesus is considered by Islam not the son of God but a prophet] and their rejection of the Prophet chosen by God [Muhammad]. . . . Truly, the word of God teaches us . . . that for a Muslim, killing a Jew [in war] or being killed by a Jew, guarantees him immediate entry into Paradise."[3]

Hatred of the Jews was an article of faith for the Wahhabis and supporters of Islamist extremism in the Arab world. The circle of close advisers to Ibn Saud was full of Arab semi-intellectuals from the Middle East who had, as though by osmosis, assimilated the worst European exports, with anti-Semitism in the forefront. Arab nationalism actively absorbed Nazi ideas.

After the First World War, "a number of clever and ambitious Arab nationalists, forced out of their own countries by British or French domination," had been taken on by Ibn Saud: "Hafiz Wahba, a former Egyptian journalist and political activist, was actually a fugitive from British justice, and Yussuf Yassin was a sharp and argumentative Syrian refugee from Palestine." There were also the Iraqi doctor Abdallah al-Damuji and the Palestinian Druze Fuad Hamza, who became a paid agent of the Third Reich and represented Saudi Arabia at Vichy. This is how they were described, in an exasperated tone, by the English emissary who negotiated with Ibn Saud in Jeddah in 1925, Sir Gilbert Clayton: "They are the familiar type of 'pinch-beck' oriental politician whose methods consist in arguing every small point, employing a certain amount of low cunning and resorting at all times to a policy of consistent obstruction."[4]

Western anti-Semitism, European and American, was not far behind. Charles Crane and his American millionaire friends displayed a "polite" WASP anti-Semitism, which sometimes turned into a campaigning mood, *a la* Lindbergh or Coughlin. Some had even played an active role in the dissemination of *The Protocols of the Elders of Zion*, the wild forgery produced by the tsar's secret services and swallowed hook, line and sinker by the likes of Adolf Hitler and Henry Ford.[5] Philby, who was close to the king as we have noted, did not conceal his Nazi sympathies. The time fostered them; a favorite jingle in the Arab world was:

No more Monsieur, no more Mister,
In Heaven Allah, on Earth Hitler.[6]

It is thus not surprising that the king granted political asylum to the pro-Nazi Iraqi coup plotter Rashid Ali al-Kilani, and to the Grand Mufti of Jerusalem Hajj Amin al-Husseini.

Nazi influence was direct. The future King Khalid, son of Ibn Saud, dined with Hitler on the very night that Czechoslovakia capitulated to the German claim to the Sudetenland, and joined in a toast to congratulate him. Long after the war, he startled a foreign diplomat by saying he believed the Führer to be "a maligned man."[7]

The obsession would never end. In 1960, the Saudi daily *Al-Bilad* ran the headline: "The Capture of [Adolf] Eichmann Who Had the Honor of Killing Five Million Jews." This did not prevent the same people from denying the reality of the Shoah.[8]

King Faisal for his part believed that the notorious anti-Semite Leonid Brezhnev was Jewish. "The communist idea was created by the Jew Karl Marx. The Jews started the Red Revolution. The communist attack on the Middle East was launched by Jews who came to Syria, Lebanon, Palestine, and Egypt to propagate communism. . . . We know that communism and Zionism are two sides of the same coin. From the establishment of Israel to today, the only beneficiary has been the USSR."[9] Faisal often greeted ambassadors posted to Riyadh and other foreign visitors with interminable anti-Jewish diatribes and gave his visitors copies of *The Protocols of the Elders of Zion*, the first of countless translations into Arabic, which had been made in 1921. He paid out of his own pocket for the printing of 300,000 copies in Lebanon to be distributed by Saudi embassies and consulates.[10] "It's all part of a great plot, a grand conspiracy," King Faisal told *Newsweek* in 1970. Author Robert Lacey, who is no enemy of the House of Saud, concludes: "This firmly held conviction was the basis of Faisal's foreign policy throughout his reign."[11]

When a deranged Australian Christian tried to set fire to the Mosque of Omar in Jerusalem in 1967, Faisal declared a *jihad* against Israel, although the authorities had quickly limited the damage: this was another anti-Islamic plot. In the space of one month, he secured an unprecedented triumph: all the Muslim heads of state with the exception of Syria and Iraq came to the summit that he had convened in Rabat. The twenty-five leaders decided for the first time to establish pan-Islamic cooperation among their governments. This was the starting point of the "conquest of Islam" by Saudi Arabia.

King Ibn Saud died in 1953 at the age of seventy-three; he left thirty-six sons and twenty-one daughters born between 1900 and 1947 from seventeen different wives. The question has been raised as to what happens to the Oedipus complex in a family of this kind; no disciple of Freud seems yet to have proposed a theory on the issue. His successor, the eldest of the surviving sons, Saud bin Saud, was to have thirty-six sons—or forty-eight, or even more likely, fifty-four—and fifty-four daughters. "He had strongly contributed to the strength of the Saudi dynasty in the same way as his father had, by copulation with a vengeance," comments one historian.[12] He would likewise consume luxury goods without restraint and show the whole family the road to luxury, gluttony, and idleness, in order to complete family mastery of the seven deadly sins. An alcoholic—like a large number of the Al-Saud offspring, despite the prohibitions shouted from the rooftops by the Wahhabis—in fragile health, his reign was a constant alternation between semi-abdications and returns to power, a frenetic explosion of luxurious expenditures, a one-way path to national bankruptcy.

At the same time, the reign of this chubby, weak, and irresolute monarch marked a turning point in the habits of the Al-Sauds. Since 1902, the dynasty had been able skillfully to play foreigners outside the peninsula one against the other. With Gamal Abdel-Nasser's seizure of power in Cairo and the rise of Arab nationalism, it had to recognize that this world overflowing with dollars, technologies, and consumer goods could also come and disturb it, put it in danger, perhaps sweep it away. The world was no longer a Turkish delight. Because he failed to adjust to this reality, King Saud was finally deposed and replaced by his brother, the austere Faisal, who in a sense founded the dynasty anew (1963–1975). He broadened the international horizon of the dynasty and launched the operation of the buying of Islam by Wahhabism. He took the initiative for the oil embargo and the quadrupling of oil prices—"the great raid"—before being assassinated.

"In the course of the twenty years following the war, Saudi Arabia had remained close to what it had been before the arrival of oil, a closed country, turned in on itself," according to the historian Anthony Cave Brown. The years in which the king managed to levy $500,000 in taxes were prosperous ones. In 1950, oil revenues reached $100 million. The rise would not stop, flooding the kingdom, or rather its masters, with untold wealth. Philby, whose long association with the family had made him into their confidant, explained: "Accustomed for generations to living from hand to mouth at the mercy of the seasons, the Arab has no compunction in dissipating his heritage on the bounteous windfalls which occasionally fall to his lot."[13]

Dissipation was given free rein. At dinner with the king, "every dish had been brought from America on a refrigerated plane." When one of his preferred wives—the king's personal harem usually had between forty and fifty women—gave birth, she received a million dollars. When one of his sons, Prince Mubarak was married at the age of twenty-one, he received his million dollars in the form of a palace.

No building, however, could rival in prodigality the king's Nasiriyah Palace in Riyadh, which combined the ostentation of the parvenu with the delicacy of the nouveau riche. "A blush-pink cement wall, eleven kilometers in circumference, six meters high, and one meter thick, surrounded what was in effect an independent town. There was a palace intended for receptions, made of the same blush-pink color as the wall, an opulent palace for the harem surrounded by exotic gardens, a two-hundred bed hospital, for the sons of the royal family and their slaves, the King Saud University, vast and comfortable houses for the families of the courtiers and the harem, a barracks, the royal garages, and acres of land-scaped gardens. There were two years of provisions in the basement larders of the reception palace," according to the king's former catering manager, who added a description of the inauguration of the palace: "The spectacle would have stimulated the imagination of the late Cecil B. DeMille. The entire façade of the reception palace, the heart of the festivi-ties, was shining with the light of huge lamps in the shape of flowers nine meters high, set along the terrace running in front of the vast building. The main entrance—with the beautiful triple arch of traditional Middle Eastern architec-ture, the openings ornamented with delicate cement trel-lises—was even more brightly illuminated by projectors. . . . Cadillac, Chrysler, Lincoln, and Mercedes limousines roared by in total disorder. . . . Rich merchants from Riyadh, mem-bers of the royal family, and counselors of King Saud came out of the cars . . ."[14] The palace had cost $25 million at the time (about 125 million in today's dollars). And the king col-lected palaces—he had twenty-five built—as did his sons, his brothers, his uncles, and his cousins. There were also the palaces abroad.

After five years of a spendthrift regime, the country was virtually bankrupt. Oil revenues in 1956 had been $340 mil-lion (about $2 billion today), but debt was climbing even faster, reaching nearly three billion in today's dollars. Inflation was galloping. Foreign banks refused to renew loans. The family customs of treating the country like a fam-ily domain, always living beyond their means, glorying in refusing to count, and wasting huge sums in the wild pursuit of luxury had finally broken the bank.

Frugal and stiff, Prince Faisal, of whom U.S. Secretary of State Dean Acheson remarked that he left "a sinister impression," was worried by the extravagance of his elder brother. He was also worried by the incoherent twists and turns of his foreign policy. In 1954, Saud had made an alliance with Colonel Nasser, the new hero of Arab "anti-imperialism." In exchange for subsidies, Egyptian military advisers, administrators, and teachers flooded into Saudi Arabia. Soviet arms were purchased through the new friend. When the Suez crisis came in 1956, Nasser nationalized the canal and was at first pushed back by the military response of the British, French, and Israelis, and finally saved by President Dwight D. Eisenhower. Saud ordered Aramco to stop delivering oil to Britain and France.

The United States then proposed that he become the "champion" of the Americans in the Arab world. When the king came to Washington on a state visit, Eisenhower went in person, for the first time, to greet him at the airport. Asked to be a moderating force and to stand up to Nasser, Saud acquiesced. Nasser was then stirring the enthusiasm of crowds like a messiah or a Mahdi. He had brought about the rebirth of the imperial dream of Muhammad Ali: Egypt would dominate the Arab world, and its leader, the *raïs*, would be the Pharaoh of the region. This fit badly with the ideas of the Al-Sauds, particularly when Nasser spoke of "our Arab oil." A life and death struggle began between Egyptians and Saudis that was to last for more than ten years through countless plots and terrorist attacks, and floods of inflamed rhetoric in which one accused the other of being "the lackey of the Jews." Mutinies and attempted military coups proliferated in Saudi Arabia.

There were assassination attempts. Saud was caught red-handed: he had paid a high-ranking Syrian officer to assassinate Nasser. The Syrian held a press conference and the Arab world laughed the king to scorn. Ridicule and the image of ineptitude created by Saud sharpened the opposition between the two brothers. In the meantime, several younger princes had become "Nasserites" and had defected to Egypt.

With the coup d'état that brought down the Hashemite dynasty in Iraq, Yemen announced its adhesion to the Syrian-Egyptian United Arab Republic: the risk of isolation and encirclement was real. Divisions multiplied and grew wider inside the royal family. This was the principal argument: Saud had to be removed for fear of a repetition of the internal fragmentation that had led to the fall of the second Saudi empire in the nineteenth century.

"One evening in March 1958, nine of King Saud's brothers gathered at . . . the home of Prince Talal . . . in Riyadh for a crisis meeting"—Abdallah (now crown prince), Abdul Mohsin, Mishaal, Miteib, Talal, Mishari, Badr, Fawwaz, and Nawwaf—and forced Saud's hand, making him appoint Faisal prime minister.[15] After several back and forth maneuvers (with Saud taking a trip to the United States for his health, Faisal taking matters in hand, imposing a—relative—austerity program, Saud returning and resuming control of the government), there was a risk of chaos. In 1964, with the country on the verge of civil war, he was finally deposed: seventy princes, sons of the founder of the dynasty, their eldest sons, a few cousins, and representatives of other branches of the family, met at the home of Muhammad bin Abdulaziz and gave themselves the imposing title of *ahl al-Hal wa al-Aql*, "those who bind and loose," denoting in Islam the highest religious authority. Two princes were charged with the task of "selling" the collective decision to the *ulamas*. The Wahhabi dignitaries Abdulmalik Al al-Sheikh and Abdulaziz bin Baz then accompanied the princes to bring the news to the departing king. On October 28, 1964, a letter from the ruling family deposed him and proclaimed Faisal king, and a fatwa from the clerics confirmed it a few days later.[16] The family council represented the "administrative council" of Saudi Arabia: seventy-two princes, twelve *ulamas*, and four head *ulamas* (some sources speak of one hundred princes and sixty-five *ulamas*). The ruling elite of Saudi Arabia, plutocrats, theocrats, and thugs, were all present.

The legacy of Saud was not entirely blank or negative for the House. After yet another military mutiny fomented by Egypt, he resurrected the *Ikhwan* and created a national force of Bedouins, half reserves, half regulars, the "White Guard," officially named the National Guard. A tribal praetorian guard for the regime, the military power of its 30,000 men rivaled that of the regular army. A quarter century after the crushing of the *Ikhwan* revolt, reconciliation was accomplished and continuity restored in the Wahhabi galaxy. In 1962, Saud appointed as its head Prince Abdullah, who still leads it with his sons.

Among the monumental errors of Saud, the "Onassis affair" was a pitiless demonstration of his incompetence and thoughtlessness, but it left a deep impression that was to contribute to the establishment of the Organization of Petroleum Exporting Countries (OPEC). Paying no attention to existing contracts with Aramco, the king contacted the Greek shipping magnate Aristotle Onassis and signed an agreement with him transferring to a joint Saudi-Onassis enterprise the transportation of oil produced by Aramco. Understanding that this was a first step toward breaking other contracts and nationalization, Aramco reacted vigorously, with the support of the American government. Secretary of State John Foster Dulles instructed the U.S. ambassador to tell "the king and [his] advisers [to] ask themselves where they would stand after three years or even one year, without the oil revenues."[17] Saud gave in. In the situation of 1954, when oil surpluses were flooding the market, consumers could call the tune. When the market changed and shortages were felt, if only for a few years in the early 1970s, it would be the turn of the producers to take the upper hand.

The oil shock of 1973–1974 was the result of what an eminent historian of Saudi Arabia, Joseph Kostiner, has called "Faisal's order," the grand design of the new king. Faisal understood better than the other Saudi princes that the oil wealth was not only for the purpose of financing a "carnival of consumption." He understood that the tribal customs of the desert were no longer adequate, that a new complexity had to be managed in a new way, as long as the tribal ideal survived and prospered. One of the "technocrats" that he promoted explained: "Adopting of some aspects of Western civilization is unavoidable if we wish to be delivered from our present backwardness." Administrative institutions were developed, some steps were taken toward technical modernization, but "Faisal and his aides did not . . . seek major sociocultural change. They were determined to maintain and even foster the role of Islam in society," to create a "higher stage of tribalism," so to speak. The power of the tribes had decreased, but tribal values had increased in strength.[18]

Faisal began by asking Aramco to support him by rescuing the finances of the kingdom. Obligingly, the company complied and issued nearly $100 million in guarantees and loans that made it possible to avoid defaulting on payments to the creditors, the major New York banks. His gratitude was limited: "The Americans are materialists pure and simple, moral considerations are of no importance to them at all; they are therefore lacking in the wisdom in human affairs that can only come from virtue," he had asserted in 1948. He had not changed his mind.

Ibn Saud, according to Benoist-Méchin, wanted Arabia to be "able to serve as a guide to the other Arab countries."[19] He moved Saudi Arabia from a passive situation in the Arab world—a strategic defensiveness—to an aggressive, expansionary position: to Wahhabize the Arab-Muslim world. With the oil crisis that he orchestrated and for which he bears primary responsibility, Faisal secured the means to carry out that strategy.

"Faisal believed it possible to transfer into the international arena the domestic principles on which the Saudi state was based. Islam provided stability, security, purpose, and discipline at home—so why not abroad as well?"[20]

There is no reason for surprise. The House of Saud uses abroad the methods and the means that have served it so well at home: a totalitarian system in which the population is indoctrinated by a ubiquitous religious inquisition, controlled by an all-powerful militia, and by the purchase, intimidation, or imprisonment, sometimes the murder, frequently the torture, of opponents. Or at least these means and methods are used in proportion to the resistance that they meet. That resistance is weak in Saudi Arabia, and the tyranny of the House of Saud is thus unlimited there. It is different abroad, except when Saudi money makes it possible to Saudi-ize or Wahhabize a society, as was the case for the Afghanistan of the Taliban.

From the moment he came to supreme power in 1964, Faisal undertook a series of journeys to Arab countries, visiting nine in nine months. "At each stop the king made the same call to his brother Muslims to join together in a pan-Islamic power bloc that could wield solid influence on the international scene . . ."[21] The circumstances favored his purpose: Nasser stupidly provoked the conflict that became known to posterity as the Six-Day War. His army was wiped out, his air force reduced to dust, and his soldiers surrendered without fighting by the tens of thousands. The only thing that saved him was an armistice imposed on Israel by the "international community." Even though Nasser withdrew his resignation after mass demonstrations shook Cairo, his hour had passed. The loss of prestige was immense and definitive. Nasserism was discredited. The center of gravity of the Arab-Muslim world began to shift toward Riyadh.

At the pan-Arab conference in Khartoum in 1967, Nasser expressed remorse and abased himself before the Saudi king.

He withdrew his troops from Yemen, where they had been conducting a ruinous war for a decade. He accepted a huge check from the king to restore Egyptian finances. The conference, marked by a new and overwhelming Saudi hegemony, agreed on a coordinated Arab policy toward Israel: "Neither peace, nor negotiations, nor recognition." Saudi Arabia was the founder and head of the Rejection Front and, in that role, one of those principally responsible for the forty years of belligerence that ensued.

CHAPTER 17

The Oil Weapon

On September 9, 1960, Saudi Arabia, Iraq, Iran, Kuwait, and Venezuela met in Baghdad to set up an organization that was destined to become a cartel, a monopoly able to control and manipulate the world oil market. Its members, according to its first resolution "can no longer remain indifferent to the attitude heretofore adopted by the oil companies. . . . [They] demand that oil companies maintain their prices steady and free from all unnecessary fluctuations."[1] The formulation is surprising: protecting prices of a commodity from *all* "unnecessary" fluctuations means removing it from the market and making prices dependent on the decisions of a political authority. This is precisely what the "Five Furies of Baghdad," as they were known, had in mind. The demands of these members of the cartel implied the breaking of existing contracts.

A decade earlier, Saudi Arabia had begun to undo past agreements: the financial rewards were turning out to be ever larger.

Aramco had to agree to split oil profits fifty-fifty. Saudi demands continued to increase. Parity caused a quadrupling in the revenues of oil-producing countries between 1950 and 1955. Not that the price paid by consumers had increased. The producing countries successfully demanded that they be paid not on the basis of production costs but on the basis of a fictitious price, the "posted price," which was "political" in nature. By 1952, the kingdom demanded that Saudis be given seats on the board of the American company Aramco, then that its headquarters be moved from New York to Dhahran.

OPEC came out of the fertile mind of Abdullah ibn Hamoud al-Tariki, director-general of petroleum and mineral resources in Saudi Arabia, a petroleum engineer trained at the University of Texas, and an "anti-imperialist" extremist determined to exact payment from the oil companies, which were accused of stealing legitimate revenues from the oil-producing countries. The very terminology was slanted: the countries in question produced nothing at all. Their subsoil held oil that the companies produced, having invested money in order to do so. The producing countries merely pocketed the royalties. Tariki's plan was not only to take control of prices but also of quantities produced and sold and, in the end, to expropriate the companies. The governments that established OPEC had "long since convinced themselves that they were being fleeced by the oil companies with the active encouragement of the governments of the Western industrial countries."[2] There was, as always, a conspiracy. The Western plot did not prevent the revenue of producing countries from doubling again between 1963 and 1968.

From 1967 to 1973, the radicalism of oil-producing countries intensified, reaching a culmination in 1973–1974, when OPEC, and particularly the Arab oil-producing countries, hit the world with the "oil shock." In the meantime, King Faisal had dismissed Tariki and replaced him with Zaki Yamani, with no change in objectives. Saudi Arabia, the largest producer in the world, was the soul of the cartel, which could not have existed without it.

With the Six Day War in 1967, the nascent cartel declared an embargo on oil exports to the United States, Great Britain, and Germany, accused of supporting Israel, but the exporters immediately violated their own embargo, before lifting it in the month of August. In January 1968, Saudi

Arabia, Kuwait, and Libya created the Organization of Arab Petroleum Exporting Countries (OAPEC). The shah of Iran further raised the stakes. Gradually, OPEC and OAPEC grew more sure of themselves. In a resolution adopted at the sixteenth ministerial conference of OPEC in June 1968, the doctrine of "changing circumstances" was set forth: when it seemed appropriate to them, the members of the cartel reserved the right to change the terms and conditions of sale, to acquire a "reasonable share" of the companies, and to change the amounts of taxes and royalties paid by those companies. All of this was justified by the "excessive profits" reaped by the companies. They were treated as captive enterprises, unilaterally. OPEC-OAPEC declared straight out that international law did not apply to oil. A great raid was in preparation against the world economy. The raiding spirit of the Bedouins had not subsided.

Western governments did not provide much support to the companies. Imperialism showed itself to be rather clumsy. The Libya of Qaddafi and the Algeria of Boumediene, armed with a sense of impunity, multiplied forced payments, but there was no major difference between these exalted revolutionaries and the so-called moderates like Saudi Arabia or pro-American regimes like the shah of Iran. The accent was increasingly placed on the available means for exerting pressure: boycott, embargo, expropriation, nationalization. Step by step, the companies capitulated to avoid the fate they were threatened with in case they refused, but in the end they were unable to prevent it. Beginning in 1971, the cartel imposed a series of measures that ate up the companies' shares, the better to digest the profits themselves. "From being the arbiters of the international oil market [the companies] faced relegation to the position of bondservants to the oil states . . ."[3] In 1972, Saudi Arabia began to brandish the threat of taking a majority ownership of Aramco. As Yamani proclaimed, the choice was between "participation" and nationalization, plague or cholera, the stake or the scaffold.

In the early weeks of 1973, the oil companies gave up all their rights and placed themselves at the mercy of the members of the twofold cartel OPEC-OAPEC. The lack of reaction or support on the part of Western governments was the decisive factor encouraging the cartel; the risk was minimal and the potential benefits unlimited.

In the United States, governed by a Nixon who was growing weaker but supposedly under the influence of Big Oil: "The State Department certainly had its quota of officials smitten with the *furor arabicus,* earnest souls who believed that they had unraveled the mysteries of the Arab psyche, and that the understanding they had gained as a consequence, combined with the sympathy they felt for Arab aspirations (or, rather, what they thought these aspirations to be), gave them an incomparable advantage over their French and British counterparts in treating with Arab governments," writes the historian J. B. Kelly with cool irony.[4] The Americans, moreover, thought that the increase in oil prices would calm the Arabs and improve Saudi-American cooperation, which had in the interim become the principal pillar of American policy toward the Arab countries. Let the Saudis become rich, as long as they continued to be clients. Or, to quote John Foster Dulles's classic quip about the bloody Nicaraguan dictator Anastasio Somoza: "Sure, he's a bastard, but he's *our* bastard."

"Raiding was considered the most noble occupation, and the dream of plunder constantly excited the Bedouin's imagination," according to a modern historian's synthesis of nineteenth-century travelers' impressions.[5] In addition, both force and custom dictate that the most powerful Bedouin tribes levy tribute from weaker inferior tribes. This is the meaning of the oil crisis deliberately provoked, at the first available pretext, by His Royal Highness King Faisal bin Abdulaziz of Saudi Arabia, with the active complicity of this Imperial Highness the Emperor of Iran, Reza Shah Pahlavi, a few minor Gulf highnesses, and secular socialist dictators hungry for blood.

Let us return to early 1973. Economic growth had increased oil consumption. Investments had not followed quickly enough, and the markets were stretched. At the margins, there was a slight shortfall in oil supplies, for the moment at least: not a shortage, but a passing problem. All kinds of prophets were extrapolating curves limitlessly and predicting a terrible shortage, an energy crisis. At the same time, it was becoming commonplace to speak of the "culpability" of the "colonialist" and "imperialist" West, which was "pillaging the resources of the Third World" and keeping it, dressed in linen and innocent probity, in backwardness and underdevelopment. It was time to pay historical debts. The hour of reparation had come. The *Internationale* called for the thief to give up his plunder, and King Faisal joined in the chorus.

A first event set off a few powder kegs. It was more and more difficult to maintain fixed exchange rates on volatile international currency markets. Anticipating a decline, Saudi Arabia and Kuwait speculated massively against the dollar, which further weakened the already fragile American currency. In February 1973, the dollar was devalued by 11.11 percent. OPEC complained about the loss in profits that it had itself helped to cause. Anti-imperialist slogans were chanted by dignitaries wearing gold-lined *djellabas* or three-piece suits, proclaiming the terrible sacrifices they had accepted to subsidize the West. Shameless.

A Saudi supporter in the United States wrote in *Foreign Affairs* in April: "King Faisal [has] said repeatedly that the Arabs should not, and that he himself would not, allow oil to be used, as a political weapon."[6] The Saudi oil minister, Yamani, warned in February that collective action on the part of the consuming countries would provoke "war." OPEC would "destroy their industries and civilization," declared this moderate.[7] In July, a communiqué from OPEC was even more assertive: "Seeking a direct confrontation with OPEC could inflict harm on the world economy." Yamani predicted that the next increase in oil prices would be huge and that it would be neither negotiated nor negotiable.

OPEC's intentions and plans had already gone into operation. It was at this point that King Faisal decided to change the game. In early May, he summoned the chairman of the board and the president of Aramco, R. W. Powers and Frank Jungers, and said to them in essence: "With regard to the deterioration of the situation in the Middle East and the dangers threatening the interests of the United States in the region because of the stalemate in the Arab-Israeli situation, [it is] absolutely mandatory that the United States be involved. . . . Saudi Arabia is the only Arab country in which American interests are safe, but Saudi Arabia could not hold out much longer against the anti-American feeling that prevailed in the rest of the Arab world."[8] It was necessary to "improve the image" of the United States in Arab eyes.

One is dumbfounded by this endless refrain played by Saudi leaders for the last thirty or forty years, brought out at every opportunity: "Saudi Arabia was becoming increasingly isolated from the other Arab states because of her friendship with the United States." The king "believed that President [Anwar el-] Sadat of Egypt intended to go to war against Israel. . . . Saudi Arabia could not afford to stand aloof from the battle. Inevitably the question of oil supplies would arise, and when it did . . . he was 'deeply concerned' that the tide of events might prove fatal to American interests in the Middle East, even in Saudi Arabia itself."[9] The nerve is once again breathtaking. Faisal financed Sadat's war, and he would have been completely unable to wage it without the huge subsidies provided by the Saudis. Faisal orchestrated, organized, and financed the war that broke out in October 1973, the "Yom Kippur War," called the "Ramadan War" by the Arabs," which it would be better to call "Faisal's War."

In late May in Geneva, Faisal received Powers and Jungers, together with the directors responsible for Middle Eastern operations of Esso, Socal, Texaco, and Mobil, just after he had conferred with Sadat in Cairo. "Time is running out with respect to United States interests in the Middle East," he told them. Saudi Arabia, the only friend the United States had in the area, was in danger of being isolated because the Americans had failed to give her positive support by taking the initiative over Israel. He was not going to allow that to happen. "You will lose everything," he warned the appalled oilmen, threatening to revoke Aramco's concession in its entirety. What Aramco must do, he said, was firstly to "inform the American public, which was being misled by biased news reports and propaganda, where its 'true interests' lay in the Middle East," and secondly, to impress upon the American government the urgent need for action. "Time is running out," he repeated. "You may lose everything."

Aramco had been a loyal servant, counselor, steward, intermediary, and propagandist for Saudi Arabia. The company had stitched together a network of clients and influences, it had invested in all kinds of foundations, learned societies, political and cultural organizations, and in the press. It had made its mark on the ideas that Americans had about Saudi Arabia. On their return to the United States, the oilmen went to the State Department to lobby the administration directly on behalf of King Faisal. Aramco and its parent companies launched a campaign of propaganda and political lobbying to try to bring about a change in American policy favorable to the Arabs. One year later, a Senate investigative committee sharply criticized it for acting as "instrument of the Saudi Arab government and carrying out Saudi orders in terms of influencing U.S. foreign policy."[10]

On October 6, 1973, Egyptian troops launched an attack on the Bar-Lev line, the fortified line of defense erected by Israel on the east bank of the Suez Canal. Iraq instantly nationalized what oil holdings had been left in the hands of foreign companies. The Gulf states doubled the price of a barrel of oil, and Iran increased its prices by 70 percent.

On October 17, the acting Saudi foreign minister, Omar Saqqaf, handed Secretary of State Henry A. Kissinger a letter from King Faisal stating that if the United States did not within forty-eight hours halt the dispatch of arms to Israel, an embargo would be placed on the shipment of oil to the United States. Washington replied that the United States was committed to aiding Israel.

That same night, the Arab oil ministers announced that they would reduce production by five percent each month "until the Israeli forces are completely evacuated from all the Arab territories occupied in the June 1967 war, and the legitimate rights of the Palestinian people are restored," who thus made their official entry into the politics of oil.[11] With this step, the oil producing countries began to shear the Western sheep, plucking the Third World chickens along the way.

The hounds had been loosed. Abu Dhabi and Qatar imposed a complete embargo on exports to the United States and simultaneously raised the price of a barrel to nine dollars, compared to the three dollars of a few months earlier. But the other oil producers waited to see what posture Saudi Arabia would adopt. On October 18, President Nixon asked Congress to approve emergency funds to cover arms shipments to Israel. On October 20, Faisal declared *jihad* against Israel, calling upon all Muslims to join it, and at the same time ordering the immediate cessation of all oil shipments to the United States, including supplies to American armed forces wherever they might be. The next day, Yamani summoned the heads of Aramco to Riyadh "and gave them detailed instructions about the implementation of the embargo": a general cut of ten percent and no oil for the United States. An American company thus acted on the orders of a foreign state to subject the United States to an embargo on a product of vital importance. The countries deemed sympathetic to the Arab cause—Britain, France, Spain, Jordan, Lebanon—were exempt from the boycott. In contrast, the "odious neutrality" of Japan was sharply criticized, and the "hostile" attitude of the Dutch to the Arab cause, that is, their refusal to surrender to blackmail, made them a particular target. The French and British governments publicly declared that they would prohibit any re-export of oil to the Netherlands. So much for European solidarity.

The embargo openly violated several United Nations declarations and resolutions, including the 1970 declaration that provided: "No state may use or encourage the use of economic, political, or any other type of measures to coerce another state in order to obtain from it the subordination of the exercise of its sovereign rights and to secure from it advantages of any kind." The embargo violated the Saudi-American trade treaty of 1933. And it also broke the contractual agreements between Aramco and the kingdom.

On November 21, a statement by Kissinger increased the pressure by indicating that "the United States would have to consider counter-measures if the Arab boycott continued for too long." Angered by this impiety, Yamani threatened to reduce production by 80 percent. "I don't know to what extent Europe and Japan will get together to join the Americans in any kind of measures, because your whole economy will definitely collapse all of a sudden. If the Americans are thinking of a military action, this is a possibility, but this is suicide. There are some sensitive areas in the oilfields in Saudi Arabia which will be blown up."[12]

Washington took no follow-up action. On the other hand, an OPEC conference on December 22 decided to increase the price of crude again, which would be raised to $11.65 on January 1. OPEC refused to institute a two-track system which would have spared the poor countries of Asia and Africa: everyone had to be shorn equally, the poor along with the rest.

The embargo against the United States was lifted in March 1974, but OPEC had won, and behind the organization, its largest producer, Saudi Arabia. Having broken all conceivable agreements, contracts, alliances, and obligations, the kingdom and its henchmen, far from being punished, made off with their booty. "It is our revenge for Poitiers," said one official of an Arab oil state. The Western *dhimmis* now had to pay the *jizya*, the tax levied on non-Muslim People of the Book.[13]

In a few months, 10 to 15 percent of world cash flow had just been diverted, drained from the veins and arteries irrigating the world economy and reinjected elsewhere, where it could not be used in a productive way.

The economic effects of the "great *ghazu*" devastated the world economy. The diversion contributed to a formidable acceleration of inflation, provoked continuing instability in exchange rates in the 1970s and 1980s, and ruined the economies of the least developed countries of Latin America, Africa, and Asia, becoming the primary cause of the major debt crisis that affected them so tragically. Compared to the 1970 price, the posted increase in the price of crude reached 800 percent in 1974, 1,000 percent in 1977, and 1,500 percent in 1979. Average inflation in industrialized countries rose from four percent in 1971 to twelve percent in 1974.

Crude oil that sold for $18 a barrel in early 1979 cost 15 cents to produce in Saudi Arabia, and it was thus sold at 12,000 percent the cost of production: an absolute record. The interests of Saudi royalty had cleverly used the Marxist rhetoric of fashionable anti-imperialist economists, whereas all petroleum wealth had become a resource only through Western investment. The monopolistic cartel was a regression to the pre-modern era of guilds, corporations, and monopolies that impose their rules on whoever does not belong to the cartel. Oil had been removed from the market thanks to the joint action of the Marxist left and the archaic Wahhabi monarchy, equally anti-capitalist. And the entire thing had been prepared, planned, and orchestrated by King

Faisal, who was able to consider the rest of the world as *dar al-Abid*, the "land of slaves."[14]

In Riyadh, real estate prices were multiplied by two thousand. Whoever owned land—the royal family and its countless servants—became almost instantly a multimillionaire.[15]

CHAPTER 18

Buying Palaces and Countries

The smallest vacant lot in Riyadh, Jeddah, Taif, or any other Saudi city, once its owner had passed Go where fortune awaited him, ran almost instantaneously through all the squares of the game; every oasis "Baltic Avenue" quickly took on the dark blue hue and the cash value of "Park Avenue."

Foreigners are not allowed to buy real property in Saudi Arabia, no doubt for religious reasons. If you wanted to rent or build, the landowners had to be paid handsomely.

To do business in the kingdom's territory, it was not enough for foreign construction firms to establish a subsidiary and set to work; first, they had to find a Saudi partner, who became a shareholder in the company created for the purpose. The shareholder, who was a member of the board of directors, had to be paid. The right to represent a foreign partner became a new form of plunder. With no effort other than lending the use of his name, the Saudi subject received a commission given the noble name of *sai* ("effort").

Given the minimal development of the infrastructure of ports, roads, and railroads, and of administrative, governmental, and municipal services—the consequence of decades of inaction—nothing was ready on time, even when the newly acquired fortune of the House of Saud gave it the opportunity to indulge in an indescribable frenzy of purchases and construction projects. It cost three or four times as much as anywhere else to build anything.

All kinds of personnel were lacking: electricians, plumbers, surveyors, masons, welders, carpenters, glaziers, furnace men, and even sweepers. Armies of modern serfs were imported from Pakistan, South Korea, and the Philippines and parked in camps. There are now five or six million of them, variously estimated at 40 to 57 percent of the kingdom's total workforce.[1] Since illiteracy—according to official figures as reliable as those for Soviet planning in the past—affects more than 37 percent of Saudis over the age of fifteen, it is clear that the contribution of foreign labor is indispensable. These serfs looked on with contempt—because they work, because they are foreigners—do everything. Saudis supervise, sign, and pray five times a day.

A foreign serf arriving in Saudi Arabia has to surrender his passport to the Saudi "sponsor" of his stay. No one can secure a visa without a Saudi sponsor, or even apply for one. The sponsor's agreement is also required to receive an exit visa, without which no one may leave Saudi Arabia. In between, the immigrant worker has no rights: no legal recourse protects his labor contract or the performance of its provisions; he is at the mercy of the sponsor, and foreign consulates have no right to intervene. Blackmail and extortion are common practices.[2]

Not only manual serfs, but also intellectual serfs are under these strict controls. Saudi Arabia, reflecting all its previous social and cultural choices, with no architects, engineers, urban planners, or landscape architects, imported high-tech serfs from the United States, Europe, and Asia. Costs rose at a dizzying rate.

Even the most basic supplies had to be imported, from the first brick to the last gram of cement, the sheet metal and the steel beams, the door handles and the locks. A huge bottleneck was created at the top of a huge funnel. Waiting time for unloading in the kingdom's ports could last three months or more. To deliver to Saudi Arabia, shippers added surcharges of 50 to 250 percent to their bills. In 1976, it was estimated that congestion in the ports added 40 percent to the cost of imports.[3]

The initial waste was enormous and took several years to be reduced. But it only gave way to further waste.

The extravagance continued. Prince Abdulaziz bin Fahd, the favorite son of King Fahd, had a $300 million palace built in Riyadh. As soon as it was completed, he came to his father to ask him to finance another one, this time in Jeddah. This was waste at the top. Lower down the scale, the waste was no less and appeared in the most absurd forms. Cows were imported by air at an exorbitant cost. Subsidies were provided futilely for agriculture that was almost impossible in that climate. Almost anyone could get a $150,000 grant to set up a farm—a fortune—and spend it all on consumer goods. The average life expectancy for a new building in the country was seven years: buildings built in 1973 were demolished and replaced by 1980. As a journalist who observed all this explains: "This building, tearing up, and rebuilding served a necessary political and economic function. . . . Members of the royal family all had concessions on various development projects or public works. Princes owned construction companies and building supply establishments and often were labor brokers or represented equipment companies exporting to Saudi Arabia."[4] Since anyone could drive without a license, the utility poles of Riyadh were constantly being hit and destroyed: the government had to spend $400 million to bury the lines. The government subsidized food commodities, and taxes were all but eliminated.[5]

The Saudi became the very embodiment of the situationist dream: living without limits and taking pleasure without restraint, or of the famous slogan of Italian leftists in the 1970s, *niente di lavoro, tutto il denaro* ("no work on a full salary"). The budget of a ubiquitous welfare state maintained a population of aid recipients for life in the framework of this redistributive economy. The allocation of funds took place in concentric circles and from top to bottom. Proximity to the royal family represented the most important factor, the closest being the most munificently rewarded. Parents and clients were fostered in this way. The political factor was also important: the tribes, mainstays of the regime, were richly endowed.

Apart from the allowance given them at birth, the princes receive huge advances on oil wealth. The king himself pockets 10 percent of the oil receipts, $8 billion annually on average for thirty years. King Fahd, who took the throne in 1982, has thus pocketed, we may estimate, $160 billion in gross revenues.

Oil earnings make one dizzy. In the five years following the oil shock of 1973, they amounted (in 2002 dollars) to more than $384 billion. Earnings for the next five years, 1978–1982, reached more than $720 billion. For the third round, so to speak, the brigands had to make do with much less: their extortions had created enough of a recession to bring about a lowering of earnings and substantial efforts to change the relationship between energy consumption and unit of GNP in the West. From 1983 to 1987, the booty amounted to only $280 billion, and the recession deepened between 1988 and 1992, so that revenues did not go beyond $220 billion. But we can be reassured that the Al-Saud family was not reduced to beggary. Earnings stagnated again over the next five-year period at $256 billion. The 1998–2002 period pointed to a rise, with more than $216 billion in four years.

The figures are so enormous that they lose all meaning. These are not financial assets taken up in cycles of investment, production, inventory, and distribution, but royalties. The use made of them is even worse. There was one "five-year plan" after another, supposed to lay the foundations for sustainable development of the country. The resemblances with the Soviet Union are deeper than religious and ideological differences would suggest. The plan was a catalogue of pious hopes, illusions, and proposals, devoid of coherence and realism. The figures had cathartic and symbolic value: they were not a matter of economic realities but of prestige. The minister of planning, Hisham Nazer, said one day that the new plan would exert all effort in "the preservation of Islamic values and the propagation of the divine faith." Had the number of conversions been planned?[6]

As in any third world country, speaking of economic planning when the most basic tools of daily life and economic accounting were lacking was a joke. In 1974, 70 percent of the population was illiterate. The government had in fact simply rejected the results of the first census ever taken in the country, in 1962, because the figures did not satisfy the requirements of national prestige. There were not enough Saudis to make up an impressive number.

The "plan" stood for modernity, a grandiose triumph over underdevelopment. Saudi Arabia had to wait until 1967 for its first paved road, from Riyadh to Jeddah. Slavery was not abolished, officially at least, until 1962. The castles built in the air were even more megalomaniacal and illusory. Because the kingdom lacked technicians, it was said with the utmost seriousness that Western countries—if they wanted to avoid future embargoes—should oblige their technicians to spend some time in Saudi Arabia to contribute to the great work. They were going to produce petrochemicals in enormous complexes built for billions of dollars, and the question of markets was not an issue; the Western clients would buy, or else they would get no more oil.[7]

After an entire generation of petro-monarchy, we can draw up a balance sheet. A period of thirty years makes it possible to draw some conclusions: what were the petrodollars used for?

If they had developed the Saudi economy, the share of oil in exports would have declined, perhaps in favor of agriculture, certainly of industry and services. But all available data show that nothing of the kind has happened. According to the Saudi authorities, the share of oil and its byproducts in exports was 91 percent in 1974, 92 percent in 1980, 89.7 percent in 1990, and 91.4 percent in 2000.[8] There has been no industrialization, no economic progress. It will be objected that an enormous infrastructure has been built. What infrastructure? A single rail line links Riyadh to Dhahran, the road network is very inadequate, telephone equipment per capita is one twentieth that of Europe, and electricity reaches barely 60 percent of the population. As for schools, 80 percent of them are located in rented premises, with no maintenance and an average backlog of five years in rent payments, and the public health system is weak and of poor quality. Does the infrastructure serve any purpose? Industry contributes less than one tenth of GNP, while the neighbor to the south, the much poorer Yemen, is approaching 11 percent, and Morocco has exceeded 26 percent. Why invest in industry—and in a productive career—when you can invest in land and buildings, in brokerage and finance?

In 1980, GNP per capita was $18,000, which placed Saudi Arabia in the front rank of nations. It is now six or seven thousand dollars, a precipitous and catastrophic decline. Dependency on oil is addictive: the patient is on a permanent IV drip, without which he would sink, since he lacks the means to support himself.

What was created was a façade of modernity, not a true modernity. Buildings of glass and steel were certainly erected: the flashy and impressive sequins of modernity. They created a Potemkin village economy, an artificial façade of a thin layer of modern installations with no foundations, a mirage soon swallowed by the sand and engulfed by the dunes.

All the world's wealth poured into Saudi Arabia in thirty years did not make it possible for infant mortality to fall below 49 per thousand. This is better than Bangladesh (68.05 per thousand) or Cambodia (64), which don't have oil, but much worse than Costa Rica (10.87 per thousand), which has no oil either.[9] Infant mortality is one of the most precise indicators of the investment a society has made in its future, its children. The verdict cannot be appealed. This is all the more true because rapid demographic growth, one of the highest in the world, increasing by 3.3 percent per year—an average Saudi woman has 6.2 children—has led to a population explosion, increasing from perhaps five to six million in 1970 to eighteen million Saudis in 2002. Seventy percent of the population is now below the age of fifteen, and they have very limited employment prospects. Domestic and foreign debt have swollen. There has been a continuing budget deficit for more than a decade.

Demographic projections predict a population of 46 million in 2030. Unless there are new oil shocks, the kingdom will be able to offer them neither employment nor the benefits of a welfare state. Students who enrolled massively in Islamic studies, much more than in technical studies, cannot turn that into a profession. The number of mosques cannot be endlessly increased: there are already 50,000, roughly one mosque for every one hundred male inhabitants above the age of fifteen. Unless they export young men in the form of preachers and terrorists—which has already begun—the kingdom cannot deal with them. The population, treated by its rulers like the plebes of the late Roman Empire, is not in a position to deal with the decline in oil revenues. The Saudi regime has staked everything on oil and on the ability of the kingdom to pressure the entire world.

The immense waste, the greedy and ostentatious consumption, the unbridled vulgarity of the plump royal family with its appetite for unlimited wealth and luxury, clearly reflect the nature of those responsible. There is no need to be a strict moralist to be offended by them. Another aspect, however, requires our attention: that is the economic nature of the waste. As we have said, total oil revenue in the years 1973 to 2001 amounted to more than two trillion dollars.

To this underlying amount has to be added the compound interest: huge sums were invested, or "recycled" as it was said in the 1970s and 1980s, through Western banks (certificates of deposit, Treasury bills, stocks, bonds, and so on). All of that produced interest, which was returned to the investor or accumulated. It is difficult, if not impossible, to determine the amount of Saudi financial assets held abroad. In the United States alone, estimates vary from $700 billion to $1.2 trillion.

In any event, the entirety of the sums paid as oil surcharges was removed from the channels of "normal" economic circulation and redirected toward economic activity conducted with unlimited losses. There was no sense and no economic benefit in developing agriculture or the petrochemical industry in Saudi Arabia. The petrochemical industry was in fact a staggering failure: everything was constructed with no concern for profitability or economic rationality. The Saudis had grown used to dictating their law to the oil market. In fact, they had tried to abolish it as a market. When they appeared on other markets, such as that for petrochemical products, the recipe ("Buy our products, or we'll cut off your supplies; your refusal to buy our products is an insult to Islam and to the sacred cause of the Arabs") had become ineffectual.

The entire diversion of resources carried out through oil surcharges thus ended up essentially in a sterilization of resources, the disappearance of resources into the "black hole" of Saudi Arabia. It was as a complete loss, in the full sense of the term, that the revenues extracted from the rest of the world were absorbed by Saudi Arabia.

To be sure, Western companies build in Saudi Arabia, and others export products, work, and produce there. But the huge costs involved are the very embodiment of true "economic horror." Of course, the advanced military technologies delivered to Saudi Arabia—which does not know how to use them—are produced. But because each economic stage is burdened by huge additional costs—imported labor, administrative chaos and incoherent organization, corruption unmatched anywhere in the world, multiple commissions for intermediaries at every link in the chain—it is as though the political capacity of Saudi Arabia to impose oil prices that bear no relation to the costs of production (unlike any other commodity) had brought about a tremendous economic distortion.

Anyone looking for a definition of imperialism will find a more accurate one there than in the obscure scrawls of Vladimir Ilyich Lenin. "A predatory political organization led by a group calling itself an elite (whether the group is ethnic, religious, or political) that establishes and preserves its ability to confiscate or impose burdens on the wealth of peoples and nations subjugated by force." If this is indeed the definition of an empire, then Saudi Arabia is an empire, an imperialist empire, if the expression may be allowed.

The Bedouins who govern Saudi Arabia today are the heirs of twenty centuries of an economy of banditry. As Ibn Khaldun showed, they scorn work on the land and as craftsmen. Work is not a positive value, not an activity that gratifies the soul. In their system of values and beliefs, it is an activity reserved for inferiors, because work, an industrial job, for example, requires conformity to rules and obedience to superiors who are not tribal superiors. Manual labor is considered degrading and repugnant. One may drive a car, but never repair it. This explains the radical failure of technical education in Saudi Arabia. "In an attempt to attract students into courses on welding, carpentry, refrigeration, car mechanics, electricity, and plumbing, the government during the Third Plan paid all educational expenses for the students and gave them a salary during training. To sweeten the attraction even further, graduates were promised a SR 200,000 ($58,823) interest-free loan to set up their own businesses. Yet there were few takers," according to an observer.[10] It was a totally different story for office work, or a job as a government official.

The relationship of Saudis to work during the oil age has been succinctly described by an Egyptian sociologist: "Probably the most devastating negative effect of the oil wealth and its chain reaction has been the near collapse of work ethics in the Arab world. Easily earned and easily spent money undermines the value of productive work."[11]

Moreover, according to a former British ambassador to Saudi Arabia, "they reject any manual or domestic labor, and balk at undertaking anything boring or routine. Plumbing is manual labor, sweeping the streets is work for a servant: those tasks are assigned only to foreigners. Making decisions is a noble task, but preparing decisions is lowly, as is collecting data, assembling statistics, checking references, and planning schedules."[12]

"Everything comes from God, and the oil is no exception," declared Prince Turki al-Faisal, son of the king and head of the intelligence services, hence an expert in economic matters. That oil might have something to do with Western engineers, Texas and California companies, the physical, chemical, and mechanical sciences developed in Europe and the United States, or with the five or six million foreign serfs who bear the burden of the only real work carried out in his country, does not seem to cross the mind of this apostle of the beneficent Allah. As a modern historian of Saudi Arabia remarks: "Saudis *know* that God gave them all the wealth and power that they currently enjoy . . ."[13]

These terse comments reveal, in their shockingly primitive candor, the deep reality of the conception of the world held by the Al-Saud family: everything comes from God. Hence, there is no process by which wealth is created. As good predatory nomads, as described by Ibn Khaldun, "It is their nature to plunder whatever other people possess. Their sustenance lies wherever the shadow of their lances falls. They recognize no limit in taking the possessions of other people. Whenever their eyes fall upon some property, furnishings, or utensils, they take it. When they acquire superiority and royal authority, they have complete power to plunder as they please. There no longer exists any political power to protect property, and civilization is ruined."

The fourteenth-century Tunisian historian goes on: "Furthermore, since they use force to make craftsmen and professional workers do their work, they do not see any value in it and do not pay them for it. Now . . . labor is the real basis of profit." The town-dwelling Arab has provided an acute analysis of the Arabs of the desert; he already knew then what they still do not know.[14]

If there is no creation of wealth through work, but only transfer of wealth by force, this is because the world is a zero-sum game in which one grows rich only at the expense of others, in which there is no productive cooperation, no fruitful exchange. This world, as sterile as the desert, is anti-capitalism.

The only constraint, the only limit on the plunder of the property of others, are the limits on the use of force and coercion by the predator. He respects force because he can neither counter nor conquer it. He crushes weakness. An excellent economic doctrine. This is a world in which economic constraints do not exist. The correspondence to economic doctrines professed by Hitler and Lenin is not accidental, proclaiming as they did that "costs do not exist," but only will, that is, brute force, military force, political force.[15] We are in a thoroughly premodern era.

The year 1973 had fundamentally changed the position of Saudi Arabia in the world. Leader of OPEC, orchestrator and principal beneficiary of the oil crisis, endowed with a treasury that was growing exponentially, and hero of the Arab world for having humiliated the despised West and reawakened Arab "honor," Saudi Arabia now occupied a central place in world affairs. The world, through thousands of journalists, hung on every word of Zaki Yamani, the oil minister who had become a media star. There was a rush to Riyadh to beg for scraps of petrodollars, contracts, hopes for contracts, allusions to some hope. The slightest syllable from the oracles of Riyadh became a matter for scholarly exegesis in the economic press. What use would be made of the brand new power acquired by the House of Saud?

Domestically, even while a swarm of foreign goods and technologies filled the openings made by oil wealth, the policy consisted of closing off minds while opening the doors. "My kingdom will survive only insofar as it remains a country difficult of access, where the foreigner will have no other aim, with his task fulfilled, but to get out," Ibn Saud had declared.[16]

As for the outside world, "Faisal believed it possible to transfer into the international arena the domestic principles on which the Saudi state was based. Islam provided stability, security, purpose, and discipline at home—so why not abroad as well?"[17] We have already quoted this diagnosis, which illuminates the motives and methods of the House of Saud abroad.

It has been said that "Abdulaziz [ibn Saud] bought the tribes. His sons bought the neighboring countries."

Egypt had opened the procession with the humble submission of the proud Nasser. Egypt's financial survival, Anwar el-Sadat recognized, depended on Saudi subsidies. He did nothing that ran counter to Saudi policies until he was certain of a solid alliance with the United States, which gave him some degree of autonomy, but left him no peace. He had to pay with his life for the Camp David agreement with Israel. Saudi Arabia has always been suspicious of Egyptian power. The memory of the troops of Ibrahim Pasha has not faded.

By 1973, Syria had become a client state of Saudi Arabia. With the October (Yom Kippur) War, this poor country, with its resources dried up by an implacable dictatorship and swallowed by a bloated military budget, needed a strategic protector—the Soviet Union—and a financial protector— Saudi Arabia. Neither Moscow nor Riyadh found fault with the arrangement.

Saudi Arabia was the primary supplier of funds to Yasser Arafat, who received more than a billion dollars from 1973 to 1981. The transformation of the killer into a diplomatic star depended a good deal on Saudi efforts. Without the oil crisis and its consequences, it would have been inconceivable that the organizer of the murder of Israeli athletes at the Munich Olympic Games in 1972 could come to the podium of the United Nations in 1974—dressed in military fatigues—to call for the destruction of Israel. The General Assembly granted the PLO observer status because an "Arab bloc" had been established and it carried some weight. The votes of poor nations were for sale, and they were bought. To its shame, the United Nations in 1975 adopted the vile resolution equating Zionism with "racism." This was the result of the diplomatic activity of Saudi Arabia and of "the rebirth of Islam" in action. "'Only Muslims and Christians have holy places and rights in Jerusalem,' said the king [Faisal]. 'The Jews have no shrines in Jerusalem. . . . The Jews have no rights in Jerusalem.'"[18]

The subsequent purchase of Pakistan was to have extraordinary consequences in the succeeding decades. On February 22, 1972, Faisal called an Islamic summit conference in Pakistan. The success was enormous in terms of participation. Allegiance, or the lack thereof, to the summoning power is demonstrated by coming or not, or sending a head of delegation of a more or less elevated rank. Presidents, prime ministers, kings, and *emirs* all appeared and pledged allegiance. Even Baathist Iraq, along with Bangladesh, Cameroon, Gabon, Guinea-Bissau—one wonders what they were doing there—Uganda, Upper Volta, and the PLO. Crowning everything, the "socialist" prime minister of Pakistan, Zulfikar Ali Bhutto, a great feudal plutocrat who originated the Islamization of law in his country, stimulated by promises of financing, proclaimed: "The armies of Pakistan are the armies of Islam. We shall enter Jerusalem as brothers-in-arms!"[19] A few years later, Prince Fahd made an agreement with the Pakistani dictator Zia ul-Haq providing for the permanent stationing of two elite battalions of the Pakistani army in Saudi Arabia in order to deal with any eventuality in the Gulf. The renting of Pakistani mercenaries had begun.

To consolidate his hegemony in the "first circle" of its strategic environment, the "Arab circle," and in the second, the "Muslim circle," Faisal had created a new body the Organization of the Islamic Conference (OIC) as well as the World Muslim League.

The time had come for Faisal to leave the stage. One of his countless nephews (of whom there were several hundred), of deranged mind, it was said, lodged several revolver bullets in his body. Only five of the sixteen successions that took place in the House of Saud from 1744 to 1975 were free of troubles—assassinations, civil war, palace revolution. The king's leave-taking was violent, but the arrival of his successor, his brother Khalid, took place smoothly.

The colorless Khalid simply continued along the path set by his elder brother. In failing health, and having a character with few sharp edges, he allowed his brothers and nephews to establish powerful fiefdoms in cabinet ministries, which enabled them to supplement their dynastic positions with political and economic functions. The reins that had been tightly held by Faisal were loosened by his younger brother, who ruled until 1982. It was under his reign that the nationalization of Aramco was completed. The company became Saudi Aramco.

It was also during his reign that Sadat shook the Middle East by going to Jerusalem in October 1977 and signing a peace agreement between Israel and Egypt with Menachem Begin at Camp David. The position adopted by Saudi Arabia, which had become the linchpin of the Arab world, would be decisive. When Saddam Hussein of Iraq organized an Arab summit to decree sanctions, Crown Prince Fahd— whom the king's ill health had left in command—acquiesced.

President Jimmy Carter, always prepared to open his heart, had greeted Fahd in Washington with a quaver in his voice: "I do not believe that we have a deeper friendship or a feeling of greater cooperation than with Saudi Arabia."[20] That did not prevent the crown prince from keeping his distance from the West, the U.S. included. He suddenly cancelled a planned state visit to the United States and, on March 31, 1979, announced that he was breaking diplomatic relations with Egypt, and that Saudi Arabia was joining the general boycott decreed against it by the Arab countries. Saudi Arabia was a participating member in the "Rejection Front." It had rejected the historic opportunity to make peace in the Middle East that had been opened up by the Egyptian leader. It allied itself with the Arab clients of the Soviet Union.

Some temporary divergences seem to have opposed Fahd to the rest of the family. The crown prince advocated imposing minimal sanctions on Cairo in order to "ensure the services of Egypt against the radical Arab states and against the Iranian revolution, and to avoid burdening relations with the United States." The policy advocated by his half-brother Abdallah, now the crown prince, favored punishing Sadat and remaining close to extremist Syria and Iraq. Fahd was placed in the minority and went for a two month vacation abroad, which he spent drinking like a fish. Abdallah, who was in charge in the interim, made sure that Saudi Arabia supported the sanctions in their entirety.

The lesson was clear: the royal family would always choose what would maintain its leadership in the Arab-Muslim world, to the detriment of efforts toward peace and reconciliation. It would always choose family unity above any other consideration. It would always make the continuation of its monopoly the principal basis of its decisions, whatever the consequences for neighboring countries, the region, and the rest of the world.

The events of the two succeeding decades did nothing but verify this diagnosis.

Conclusion: Taking Saudi Out of Arabia

The Arabia called "Saudi" is a pseudo-state: the weight of the evidence is overwhelming. A subtribe, with unlimited appetites, has seized control of the Arabian peninsula and treats territory, resources, and population as its private possessions. The modern buildings of Riyadh cannot conceal the reality: they are a cardboard façade, a Hollywood back lot transported to Arabia in which, seen from a distance, the cast plays with the tools of modern civilization; there are cabinet offices, an economic plan, a central bank, businesses, and banks. Seen close up, Saudi reality is defined by the bearded thugs of the religious police and by the unconditional and unlimited stranglehold of the Al-Sauds and their tribal and religious allies on power.

Saudi Arabia is also an outlaw pseudo-state. Domestically, the princes are above and beyond the laws that are harshly imposed on all the others, the inferior species of ordinary Saudis, Saudi women, foreign serfs, and Shiites. This multifaceted apartheid is a constitutive element of Saudi Arabia. *Bas Saudi* (not Saudi) is the equivalent of *nee wit* (nonwhite) of South African apartheid. The possession and consumption of alcohol, as we know, are considered hanging offenses. But behind their high walls, the Al-Saud princes, alone sheltered from the *mutawiyin*, drink heavily and have made cirrhosis a family disease. The example comes from on high: King Saud drank himself to death, and King Fahd followed without restraint. Immunity covers not only the crime of alcohol consumption: no one may touch the Al-Sauds except the Al-Sauds themselves.

The head of the *mutawiyin*, we should point out, has ministerial rank, but the "minister" does not have the right to investigate the princes. This says all that needs to be said about the absence of law and the nature of the Saudi "state," an agreed-upon façade enabling it to behave like others on the international stage. Tribal chieftainship is a parody of a state, the tribal chief plays at being a cabinet minister.

But Saudi apartheid is not satisfied with its vast territory; it takes advantage of its huge oil wealth to conquer other territories. The absence of law that characterizes Saudi Arabia has pretensions to spread to the rest of the world, as though the Saudi outlaws were entitled, wherever they go, to a kind of extraterritorial status. When Prince Bandar bin Sultan, ambassador to Washington, uses his personal jet to travel to his home in Aspen, or when Crown Prince Abdallah goes to see the president of the United States, their pilots refuse to talk to air traffic controllers if they are women: "No females, we're Saudis." The anecdote, angrily disclosed by air traffic controllers, is revealing about a system, about the refusal to accept the law of others, and the imperious will to impose their own law. Examples of this thuggish behavior are countless: Prince Turki bin Abdulaziz illegally confines and beats a slave in Miami, and when the police come asks for diplomatic immunity to which he is not entitled. And Saudi pressure, joined with the craven support of the Saudi lobby in Washington, secures it for him a week after the event.[1]

The immunity is not diplomatic, but princely: the Al-Sauds consider themselves a species superior to the rest of the human race. As long as they were only starving camel drivers, that was of no importance. It was the great oil raid of 1973 and its consequences that turned these exorbitant pretensions into accepted demands. A Saudi prince does not obey your laws, infidel churls! Nor does he obey the laws of other Muslims. A very particular form of hatred surfaces in Arab countries in reaction to the manners and the contemptuous arrogance of those who think they can buy everything and everyone.

Let us admit further that the title "prince" is purely formal. Even if one were to respect the right of illiterate and coarse nomads to call their chiefs princes—we have no reason to be gratuitously discourteous—the demographic explosion of the Al-Saud family has created an endless supply of pseudo-princes. It even seems impossible to count this subspecies, which multiplies uncontrollably. Are there three or eight thousand Saudi "princes"? No one knows. If necessary, it was agreed—politeness to foreigners—to call a dozen bearded men in *jellabas* "princes." But five or eight thousand? Inflation, as is well known, devalues currency. The inflation of princes has devalued the title. Each prince thus bears the title of only one five thousandth of a prince, so that at diplomatic receptions, the introduction might go: "His Royal Highness the five-thousandth of a Prince Bandar," which would be closer to reality.

And what do these fragments of princes say when they talk to each other? In this area we have fragmentary but invaluable documentation. The "big ears" of American intelligence, the National Security Agency (NSA), intercepts conversations among members of the royal family and collates them. Some transcriptions were disclosed to Seymour Hersh, an American journalist who specializes in being used as an intelligence man's duct.[2] His introductory comment is damning: "The intercepted [conversations] reveal a regime that is more and more corrupt, which has alienated its religious base, which is so weak and afraid that it tried to secure the future by providing hundreds of millions of dollars in tribute to fundamentalist groups that want to overthrow it so that they would leave it in peace." The intercepts also reveal that "since 1996 Saudi finance has been supporting Bin Laden and al-Qaeda and other extremist groups in Afghanistan, Lebanon, Yemen, and central Asia, and throughout the Gulf region." Hersh quotes an American intelligence official: "The Saudi regime has gone over to the dark side."

As for the princes, "they speak openly [on the telephone] about looting the state, and even quibble about acceptable percentages to skim off." Other transcripts "indicate that Prince Bandar, the ambassador, was a party to contracts for arms sales in London, Yemen, and the Soviet Union. It is true that the huge "Yamama" contract with Great Britain for several billion pounds sterling included commissions at the rate of approximately 40 percent. The same Bandar, in answer to a question, was irritated that anyone dared even discuss the problem: "If you tell me that building this whole country, and spending $350 billion out of $400 billion, that we misused or got corrupted with $50 billion, I'll tell you, "Yes." But I'll take that any time. . . . But, more important, more important—who are you to tell me this? . . . What I'm trying to tell you is, so what? We did not invent corruption. . . . I mean, this is human nature. But we are not as bad as you think."[3] But it is practiced on an industrial scale, the only industry in Saudi Arabia where the natives display technical proficiency.

Relying on the NSA documents, Hersh adds that they "reveal the hypocrisy of many members of the Saudi royal family" and why it has alienated the majority of its subjects. For years, the Saudi princes have filled the pages of the tabloid press with stories of their alcoholic orgies and their partying with prostitutes, while draining millions from the budget. The NSA transcripts give details. A call from a prince, who has been a cabinet minister for twenty years, orders one of his subordinates to conceal from the police evidence of payment for the services of prostitutes, apparently by members of the royal family. According to the transcript, the prince said that "under no circumstances" did he want the "list of clients" to be transmitted.

One "hears" in these documents the higher princes, Aballaf, Nayef, Sultan, Salman, anxiously asking about the health of King Fahd after his stroke. On January 8, 1997, Sultan speaks to his son Bandar about a plane trip with Salman and the king: the latter is "barely able to speak to anyone," being "stuffed full of drugs." Hersh comments: "These words took on all their meaning a few days later, when the NSA intercepted [another] conversation in which Sultan said to Bandar that the king had given his consent to a very complex agreement of exchange of fighter jets with the United States so that F-16s could be incorporated into the Royal Saudi Air Force. Fahd was obviously unable to give his consent to such an agreement, or to prevent anyone from covering a lucrative contract with the authority of his name."

It is clear that only extreme medical and pharmaceutical efforts keep a spark of life in the worn out carcass of King Fahd. The only reason for this medical excess is to prevent Crown Prince Abdallah from taking the throne, because of the furious battles dividing the thieves over the division of the spoils. It is not that the succession has any serious political stakes: no one in the family is "pro-American" or "pro-Western." What Voltaire said about the Geneva banker—"if you see him jump out a window, follow him; there is money to be made"—applies: the Al-Sauds are pro-Al-Saud. They will go where their interest leads them, and nowhere else.

The succession resembles the artificially maintained existence of King Fahd, like the vegetative existence of the last years of Leonid Brezhnev, Yuri Andropov, and finally Konstantin Chernenko, who ate, drank, and breathed thanks to machines. Hearts beat and organs functioned only artificially, because the system was totally unable to carry out an ordered succession. All the rival factions needed time to maneuver and weaken their opponents. The Saudi succession, equally totalitarian, resembles Soviet succession, or the succession of Mao in the few years before his death in 1976: a drooling mummy in the hands of a manipulative entourage.

Who will be king? The answer is as clear as desert mud. Crown Prince Abdallah, as his title indicates, is the designated heir. With King Fahd, his six brothers, sons of Mrs. Abdulaziz, wife number twelve(?), née Al-Sudairi—Sultan, Salman, Nayef, and the others, Fahd being the oldest—form the powerful sibling group known as the "Sudairi seven." Abdallah is not a part of it and he has no half-brothers. In the world of palace intrigue, the abundance of brothers, and hence of cousins and nephews, is an element of power. These alignments have absolutely no value from the point of view of political opinions. If a faction believes that it can benefit from a temporary external alliance to counterbalance a rival faction, the agreement will be made. It is only from this point of view that one faction or another will enter discussions with other Arab regimes, with the Americans, or with any other outsider.

Saudi leadership does not have as its purpose the definition of a given political or ideological course. Quite the contrary, the factions choose as standard bearer or insignia or emblem one or another ideological variant. They choose an identifying marker. The idea is put about, for example, that Prince Abdallah, by contrast with King Fahd, is anti-American and anti-Western. If being pro-American means covering with your authority the unprecedented stream of hatred against the United States and the West that has swept through the kingdom for at least a decade, then the idea of pro- or anti-American has no meaning. Prince Abdallah, we are told, is pious and austere, unlike his playboy half-brothers. But the available information seriously contradicts this image. A very well informed Saudi dissident tells the following story: the crown prince had a palace built, yet another one, decorated with waterfalls and fountains, for the modest sum of $15 million. At the time—this was in 1998—the crown prince made a diplomatic visit to China, where he saw a landscape garden.

On his return, he immediately demanded that the little jewel that had just been built be demolished and that they build the same thing that he had seen in China, at the equally modest cost of $20 million. Truly austere behavior, or are the others so much worse that the label can be applied to him? Perhaps it is because Abdallah has been head of the National Guard for forty years, the Bedouin army, the family's praetorian guard: he identifies with the position and behaves as it requires.

Saudi leadership is not defined by political content properly speaking. Then what is it? "The daily task of the Saudi monarch and his associates consists in weighing the strength day after day of his friends and his enemies, and then [on that basis] buying them or preventing them from acting, calculating and distributing subsidies, tips, and grants, in short the whole gamut of transfer of overt and covert funds," aptly writes David Pryce-Jones.[4] And in the contest for power and booty, each important prince counts not only on his relatives and clients, but also on his private army: each of them has one.

The fate of Saudi Arabia is traditionally the stake in a game involving about one hundred players: brothers, half-brothers, uncles, cousins, nephews, and the higher *ulamas*. The highest layer of Saudi society represents about 85,000 individuals, according to Raymond Seitz, former U.S. ambassador to London and vice president of the investment bank Lehman Brothers. On average, these rich Saudis have invested three quarters of their assets in the United States, the rest in Europe and Asia. That represents $500–700 billion for the United States alone. Bard Bourland, an expert in the Saudi American Bank (in which Citibank holds a one fourth interest), estimates that the assets of the upper layer of princes and courtiers are within the range of $500 billion to one trillion dollars.[5] In addition, one hundred thousand Saudis own a house or apartment in the United States.

For the kingdom to survive, all of them need the price of oil to be high. Revenue per capita has been falling steeply for a decade. Unemployment is extremely high, particularly among young people, particularly young graduates, few of whom have acquired any real qualification. Recall that one third of the students are enrolled in "Islamic sciences" and are thus dependent on the rest of society throughout their lives, and that for the other two thirds, "Islamic sciences" represent one third of the curriculum, as Marxism-Leninism used to in the USSR and the satellite countries. The kingdom is in a deep economic, budgetary, and financial crisis. Without the constant repeated injections of liquidity that only oil can engender, the ruling tribe can no longer buy the loyalty of the inferior and external tribes. The emperor has no clothes, or at least they are growing ragged.

As we have explained in detail, in history's roulette game, the ruling tribe has bet almost everything on one color, the Islamic green. The founding king, Abdulaziz ibn Saud, had raised up the fanatical legions of the *jihad*, the *Ikhwan*, to seize power and to consolidate it. The successor kings, Faisal in particular, raised up external *Ikhwans* to spread their *jihad* to the Arab world first, and to the Muslim world thereafter. The twists and turns of history have made them raise the stakes: the Soviet threat and the first Afghan war accelerated, amplified, and exacerbated a natural tendency in the genes of the dynasty and the tribe. A creator often thinks he can control his creation. In this case, the creation greatly surpassed its creator, who was never willing or able to disavow it. In Mary Shelley's novel, Doctor Frankenstein, horrified by the monster he has created, tries to destroy it by any means possible. The Saudi kingdom does not seek in any way to destroy its monstrous offspring. It barely goes so far as to treat it as an illegitimate son.

The great sterile desert from which the al-Sauds and their Wahhabism arose had always been Arabia's wasteland. There one was protected from the external world, from its culture and diversity by the arid ferocity of the desert. Once they had left their sand dunes, the Al-Sauds could survive only by spreading Wahhabism everywhere, by transforming the world into a similar desert. To Wahhabize the world was to Bedouinize it, and turn it into a desert. Periodic eruptions of fanatical religious fervor are typical of Arabia. Wahhabism itself comes from that source. These feverish outbursts that seize the tribes create the "industry of death" and its corollary, "the profession of [giving] death" praised by the *khutba*, the sermons in Saudi mosques.

In the face of the unified chorus coming from the ranks of Islamic radicalism that Saudi Arabia fosters with its state ideology, promotes through its machinery of religious agitprop, subsidizes through all the bank accounts of "charitable organizations" and the front organizations of its secret services, that it supplies with leaders and foot soldiers, in the face of this chorus coming from the voluble mouths of Hamas, Islamic Jihad, Osama bin Laden, and countless others, from Hezb-e-Islami in Afghanistan, Harakat and Jamaat-e-Islami in Pakistan, Abu Sayyaf in the Philippines, Jemmah Islamiya in Indonesia, and other beneficiaries of Saudi largesse, from the Saudi *ulamas* themselves and their flock, from the thousands of mosques in the Arabian peninsula—this chorus that cries "Long live death!"—how can we not think of the modest and moving heroism of the Spanish philosopher Miguel de Unamuno who, on October 12, 1936, forced to witness the profanation of the venerable University of Salamanca, cradle of Spanish art and philosophy, having heard the fascist General Millán Astray, dressed in black leather and surrounded by his jackbooted troops with their submachine guns, bellow the blasphemy "Long live death!", and then stood up, overcome with sorrow, and replied, with an old man's slowness and dignity: "There are circumstances in which keeping silence means lying. I have just heard a morbid and senseless cry: Long live death. This barbaric paradox is repugnant to me. General Millán Astray is mutilated. This is not insulting, so was Cervantes. Unfortunately, in Spain today there are too many who are mutilated. I suffer at the thought that General Millán Astray could lay the groundwork for a mass psychology. A mutilated man who does not have the greatness of soul of a Cervantes frequently seeks relief in the mutilations that he can inflict on those around him." Then he turned to Millán Astray: "You will conquer because you have more brute force than you need. But you will not convince. Because to convince, you would have to persuade. And to persuade, you would have to have what you lack: reason and right in the struggle. I consider it futile to urge you to think of Spain. I have finished."

Saudi power is the result of two accidents: an accident of geology that concentrated vast reserves of easy to extract hydrocarbons in a limited area of the Persian Gulf, and an accident of history that allowed King Faisal to use the boom in oil consumption provoked by the expansion of Western capitalism to impose an embargo and a price explosion, giving extraordinary power to a few people. A third accident exacerbated the situation: the lack of a counterforce in the region. The Ottomans were no longer there, the ruling elites of other Arab countries, Egypt above all, had failed miserably, the British and French had withdrawn, and the Americans had no desire to occupy any territory, only to keep things from getting out of hand. The balance of power was destroyed. The result was the birth and expansion of a monstrous pathogenic body that has spread its own evil to the rest of the world. Of course, Saudi Arabia is not the only terrorist state: Iran, Iraq, and Syria are all in competition, and Pakistan, with Saudi help, spreads a virulent pathology. But Saudi Arabia is the theological piggy bank and the Fort Knox of terrorism. What various accidents—and the weakness, cowardice, and propensity of Westerners to be corrupted—have created must be defeated by action, rather than through the unpredictable operation of other providential accidents.

Let's begin with a Middle Eastern twist to a classic fable: As fire is raging on the bank, the scorpion asks the frog to take him across the river on his back. "But I know you," protests the frog, "you'll sting me and I'll die." The scorpion reassures the frog: "No, that would be stupid of me. If I kill you, I'll drown." Persuaded, the frog accepts. In the middle of the river, the scorpion stings the frog. Feeling the poison fill his veins, the frog asks: "But you told me..." "Yes," answers the scorpion, "but we're in the Middle East."

We have to turn collectively to the Saudi royal family and as Teddy Roosevelt said, "speak softly and carry a big stick." The Al-Saud family has to be given an ultimatum. It has to satisfy point by point a long catalogue of nonnegotiable demands:

Put a definitive and unconditional end to all anti-Western and anti-Shiite sermons in all the mosques, buildings, and religious installations in the country, as well as in universities and schools.

Withdraw from circulation all schoolbooks and other "pedagogical" materials filled with the same content.

Bar Wahhabi preachers, theologians, authors, and propagandists from speaking publicly, and permanently dismiss teachers guilty of inciting hatred.

Prevent the publication in the press and the distribution by the electronic media of any form of incitement to hatred.

Punish those guilty of the acts mentioned with imprisonment and exile.

Cut off without exception the public and private funding of all sources of "education" and propaganda for hatred.

Shut down the "charitable works" that finance fundamentalist propaganda and Islamist actions inside and outside the kingdom.

Confiscate the assets not only of these bodies, but also of their principal donors, who are guilty in the same way as those who pull the triggers of terrorist guns.

Disclose the accounts in the principal banks of the kingdom to the international authorities; expropriate them for the benefit of victims of terrorism in every case in which they are compromised.

Similarly, disclose the files of the intelligence services, the interior ministry, the police force, and the National Guard, and hand over the officers, whatever their rank, who are compromised in one way or another in international terrorism.

Hand over to an international tribunal all Saudi officials similarly compromised, whatever their rank.

In a word, what is required it the dismantling and eradication of the Saudi-Wahhabi war machine. The measures are clear and verifiable. If the regime were to resist, retaliatory measures would have to be prepared. Threats are necessary to compel compliance. To threaten effectively, you have to cut to the quick. In the case of the Al-Sauds, four things are precious to them: their oil, their financial assets outside the kingdom, their political power in the Arabian peninsula, and their role as guardians of the holy places of Islam. What can be done?

Oil is Saudi by accident. The use that has been made of this black gold mine is so contrary to the public good that the international community owes it to itself to take it away from the abusive owner. Without those resources, the pathogenic monster would be weakened. Once the dynasty had been deprived of its oil wells, the oil province of eastern Arabia, Hasa, could revert to its rightful owners, the vast majority of whom are Shiites. Because some might be alarmed by a conjunction of the neighboring Shiites of southern Iraq with the inhabitants of Hasa and nearby Iran, an autonomous state protected by the international community could be established, perhaps under a mandatory regime, but not subject to foreign occupation. It would have the right to a significant proportion of the oil revenues, if only to compensate for the 250 years of bad treatment inflicted by the Wahhabis, but also a half century of Saudi failure to invest in the province's inadequate infrastructure: hospitals, universities, and so on.

Even so, the huge financial resources coming from oil would instantly saturate this under-equipped and underdeveloped province, producing there what they have caused everywhere, in all underdeveloped countries that suddenly gain oil wealth: gangrene. Wouldn't it be better, after a margin of perhaps 25 percent had been paid to the autonomous state of Hasa, for a regional Middle Eastern oil authority to co-manage the province's oil wealth and redistribute it? A redistributive formula could be based on a ratio, by country, favoring those with large populations and little oil production. Major producers with small populations, such as the Gulf States, would have no claim to a share of the wealth thereby redistributed. A country like Egypt, with a large population and little oil production, would in contrast receive substantial revenues. Jordan, with no oil and a rather small population, could count on moderate amounts. Israel, with a comparable population and no oil, would fare similarly. Yemen, with a larger population but no oil, could expect to receive significant amounts.

Without underestimating the practical and political difficulties in applying it, this would be a way of helping to create a common interest among the countries of the region, not to mention the general moral satisfaction created by this just reversal of fortune. A disinterested offer on the part of the Western powers—an offer that would involve no Western control over the province or its oil—could also lay more solid foundations for cooperation between the Arab countries and the West.

The fate of the oil fields of Hara has long been a matter of concern for military authorities. We know that demolition experts would need only a few dozen pounds of explosives to put Saudi wells out of commission for two years. In fact, in the mid-1980s, the CIA carried out a detailed and obviously secret study of the question, which was considered so "explosive" that it was not even entered into the agency's computers but typed on typewriters. The idea of a preventive or preemptive occupation of the oil fields goes along with their protection from regional predators or terrorist operations, and with their preservation. If the Saudi regime were not to comply with the conditions of the ultimatum, those fields should be occupied. The Saudi army, with all due respect, is a joke. "The day I saw lieutenants with their little paunches, I understood everything," an American officer told the author. Light airborne and amphibious forces would be enough to do the job.

We may strongly doubt that the governments of the region—humiliated and crushed by Saudi contempt—that the peoples of the region—witness to Saudi arrogance, to their debauchery, to their haughty and cavalier treatment of other Arabs—would rise up or even lift a finger to protect them or to protest against the misfortune befalling them. All Arabs, or almost all, including many individuals whose services have been bought or hired by the Saudis, are not lacking in resentment against them. The nasty "joke" played by history and geography—giving oil to the "Arabs of the desert" and keeping it from the "Arabs of the cities"—would come to an end.

The second treasure of the royal family is money, beginning with the huge financial assets invested in the West. A legislative arsenal exists enabling the freezing, or even the confiscation, of the assets of an enemy country which is in a state of war with the United States (or the countries of Europe) and its nationals, in the event the nationals of a country are at war with the United States. The product of activities in violation of international law, the private and public fortune of Saudi Arabia can and should be subject to confiscatory measures, as a precaution to dry up at the source the financing of terrorism and Wahhabi fundamentalism and as reparation for the countries and individuals that have been their victims. The idea of an international tribunal charged with judging the guilty and awarding reparations could make some headway.

The third asset of the Al-Sauds is their political power. As we have said from the outset, Arabia became "Saudi" only a short time ago. It is the result of imperialist wars waged by Bedouins of Najd. But the regions of Arabia swept through and annexed by Abdulaziz ibn Saud's bandits have their own identities: Shiite Hara, a Persian Gulf land; Hijaz, on the shores of the Red Sea, an old transshipment region touched by the great waves of international trade, whose elites were hunted down and humiliated by the *Ikhwan* and its master; their descendants still consider the Al-Sauds to be occupiers and usurpers. The independence of Hijaz is not impossible. As for the province of Asir, further south, bordering Yemen, it was seized from Yemen by force of arms in 1932–1934. Its fate is not written. There would remain Najd for the Al-Sauds and the Wahhabis, if they wanted to preach in the desert, cut off from oil, money, and political control. We wish them Godspeed, because for the first time in a century, the Al-Sauds would have to work. This idle, profiteering, pleasure-loving, and predatory society, in the image of its ambassador to London, who wrote a poem to the glory of a suicide bomber and who, explaining in an interview that he himself would have wished to experience martyrdom, added: "My weight does not allow me to do it." This society that produces a $50 million telethon to pay for the assassination of civilians in another country deserves to be drummed out of the community of nations. Let it be so.

There remains a problem of extraordinary importance: that of the holy places of Islam, *al-Haramayn*, Mecca and Medina. Their usurpation by the Al-Sauds necessarily conferred on them unwarranted Muslim legitimacy. A cleric from Al-Azhar, revolted by the subversion of his alma mater by Saudi money, proposed that, rather than turning it over to another family, however prestigious, the management of the holy places should be turned over to an international Muslim college, appointed by the Muslims of the entire world, without distinction among schools—Malakite, Hanafi, Shaafi, or Hanbali—or sects—Sunni, Shiite, Sufi, or Ismaili—or countries, since the center of gravity of Islam is now located in the Indian subcontinent, where Bangladesh, India, and Pakistan are three of the largest demographics of Islam, and the fourth, Indonesia, is also Asian. A collegial management would make it possible to avoid the confiscation of Islam that Wahhabism has undertaken to carry out, and to re-create the spirit of intra-Muslim tolerance that prevailed in Mecca before the Wahhabis.

Oil, money, political control, religious control, these are the means available to us to make the sated and felonious dynasts of Riyadh give up their ill-gotten gains. It is possible, although improbable, that the extraordinary instinct for power that is the defining characteristic of the Al-Sauds will make them aware, at the edge of the abyss, of the urgency of the situation. If it happened that some members of the royal family, reacting to intense external pressure, understood and undertook to carry out fundamental reforms, beginning by meeting the list of demands formulated here, these Saudi "Gorbachevs" would be welcome. We could then work fruitfully to trim the excesses, use drastic means to clean out these Augean stables. This would be the last chance open to the family before definitive "de-Saudi-izing." Experience, however, leads us to doubt the presence of a potential Gorbachev among the Al-Sauds. It also teaches us of the dangers that await a reformist autocrat who alienates both established interests and those that are attempting to make themselves felt.

On the other hand, it would be a historic opportunity for the entire region of the Middle East, freed from Saudi-Wahhabi oppression and subversion, which would constitute, after the liberation of Iraq by the coalition forces, a second stage in the reform of the Arab world. The Syrian regime, a client of the Al-Sauds, would not withstand the collapse of its benefactor after that of its Baathist rival, and would have to leave Lebanon, before leaving the stage for good. The terrorists of Hamas, deprived of subsidies, would have to, if not shut up shop, at least lower their sights: the decline of the Al-Sauds would logically produce improvement in a regional situation that they have done so much to corrupt.

The dynasty would then have gone through in a century the cycle that Ibn Khaldun discerned in and predicted for all the Bedouin empires, each of which, he says, lasts for only four generations: "The builder of the glory of the family knows what it cost him to do the work. . . . The son who comes after him . . . is inferior . . . to his father, in as much as a person who learns things through study is inferior to a person who learns them from practical application. The third generation must be content with imitation and, in particular, with reliance upon tradition. . . . The fourth generation . . . is inferior to the preceding ones in every respect. This member has lost the qualities that preserved the edifice of their glory. He actually despises those qualities. He imagines that the edifice was not built through application and effort. He thinks that it was something due his people from the very beginning by virtue of the mere fact of their noble descent."

Let us grant the Saudi empire five kings rather than four generations: Ibn Saud, Saud bin Abdulaziz, Faisal bin Abdulaziz, Khalid bin Abdulaziz, and Fahd bin Abdulaziz, on his death bed, after whom the empire will collapse. Fahd's successor might be the last king of Arabia. Ibn Khaldun also says: "The rule of four generations . . . usually holds true. It may happen that a 'house' is wiped out, disappears, and collapses in fewer than four generations."[6]

Epilogue

A Saudi Invitation

This was the book that appeared in France in the Fall of 2003. The press was good: within a month of its appearance, all major newspapers, TV channels, and radio stations in the country had covered it.

On February 25, 2004—barely three months after publication—I received from Riyadh a fax transmission from Muhammad Ibn Saad Al-Salim, president of the Al Imam Muhammad Ibn Saud Islamic University inviting me to participate in an international conference related to the subject of extremism and terrorism.[1]

Given my "radioactive" reputation, as the *Washington Post* had kindly put it, and since the Imam Muhammad University is a strictly Wahhabi institution, which only graduates students in Islamic theology, I was more than mildly surprised. After consulting with a few Washington friends and experts, who generally advised me to demand VIP security, an understandable concern for my family and myself, I answered positively, also asking my hosts to arrange meetings with senior Saudi policy-makers. Since I had been blamed for my ignorance of the Kingdom, what better opportunity for its senior representatives to enlighten me?

I received no reply. By March 9, puzzled by my putative hosts' silence, I sent an e-mail to Dr. Ibn Saad Al-Salim inquiring about the identity of the other conference speakers, security arrangements, and other details.[2]

The plot was not allowed to thicken much more. On March 16, someone called "Al-Nasser" indicated that it was now too late for my participation in the conference and as such withdrew the invitation.[3]

I was somewhat gratified to have graduated—at least rhetorically—from "low-class prostitute," as I had been described by the lapdog journalist of the dynasty, to a potential "good people," the reasons for both the issuance of the invitation and its amusing non-outcome, were unclear. "The Wahhabi are trying to look good, and tolerant," said the one; "they want to see if you can be bought, and at what price," said another. "Maybe some people want to build bridges with Washington Neo-Conservatives," added yet another. "You'd be the token opposition." And why if not rescind, at least waffle on the invitation until it was indeed too late? "Well, the guy who invited you probably was put on hot coals by higher-ups, like «*you invited whom?*» and he's probably in a salt mine somewhere, or peeling potatoes or whatever it is they do for penance there," a knowledgeable friend commented.

The back-and-forth internal to Saudi Arabia was occasionally reported to me. A West European member of Parliament mentioned that he had been asked endless questions in Riyadh about the Pentagon briefing, the book, the debate that both had set off. A prominent German academic told me of reverberations at the highest level in the kingdom. "You're the talk of the town," a government minister said.

Talking Turki

All the while, some Saudi leaders—perhaps the same that worked at getting me uninvited—were decidedly unhappy. To take but one, Prince Turki al-Faisal, former head of intelligence and now Ambassador to the United Kingdom, was very forlorn, if not downright melancholy, that his hitherto spotless reputation had been sullied by the terrible, terrible words I had written. Now, the despondent prince would not issue rebuttals, or even sue, on account of the book's contents: while not as favorable as America's to defendants—politicians, writers, journalists—French libel laws have their guidelines. To sue a major French publisher in Paris for libel can be a dicey affair. The plaintiff, for instance, may lose, on account of the local equivalent of the First Amendment. French law stipulates that malicious intent must be proven as well as deliberate untruthfulness of content.

No, His Highness would take no such risk. Instead, Prince Turki sued—in London. But he did not sue the book—he sued a leading *French* newsmagazine, *Paris-Match*, for words of mine printed in an interview they had published. Turki's lawyers, who demanded apologies and damages from *Paris-Match,* argued that, since a few hundred copies of the magazine are sold every week in Britain, the damage inflicted upon Mylord's repute and good name was incalculable.

In fact, it was calculated to be calculable. Britain's libel laws are notorious: the defendant is bankrupted by costs in the first place. A standard libel case in British justice costs *forty times more* than one in France! So the Saudi's lawyers waited *six months* after the book appeared in Paris... to sue a French newsmagazine in London. In Saudi Arabia, the authors of unwanted comments and distressing criticism are coerced, bribed, jailed, tortured, or killed. Since Turki was not really able to do any of the above—or not without high penalties—the solution was obvious: intimidate in order to shut up, use the (otherwise execrated) laws and courts of a democratic nation to pursue the malicious ends of the Saudi dynasty.

This, incidentally, is not an isolated case. Take, for example, the case of Khalid bin Mahfouz, a Saudi financier, who until 2003 owned and ran the National Commercial Bank (NCB), the largest bank in Saudi Arabia. After the September

11, 2001 attacks, Mahfouz, his son Abdulrahim, and the NCB were parties to the 9/11 litigation (the suit against Abdulrahim was dismissed by the U.S. district court in January 2005).

In sharp contrast to most Western countries, Britain's libel laws place the burden of proof not on the purportedly injured party but on the side that leveled the allegations. That is, in Britain a party accused of libel is guilty until proven innocent. And proving oneself innocent is extraordinarily difficult, as the jurisprudence of British libel laws demonstrates.

Mahfouz has deep pockets. His personal net wealth is estimated at over $3 billion, so he can afford to litigate forever, unlike the targets of his lawsuits. Most of them have abandoned their attempts to look into his alleged terror links. Major publications and newspapers have opted to rescind their allegations most likely because of the high court costs of battling Mahfouz in the UK. Mahfouz's most recent target is New York-based terrorism researcher Rachel Ehrenfeld, who directs the American Center for Democracy. She documented the allegations against Mahfouz, his family, and the NCB in her 2003 book *Funding Evil: How Terrorism is Financed and How to Stop It*. Mahfouz filed suit against her in Britain in October 2004.

Ehrenfeld, who like Mahfouz's other targets lacks the financial means to defend herself in Britain, and who like the others understands that she would be hard-pressed to emerge victorious given Britain's pro-plaintiff libel laws, has through necessity decided to turn the tables on Mahfouz. She scraped together the money to file a countersuit in New York. In her suit, Ehrenfeld asks the court to find that Mahfouz's libel charges would not pass muster in America. She further asks that the court declare unenforceable any award granted to Mahfouz in Britain.[4]

There is a pattern of rich, powerful, and guilty-as-charged Saudis who manipulate Britain's medieval, or absolutist *lèse-majesté*, libel laws to chill and silence critics and researchers. Justice for billionaires, I said: the court costs *alone*, prior to any case being opened, amounted to 980,000 pound sterling, or $1.5 million! The suit absurdly claimed that the *Paris-Match* interview had ascribed direct, tactical control of al-Qaeda to Turki. The French journal, frightened of escalating costs, decided to throw in the towel, allowing Turki's army of scribblers and PR men to claim "victory," and reportedly a large sum of money changed hands.[5] Shakespeare's Macbeth asks himself if all the water in the world can wash away the blood: "Will all great Neptune's ocean wash this blood / Clean from my hand?" And he answers his own question: "No, this my hand will rather / The multitudinous seas incarnadine, / Making the green one red."[6] Nor would money.

On May 31, 2004, an article written by John Crewdson appeared in the *Chicago Tribune* under the headline: "German Intelligence Points to Two Saudi Companies As Having Al Qaeda Links." The piece, datelined Hamburg, Germany, started:

> Two private Saudi companies linked with suspected Al Qaeda cells here and in Indonesia also have connections to the Saudi Arabian intelligence agency and its longtime chief, Prince Turki bin Faisal, according to information assembled by German intelligence analysts. The Twaik Group and Rawasin Media Productions, both based in Riyadh, the Saudi capital, have served as fronts for the Saudi General Intelligence Directorate, according to an inquiry by Germany's foreign intelligence service, the BND.

The article reported that "In a March 18 letter faxed to the *Tribune*, Prince Turki stated only that 'I have not developed any relationship with either group.'"

One last note of passing interest: I mentioned in the introduction the journalist who had crassly insulted me. This Jamal Khashoggi, after he stopped working at the Beirut

Daily Star, became no less than a media adviser to the Saudi Ambassador in London, one Prince Turki![7]

Saudia Unraveling

Events, in the Middle East no more than elsewhere, have their own impetus. They move fast, regardless of authors' and publishers' intent. This book was written at the very beginning of 2003, and appeared in France in the Fall of the same year. So much has occurred since in and around Saudi Arabia that more than an afterthought is required to analyze events.

Were the book's conclusion hasty or overly alarmist? "Saudi Arabia has descended into a cauldron of hatreds and divisions," commented Dr. Mai Yamani, a Saudi researcher at London's prestigious Royal Institute of International Affairs ("Chatham House"), a bastion of analytical moderation. In June of 2004, the daughter of the former Saudi Oil Minister Sheikh Zaki Yamani was writing a cold and disquieting evaluation of the kingdom's position in the British daily *The Guardian*.[8] Her piece is worth quoting at length:

> Long before the latest violence erupted, Saudi Arabia's immaculately suited spokesmen were out on the stump, telling anyone who would listen that the situation in the country was completely under control. They're now doing it again—only this time nobody believes them.
>
> All the signs suggest that in the face of mounting violence and international pressure, the House of Saud has sunk into terminal denial and paralysis. Convinced that their enemies are all around them, they are nevertheless unable to locate them. Even when gunmen are totally surrounded in a building, three of them succeed in escaping. Last year the aged King Fahd threatened militants with his "iron fist", but they have gone on killing regardless. While the princes have insisted reforms are in progress, they continue to fling reformists themselves into jail—and intimidate others into keeping quiet. The government maintains its oil

installations are completely safe from attack—and yet high-level oil analysts insist the Saudi security forces which guard them are infiltrated by extremists.

Such contradictions suggest that very little is currently under control in the Saudi kingdom.

While expatriates consider whether to depart en masse, reports from the Gulf say that staff members of one of the more entrepreneurial princes have asked officials in Dubai to find them living space. They might well be re-locating in the near future.

But it would be wrong to predict any immediate collapse of the state. Despite a marked cooling in relations, Saudi Arabia remains the key ally of the US in the region. With continuing violence in Iraq, Washington's priority is to prevent Saudi Arabia descending into similar anarchy, even if it means propping up a regime it no longer likes or trusts. American demands for reform have quietened in the past few months, which may explain their muted response to the clampdown on Saudi liberals last March.

While oil prices remain exceptionally high and with a US presidential election in November, Saudi Arabia is the pump that cannot be allowed to run dry. Predictably, the kingdom is determined to remind the Bush administration of its central role in the world economy and politics, aware that if peace breaks out in neighbouring Iraq, it will lose some important leverage.

Already its influence in the Gulf has been badly shaken. The smaller states no longer need Saudi Arabia for protection and security, and no longer look to Riyadh for a lead on the international stage. Moreover, some have clearly replaced the Saudi state in Washington's affections, especially as they move ahead with political and economic reforms, outstripping the kingdom's own meagre efforts.

It is now known that a number of those Gulf rulers have been lining up to tell the Saudis that reform is their only chance of survival, and that it may already be too late. But even those princes who accept that notion—such as Crown Prince Abdullah—no longer appear to hold sway in the cabinet.

In any case, the Saudi state has become such a cauldron of hatreds and divisions—many now highlighted by the war in Iraq—that reforms favouring one group would almost certainly be rejected by another. Regional rivalries have been sharply exacerbated. The Asir region is viewed by many as partly Yemeni. The Hijazis see themselves as a separate cultural and religious entity. After decades of exclusion from key jobs, the Shia in the oil-rich province are deeply ambivalent about their Saudi identity and feel newly empowered by Shia advances in Iraq. Conceivably, they could begin to demand their own state. Some even talk about Shia political power as a disease that could spread into Saudi Arabia and engulf it. If Iraq were ever to sink into civil war, the Saudis themselves would be hard-pressed to hold their nation together.

To the Saudi royal family nothing is more troubling than the Shia questions. All Saudi Shia are followers of the Iraqi Grand Ayatollah Ali Sistani—so they already look across the border for guidance. Bearded, turbaned and cloaked Shia clerics, now far more visible in Iraq, terrify the minority Saudi Wahhabis. From being the region's big losers over the last few decades, many Shia now feel they can redress the balance, settle old scores and control the oil wealth.

As they review their options, the Saudis have probably concluded that they can live with a Shia-dominated government in Iraq, but only if it contains prominent Sunni faces. All the same, relations won't be easy. Shia ideology is in direct collision with the Sunni Wahhabi doctrine that underpins the Saudi state and frequently labels the Shia as "heretics".

For months, the Saudi government has trumpeted its "national dialogue" which brought together Ismaelis, Sufis, Shia and Salafis for unprecedented talks, chaired by Crown Prince Abdullah. But this is little more than window-dressing. The Wahhabi establishment has no appetite for the discussions and has made clear it is not in the reform business. For the first time, leading Saudi figures are talking privately of schism and the possibility of religious war.

So there are no comfortable options for the Saudi royal family. Announce a hurried series of reforms and the princes will be seen to have bowed to American pressure and will face the wrath of the clergy. Do nothing, and even the moderates will turn against them and into the arms of the extremists. Offer government posts to the Shia, curb the powers of the ubiquitous religious police—the Mutawa—and another backlash would follow.

Meanwhile, al-Qaida attacks with relative impunity. Some security experts believe that key installations like Ras Tanoura and Abqaiq, the world's largest oil processing complex, are vulnerable to attack. Questions about the competence and loyalty of elements within the security forces are denied by the authorities. Nevertheless, recent attacks have revealed intricate personal and tribal links between those forces and the violent jihadis.

Revolution may not be imminent, but the security situation seems bound to deteriorate, provoking fresh splits in the kingdom's complex political and religious architecture. Without a clear plan of action, it's not surprising that the Saudi leadership has put its head in the sand.

By and large, I concur with Dr. Yamani's views. Looking at the Middle Eastern region as a whole, I may nonetheless venture a different sense of the timing of events yet to unfold. Shortly after my Defense Policy Board briefing, an Arab foreign minister told me that the buzz even amongst "card-carrying" members of the Saudi Lobby in Washington gave the kingdom no more than five years of life expectancy. At a dinner, a lobbyist for Saudi Arabia from Patton, Boggs even told me he tended to agree with my perspective and the calendar I was trying to outline for the fall of the dynasty.

Careening into the Unknown

Pressure is mounting relentlessly. As shown by the wave of terrorist attacks, the stress on the kingdom's domestic fabric has been increasing, closer and closer to the breaking point. The external pressure has not been less unremitting: in Middle Eastern affairs, the Saudi royals threw their weight against President George W. Bush in more ways than one.

President Bush upset the regional apple cart when he ordered the U.S. troops into Iraq: for the first time in modern history, Washington revoked the tacit order of things in the region—an equation that placed Saudi Arabia and its rulers in the center of U.S. policy: petroleum in the Persian Gulf is abundant and cheap; in order to benefit from it and preserve it, America must make friends with the landlords that own the fields, and their periphery. Hence, America will shy from no friendship with any Arab dictator and despot. Arabistan writ large will be spared pressures exerted elsewhere for modernization and democratization. John Foster Dulles's foolish dictum about Nicaraguan dictator Somoza— "he's a bastard, but he's *our* bastard"—was applied, starting with the unfortunate and ill-starred American salvaging Egyptian dictator Gamal Abdel Nasser from the consequences of his follies in 1956. America as a result "had" many bastards in the region, which, with Dulles, it misguidedly believed were "ours."

Hence, various Arab leaders were given, if not an outright veto right, at least a strong say in U.S. policy in the region. President Bush concluded from the September 11, 2001 attacks that this doctrine had become obsolete: as long as the Middle East remained mired in a mixture of backwardness, regression, resentment, despotism, and dictatorship, terrorism would endlessly be invigorated. To eradicate the danger, he ordered the destruction of Saddam Hussein, the Sunni dictator: this was unprecedented. Sunni dictators had the favors of both the State Department and the CIA. They were also the favorites of the Saudi royals. When Ahmed Chalabi some years ago visited Saudi Arabia, he was offered full support, financial and all, by the royals, under one condition: that he give up any notion of democracy in Iraq. Saudi Arabia, for all its religious pretenses, supported the "secular" Baathist dictators of Iraq and Syria both, and many others.

Riyadh threw its weight against the president. Its diplomats cooked up scheme after scheme to save Saddam—in vain. Its Washington lobbyists took place of pride against any offensive on Iraq, starting with former National Security Adviser Brent Scowcroft, who spared no public or private forum to drum up opposition—thus burning his bridges with the president. All to no avail: both the Saudi government and their faithful retainers in the U.S. capital, including the great bearer of gifts and graft Prince Bandar, ambassador-for-life, spent and lost enormous political capital in Washington. Defense Secretary Donald Rumsfeld, in a well-publicized prewar tour of the Gulf, announced the spectacular pullout of U.S. forces and facilities from Saudi Arabia, and their relocation to Qatar.

What was the Saudi reaction? It was unadulterated, if muffled fury. Hundreds of Saudi clerics issued repeated calls for Saudis to go wage *jihad* against the U.S. and Coalition Forces in Iraq. The Saudi media and websites were soon publishing pictures and sympathetic biographies of the "martyrs." A study of 154 Arab volunteers killed in Iraq showed that 94 were Saudis (or 61 percent); the next largest contingent, Syria, was a very distant runner-up with 16 volunteers (or 10 percent). Two-thirds of the Saudis were Nadjis, 64 volunteers, from the fief of the al-Saud and the Wahhabis.[9] In conclusion of the study, its author, respected analyst Reuven Paz, wrote:

> The intensive involvement of Saudi volunteers for Jihad in Iraq is . . . the result of the Saudi government's double-speak, whereby it is willing to fight terrorism, but only if directly affected by it on its own soil. Saudi Arabia is either deliberately ignoring, or incapable and too weak, to engage in open and brave opposition to Jihadi terrorism outside of the Kingdom . . . Their blind eyes in the face of the Saudi

Islamic establishment's support of the Jihad in Iraq may pose a greater threat in the future, as the hundreds of volunteers return home.

After a car bomb killed 125 at Hilla, Iraq, on February 28, 2005, several thousand demonstrated in anger chanting "Down with Baathism and Wahhabism." They knew. Right before U.S. and Iraqi forces slammed into Fallujah to crush the terror insurgents, 26 "prominent [Saudi] scholars and preachers urge[d] Iraqis to support the militants fighting U.S.-led forces."[10] These none-too-scholarly scholars, amongst the cream of Saudi Wahhabi extremism, included Safar al-Hawali, Nasir al-Omar, Salman al-Awdah, Sharif al-Hatem Aouni, Awad al-Qarni, and others. Killing Americans was "legitimate," the *jihad* against them a "duty for all." In brief, the Saudi regime not only tried to prevent, slow down, and hinder the U.S. overthrow of fellow Sunni dictator Saddam Hussein, but set no obstacles to the flood of *jihadis* intent to go there to kill Americans—and Iraqis in large numbers, Shiites in particular.

Nothing had changed. As Saudi critic Mansour al-Nogaidan wrote at the beginning of 2005: "Saudi Arabia is bogged down by deep-rooted Islamic extremism in most schools and mosques, which have become breeding grounds for terrorists."[11] Hoover Institution scholar Arnold Beichman thus could quote recent words from Saudi Cleric Musaa Al-Qami: "The chaos evident today in the human race," killing, attacks, rape, robbery, and so on; "the cause of all this is that the flags of the Jews, the Christians, and other faiths are raised higher than the flag proclaiming, 'There is no God but Allah, and Muhammad is His Messenger. . . .'" Further, the cleric added: "What position should we adopt toward Allah's enemies? There are those who don't want us even to use the term 'Allah's enemies.' They don't want us to say that the Jews and the Christians are Allah's enemies. They don't want us to say that the Jews and Christians are the enemies of the

Muslims and Islam."[12] Fighting words meant to become action. On December 21, 2004, Saudi med school drop-out Ahmed Said Al-Ghamdi—from a clan from Asir province that had contributed several of the 9/11 musclemen, and a wealthy family, his father a Saudi ambassador—killed himself and 22 American servicemen in Mosul, Iraq, in one of the bloodiest homicide bombings perpetrated there. The Saudi government newspaper *al-Watan* reported that U.S. troops were "savagely harvesting" the organs of Iraqi insurgents for sale in the U.S., and gave the prices fetched by such fictitious transactions.[13]

It is reported by the Israeli Ministry of Defense—based upon documents seized in Ramallah—that the Saudi Royal family had contributed no less than $4 billion from 1998 to 2003 to Palestinian killers and the families of the "martyrs."[14] And one Fahal Ral Bali, a member of Defense Minister Prince Sultan's Special Committee for Relief, was arrested in Malawi in the framework of a vast international organization for having funneled masses of money to al-Qaeda.[15] The "Sudairi Seven"—of whom Prince Sultan is an eminent member—are involved.[16] In an allegation made by the Israeli daily *Maariv*, "Western intelligence reports that some of the Sudayri princes have knifed their half-brother Abdullah in the back by resuming back-channel contacts with al-Qaeda. The reports specifically mention Prince Nayef, Prince Salman and King Fahd's youngest son Abdulaziz."[17]

But, wasn't Saudi Arabia itself the butt of a terror campaign? Did the government not dissolve the *Al Haramayn* Foundation and amalgamate several "charities" into a Saudi National Commission for Charitable Work Abroad?[18] Did not a prominent government member, Minister of Labor, Dr. Ghazi Al-Gosaibi, unequivocally state that "extremist teachings cause terrorism"?[19] Well, he was the very former Saudi Ambassador who had fulsomely praised homicide bombing by Palestinians and regretted that only his personal girth prevented him from emulating them. . . . Terrorism is so much nicer when it hits others. Western intelligence agencies, including especially a CIA investigation, had determined that at least ten branches of the *Al Haramayn* Foundation, including India, Pakistan, and Somalia, "were providing arms or cash to terrorists."[20] The U.S. Treasury in September 2004 designated the U.S. and Comoros branches of the Foundation as financiers of terrorism; its U.S. director was designated as financier and facilitator of terror. The investigation "showed direct links with al-Qaeda."[21]

Whatever change was occurring in Saudi Arabia was more trumpeted public relations for foreign consumption than substance. For instance, the Saudi government organized another international jamboree parading as a "conference on terrorism."

On the last day of the conference, *Arab News* reported that Saudi Islamic Affairs Minster Saleh Al-Sheikh had issued an edict condemning suicide bombings against Muslims as an act of terror. But he added that those fighting occupation are not terrorists. As Saudi cleric Sa'd Al-Breik stated in a TV interview: "[Waging jihad is permitted] only when there is a worthy cause. As for Iraq, this is a [worthy] jihad to get rid of the occupier and to confront the enemy." Another example of incitement included Saudi cleric Aed Al-Qarni, who gave an interview on Saudi TV Channel 1 on February 7, speaking from the conference itself. Stating America was behind the September 11, 2001 attacks, he explained: "The first to kill and use terrorism in the world were the Jews and America. They began to act this way 200 years before us. The blowing up of the buildings in Washington, opposite the Pentagon, was an American terror attack. There are world Zionist circles that want to create for us constitutions that are illegitimate. But we won't accept the Zionist rule or that of the White House—which is, in fact, a Black House."

Also from the influential Al-Qarni clan, preacher Musa Al-Qarni, who said: "We ask Allah to strengthen the spirits of the jihad fighters in Iraq, and to help them against their enemies the Jews and the Christians."[22]

In a remarkable column published in the Saudi daily *Al Riyadh* on February 24, 2005, a lecturer in social science at King Saud University named Badria bin Abdallah Al-Bishr described her astonishment at discovering that her son's teacher was one of the perpetrators of the December 30, 2004 car bombing of the Saudi Interior Ministry in Riyadh. She also recounted that after 9/11, her fifth grader was taught at school that Osama bin Laden was a hero, while her third grader was instructed to draw a picture of the two planes hitting the twin towers.[23] Some change.

Was there a full-scale war between al-Qaeda and the dynasty? It appears that Osama bin Laden had ordered his local affiliates to launch into the 18-month campaign of bombings, which mostly targeted Americans, Britons, expatriate workers, and low-level Saudis—American contractor Paul Johnson, beheaded on June 18, 2004, and Korean worker Kim Sun-Il, for instance. The oil-related facilities at Yanbu, on the Red Sea, oil-worker residential compounds in al-Khobar, on the Gulf, the U.S. Consulate in Jiddah, were attacked. Aside from one car bomb that exploded outside the Ministry of the Interior in Riyadh, the terrorists carefully avoided harming or attacking the Royal family. The terror campaign challenged the façade of normalcy and control the dynasty had painstakingly erected. The regime reacted with fury—reportedly, 17 of the 26 most-wanted members of al-Qaeda in the Kingdom were arrested or killed. Various analysts believe that bin Laden's decision was premature, owing to a lack of preparation on the part of the four reported cells of al-Qaeda in the Kingdom. At any rate, politically, the gunmen's attacks and the car bombs never amounted to more than painful pinpricks. In August 2004, Crown Prince Abdullah had declared victory in the Saudi fight against the active domestic terrorists.[24]

But what is the meaning of victory? The day after the May 1, 2004 attack in Yanbu, the Crown Prince told a gathering of Saudi dignitaries:

> You all know who is behind it all. Zionism is behind it. It has become clear now. It has become clear to us. . . . It's not 100%, but 95% [certain] that the Zionist hands are behind what happens. We are convinced that Zionism is behind everything. This has been established. I am not saying by 100% but by 95%.[25]

Amusingly, asked to clarify this statement—which needs no clarification at all, really—the propagandist of the royals, Adel al-Jubeir, charged me personally with being responsible for terror in Saudi Arabia.

The entire royal family was united. Prince Nayef told the Yemenite weekly *September 26* that Israel and Zionism were behind al-Qaeda. Prince Salman stated that "these terrorist acts . . . are being supported by extreme Zionism." And Prince Turki, the soul of offended innocence, in London at least, was reported by the royal website and daily *Ain al-Yaqeen* to have told *al-Akfar* magazine that "the Jewish lobby which has spread illusions and delusions far from the truth in the West, is the main obstacle facing our presentation of the Arab causes in a way that can prevent this lobby from hiding the truth, forging history and stigmatizing Arabs as terrorists, killers and fanatics."

It turned out that the Saudi National Guard (SANG) was complicit in the May 2004 attack on the Riyadh housing compound which killed 35 and injured 200: the SANG had removed 50 or 70 security staff from the compound on that day for an unscheduled and unusual exercise.

In an opinion article they published in the *Washington Times*, Senator John Kyl (R-Az.) and Senator Charles Schummer (D-NY), both members of the Judiciary Committee of the Senate, accused Saudi Arabia of deceiving its American allies: "The House of Saud has for decades played a double game with the United States, on the one hand acting as our ally, on the other supporting a movement—Wahhabism—that seeks our society's destruction," they wrote.[26] Saudi-American relations have been undergoing a slow-motion divorce. In March 2005, another fifteen Senators drafted and sent a letter to Secretary of State Condoleeza Rice—herself the target of a vicious, racist, and sexist campaign in the Saudi media—where they demanded that the bilateral relationship be "defined more clearly."[27] The official daily paper *Al-Riyadh* even went as far as to publish an editorial entitled "Bush the Nazi."[28] The equally official *Saudi Gazette* published an op-ed piece by one Maqdoom Mohiuddin "revealing" an American "plot" to invade Pakistan, Sudan, Indonesia, Nigeria, and Turkey!

The "divorce" has produced various effects that are as many novelties in U.S.-Saudi relations: the State Department revoked the diplomatic immunity of 70 "diplomats" at the Saudi Embassy in Washington, D.C.: they were not diplomats but Wahhabi agitators, missionaries, and predicators. Further, the FBI subpoenaed part of the Embassy's bank accounts to investigate connections with terrorists. The same FBI raided Qorvis, the K-Street public relations firm, charged with orchestrating an illegal Saudi ad campaign in violation of the Foreign Agent Registration Act.[29] The U.S. Commission on International Religious Freedom successfully pressured the State Department into designating Saudi Arabia as a "country of particular concern" (CPC)—a small step for a decent U.S. policy, a giant leap for the State Department.[30]

Granted, the Kingdom lent minimum service during the Iraq War: it grandly allowed the U.S. to use three air bases and for Special Forces to launch attacks from Saudi soil; provided cheap fuel to U.S. and Coalition aircraft launching reconnaissance and intelligence missions; 250 to 300 Air Force aircraft staged from Saudi Arabia, including AWACs planes, C-130s, refueling craft and others. Riyadh could not have done less without incurring the risk of a public break.

The Bush Administration has not followed a straightforward path on the Saudi question, lending itself to much justified, and much unjustified, criticism (think of the idiotic forecast issued by the Democratic Party's strategic affairs expert, one Michael Moore, who predicted that the Saudi Royals would lower the oil price in order to facilitate George Bush's reelection!) The administration's willingness to move on Iraq but not on Saudi Arabia, ended up moving in a cumbersome and weighed-down fashion. It walked the walk of a policy crab, in zig-zags. By invading Iraq, by overthrowing Saddam, the president took the momentous decision of overthrowing the nefarious Middle Eastern "order" that had prevailed since 1945, and ultimately caused the soaring terrorist war against the United States. This was a decision of historic import, as it finally ran that pseudo-order out of a region it had condemned to stagnation and violence. As the reader knows, the effect of the president's decision went well beyond the borders of Iraq. While hypocritical Cassandras were bemoaning the "creation" of a haven for terrorists, the real events were bypassing the critics. The Syrian regime, for all its help to the insurgency in Iraq, was put under pressure and deeply destabilized. So much so that it made the colossal blunder of threatening, sacking, and finally assassinating their former asset in Lebanon, ex-prime minister Rafiq Hariri. The Lebanese people, who had just witnessed free elections in Iraq, rose up. Syria had to backtrack and retreat. The Egyptian dictator Hosni Mubarak was under pressure, too. Instead of calmly installing his son as dictator-to-be, as planned, he had to make a series of rather cosmetic concessions, minimally to appease the mounting demand for some dose of democracy. The notion of an "Arab Spring" gained currency.

What enraged many regional leaders about the events in Iraq was the enfranchisement of the country's Shiite majority—after 80 years of exclusive, brutal, and arrogant Sunni confiscation of power. The "Sunni Axis," which ruled the region, was broken. Strange rumblings came from Amman, Jordan, but even more, from that Saudi Arabia to which Shiites are apostate enemies of Islam, worthy of being slaughtered whenever one can, trampled underfoot whenever one may. The perspective of the Shiites of the oil-rich north-eastern quadrant—many of whom are closely identified with Iraq's Grand Ayatollah Sayyid Ali Husaini Sistani—scared the daylights out of the masters of Riyadh, who were already greatly upset at the democracy they saw in action in Iraq. The political universe shaped in large part by the Al-Saud, the *pax Britannica* into which they had so cleverly found their imperial niche and spread their oil-soaked influence, was unraveling. The events in Lebanon themselves testified to that: Hariri had not only been Syria's asset—he was a Saudi citizen, had made his multibillion fortune in Saudi Arabia, and was an asset of Crown Prince Abdullah. The Syrian regime, a brutal thuggocracy which had ruined the country in more than 30 years of rule, was critically dependent on two countries for survival: Iran, with which it shared much of the terrorist assets under its operational command, and Saudi Arabia. The Saudi response to the murder of Hariri was one of untrammeled rage. The Crown Prince crowned a series of bloody-minded official statements by saying that he "warned Syria that it is at risk of damaging relations with Saudi Arabia if it does not begin removing its troops from Lebanon."[31] In the parlance of Arab diplomatese, where a smile is a threat and soft words a menace, this is tantamount to a declaration of political war.

The succession of events shaking the region, in other words, has undermined all the false security upon which the despots and the dictators stood. This is eminently true of the Saudi regime, which had needed the entire region to be ruled despotically and dictatorially, in order to impose its own radical Islamic agenda, that of Wahhabism. Modernity and democratization are deadly poisons to the Wahhabi parasite and its Al-Saud carriers. The more the region veers in the direction of greater accountability, transparency, and democratization, the weaker any regional despot becomes.

One factor, however, had given the House of Saud a new lease on life. The lease is precarious, but it is real: at $25 a barrel of oil, the Saudi ability to buy support at home and allies abroad was dangerously corroded. At $50, it creates new margins to maneuver. It is no accident that Osama bin Laden himself called for a $100 a barrel price "minimally."[32] At about $25 a barrel, Saudi oil income for the year 2002 was about $61 billion. In 2003, as prices rose, it mounted to more than $105 billion. At $50 a barrel, the annual rent may top $150 billion. The steep increase in prices—which is relative, since inflation-adjusted figures bring the "real" prices down, more in line with historic trends—is not only due to a "risk premium" caused by instability in the region. Oil industry insiders argue that the world, the Gulf, and Saudi Arabia itself are rapidly running out of cheap oil. The rosy scenarios according to which the oil kingdom can produce more oil, and more oil can easily be found, and unexploited oil fields are just waiting to come online, are just mistaken. After the mid-1950s, few giant oil fields have been found, they argue, and many giant oil fields are nearly depleted. Seven key fields produce more than 90 percent of Saudi crude. Their average "life" is 45 to 50 years, and their "sweet spots" are "almost depleted." But secrecy shrouds the real story: "How much oil is produced; how much spare capacity really exists; how many 'proven reserves' are really proven; what are the production volumes of each field? What is the average well productivity? What will the decline by field be?" asked Matthew R. Simmons, an authoritative industry insider.[33] Expert estimation on even historical production vary by more than 15 percent whether the source is Saudi Aramco, OPEC, the International Energy Agency, British Petroleum, or the U.S. Dept. of Energy! The Saudi official figure for proven reserves is an arbitrary fairy tale. As Simmons put it, the "Ghawar [field] has provided 55 to 65% of all Saudi Arabian oil from 1951 to 2004. When Ghawar's oil output declines, Saudi Arabia's output will have peaked."

The other key fields are all "mature." Huge new investment will be required to pump the reaming crude: costs inexorably will run up, whether OPEC or OAPEC of the Saudi rulers want it or not. Being nice to them will not stop prices from soaring. The "swing" position the Saudis have carefully husbanded since 1974 is fast disappearing.

The more expensive crude oil becomes, the greater the pressure on consumer to switch to alternative sources of energy, as the aftermaths of every major spike in oil prices since 1973 demonstrates. The same will happen now. Short-term benefits can be "bought" at the expense of medium and long-term wealth. The House of Saud is presently eating into its own future.

Thirty years ago, the fundamental choice made by the dynasty was to use the proceeds of their gigantic raid on the world economy to make themselves powerful, to buy the world, as it were, especially in purchasing the world of Islam, to buy protection by offering their own protection racket on the oil prices and supplies, and to consume without restraint. Thirty years later, the failure to modernize the Kingdom is striking, beneath the veneer of steel and glass and gold. One of the modernizations that has not even begun is that of institutions, mores, and the Saudi polity itself: democracy is not just some Western luxury. Empowering large numbers of people is necessary to run a modern economy. A *rentier* economy needs accountants, not decentralized decision making.

The holding of "municipal elections" in February 2005 was the hypocritical homage paid by vice to virtue. After decades of clamoring that democracy is un-Islamic, that the Saudi mode of government is perfect and needs no heretical innovation imposed from the outside, and that elections are an abomination, the Saudi regime organized an amicable farce whereby after a ten-day campaign, an undetermined number of possibly registered voters cast their ballots for candidates who would fill half the seats in the councils of 178 towns, and be members of city councils the powers of which are not determined and the budgets of which are out of their control. Some liberalization.

It is not that there are no advocates of an opening, of a loosening of the stifling grip of the religious police, of the absolute clutch on power exerted by the lawless royal family. Amongst the educated middle-classes, such "liberalizers" are numerous. Sometimes, their voices even make it in opinion articles published in the newspapers of the country. But they are outgunned by the Wahhabis.

In January of 2003, a dozen of these advocates of the modernization of the country's institutions and governance were told by the authorities that they were allowed to present demands—but only to the Royals. When a hundred of them met in Riyadh in February 2004, the police arrested twelve of them. The lawyer protesting their detention was arrested. "In jail the reformists were told that they would be released on the condition that they sign statements pledging to direct their demands to official ears only and not talk to the press. One by one they accepted the government's offer and went home," a journalist narrates.[34] Except three, who refused the "offer," two academics and a poet who are being tried for holding a public gathering, for claiming that the Saudi judiciary is not independent, and for asking for a Constitution, and "undermining national unity and principles of the Islamic-based fabric of society," high crimes if ever there were any.[35] The pretend-liberalism displayed by the Crown Prince, who had received some of the "dissidents" and regally accept to receive a petition from them, was too much for his half-brother, the Minister of the Interior Nayef, even if it was just for show—as when the Chinese dictators release one amongst hundreds of thousands of political prisoners to display how sensitive they are to Western human rights concerns. Hence the arrests. Who is it that runs the show?

The lie was soon given to the entire charade. Elections are but one element that forms a modern, democratic polity. They are, as Natan Sharansky insisted, "one man, one vote, more than once." But they come as a crowning achievement, not an end in itself: popular participation in representative government ensures that society as a whole gives its informed assent and deliberative consent to governance, and those entrusted with government. On February 5, 2005, a new Saudi Minister of Education was appointed. Abdullah bin Saleh al-Obeid is a hard-core Wahhabi. From 1995 to 2002, incredibly enough, he was the head of the Muslim World League, this world-wide terrorist infrastructure we have encountered at every corner of international mischief. He later became the head of a quaint Saudi organization called the "National Commission for Human Rights," the main object of which is to negate its very name. He was the head of it when the U.S. State Department decided to designate Saudi Arabia a "country of particular concern" for its utter rejection of the most elementary religious freedoms.[36]

Al-Obeid's predecessor had commissioned a study to review the contents of the religious curriculum in boys' schools. At the Forum for National Dialogue held in December 2003, he had recommended that the denigration of other religions, and incitement against their faithful, should stop. Inevitably, the would-be reformer got the sack and was replaced by an extremist.

Once again, the Saudi-Wahhabi nexus had demonstrated its nature: it is like a self-sealing tube, which quasi-instantly reconstitutes itself, preventing interchange between itself and the outside world. Small punctures, mini-reforms or infra-changes, are quickly reabsorbed, negated, swept away. The survival of the partnership established in 1744 between the Al-Sauds and Wahhabism demands it. Saddam Hussein did not reform himself or his regime. The Assad dynasty will not. The Iranian Ayatollahs will not liberalize. Kadhafi will not free his people. The Algerian military kleptocracy will hang on to power until its dying breath. Dictators and despots do not, until and unless they are pressured, "till the pips squeak."

Such was the diagnosis I presented to the members of the Defense Policy Board in July 2002. I see no reason, three years and many events later, to alter that judgment. Rather, the policy recommendations I offered then are even more topical now that an Arab Spring has, oh so tentatively, started. Springs can be stifled. They need to be nurtured. The ill winds blowing from the Arabian desert would smother Spring: they need to be squelched. This is a necessary part of the strategy the United States must have in order to win the War on Terror.

I will borrow my conclusion from the wise Fouad Ajami, who wrote in his article "Reaping the Whirlwind":

> It was a matter of time before the terrible wind that originated in the Arabian Peninsula returned to its point of origin . . . The jihadists have struck far and wide. They have taken the Wahhabi creed, stretched it to the breaking point, and turned it into an instrument of combat. Where the creed had once taught obedience to the rulers, it now turned its wrath on the "infidels" defiling the sacred earth of Arabia, it was now a time of denial. In the years behind us, the bubble in which the Saudi Kingdom was sheltered burst.[37]

Notes

Introduction

1. Press release from the royal embassy of Saudi Arabia, Washington, D.C., August 6, 2002.
2. *Saudi Arabia*, July–August 2002.
3. Even so, Rumsfeld had made the obligatory soothing phone call to his Saudi counterpart, Sultan bin Abdulaziz, although, I was told, he said something entirely different in private. He also wanted it to be known that: "I appreciate the clash of ideas."
4. Nicholas M. Horrock, "Rumsfeld Reaffirms Saudi Friendship," *Washington Times*, August 7, 2002.
5. Mark Thompson, "Inside the Secret War Council," August 19, 2002.
6. David Ignatius, "Dissing the Dissenters," *Washington Post*, August 23, 2002.
7. Robert Novak, "Trashing the Saudis," *Washington Post*, August 22, 2002.
8. *Washington Times*, August 22, 2002.
9. *The Daily Star*, August 15, 2002.
10. "Estranged Allies," *Al-Ahram Weekly online*, August 29, 2002.
11. Zogby International, December 1, 2002, http://www.zogby.com/Soundbites/ReadClips.dbm?ID=4893.
12. *National Review online*, August 9, 2002.

13. "Our Enemies the Saudis (continued)," *U.S. News online*, August 7, 2002.

Chapter 1

1. Judith Miller, *God Has Ninety-Nine Names* (New York: Simon & Schuster, 1996), p. 104.
2. Alexei Vassiliev, *The History of Saudi Arabia* (London: Saqi Books, 1998), pp. 56–57.

Chapter 2

1. Alexei Vassiliev, *The History of Saudi Arabia* (London: Saqi Books, 1998), p. 397.
2. José Arnold, *Golden Swords and Pots and Pans* (New York: Harcourt Brace & World, 1963), pp. 163–165, summarized and quoted by Anthony Cave Brown, *Oil, Gods and Gold: The Story of Aramco and the Saudi Kings* (New York: Houghton Mifflin, 1999), pp. 234ff.
3. Arnold, *Golden Swords and Pots and Pans*, p. 163–165.
4. Joseph Kostiner, "Transforming Dualities: Tribe and State Formation in Saudi Arabia," in Philip S. Khoury and Joseph Kostiner, eds., *Tribes and State Formation in the Middle East* (Berkeley: University of California Press, 1990), p. 246.
5. On this question, see the two definitive books by Juliette Minces, *La Femme voilée, l'islam au féminin* (Paris: Hachette, 1990) and *Le Coran et les femmes* (Paris: Hachette, 1996).
6. http://news.bbc.co.uk/2/hi/middleeast/1874471.stm.
7. Antoine Basbous, *L'Arabie Saoudite en question, du wahhabisme à Ben Laden, aux origines de la tourmente* (Paris: Perrin, 2002).
8. Judith Miller, *God Has Ninety-Nine Names* (New York: Simon & Schuster, 1996), pp. 106–107.

9. The Saudi Institute, "Suggestions to Improve Saudi Religious Freedom," February 3, 2003, www.saudi institute.org.

10. Yaroslav Trofimov, "Saudi Shiites See Hope in an Invasion of Iraq," *Wall Street Journal*, February 3, 2003.

11. J. B. Kelly, *Arabia, the Gulf and the West* (New York: Basic Books, 1980), pp. 250–251.

12. Sandra Mackey, *The Saudis: Inside the Desert Kingdom* (Boston: Houghton Mifflin, 1987), pp. 30, 103.

Chapter 3

1. All the *fatwas* cited are listed at www.uh.edu/campus/ msa/articles.

2. Gerald de Gaury, *Faisal: King of Saudi Arabia* (New York: Praeger, 1966), pp. 166–167.

3. Antoine Basbous, *L'Arabie Saoudite en question, du wahhabisme à Ben laden, aux origines de la tourmente* (Paris: Perrin, 2002), p. 105.

4. Quoted by David Holden and Richard Johns, *The House of Saud* (New York: Holt, Rinehart and Winston, 1981), p. 262.

5. Sandra Mackey, *The Saudis: Inside the Desert Kingdom* (Boston: Houghton Mifflin, 1987), p. 263.

6. Basbous, *L'Arabie Saoudite*, p. 149.

Chapter 4

1. Robert Lacey, *The Kingdom: Arabia and the House of Saud* (1981; New York: Avon, 1983), p. 374.

2. MEMRI, Special Dispatch Series #389, "Saudi Ambassador to London: 'I Want Peace with Israel; I Long to Die as a Martyr; Stoning and Amputating Hands Are at the Core of Every Muslim's Belief,'" accessible at http://memri.org/bin/ articles.cgi?Page=archives&Area=sd&ID=SP38902.

3. Sandra Mackey, *The Saudis: Inside the Desert Kingdom* (Boston: Houghton Mifflin, 1987), pp. 264–265.
4. Gilles Kepel, *Jihad, expansion et déclin de l'islamisme* (Paris: Gallimard, 2000), p. 70.
5. Kepel, *Jihad*, p. 137.
6. Alexei Vassiliev, *The History of Saudi Arabia* (London: Saqi Books, 1998), p. 155.
7. E. Rehatsek, "The History of the Wahhabys in Arabia and India," *The Journal of the Bombay Branch of the Royal Asiatic Society*, vol. 14 (1880), p. 361, quoted in Vassiliev, *History*, p. 156.
8. Kepel, *Jihad*, p. 56.
9. Quoted by Stephen Schwartz, *The Two Faces of Islam: The House of Saud from Tradition to Terror* (New York: Doubleday, 2002), p. 132.
10. Adam Parfrey, ed., *Extreme Islam: Anti-American Propaganda of Muslim Fundamentalism* (Los Angeles: Feral House, 2001), pp. 69–71.
11. In this connection, see the fundamental work by Daryush Shayegan, *Le Regard mutilé* (Paris: Éditions de l'Aube, 1995).
12. Richard P. Mitchell, *The Society of the Muslim Brothers* (London: Oxford University Press, 1969), p. 14.
13. Mitchell, *Muslim Brothers*, pp. 232–333.
14. Judith Miller, *God Has Ninety-Nine Names* (New York: Simon & Schuster, 1996), p. 119.
15. Olivier Roy, *The Failure of Political Islam*, trans. Carol Volk (Cambridge: Harvard University Press, 1994), p. 79.
16. Parfrey, *Extreme Islam*, pp. 61ff.

Chapter 5

1. Antoine Basbous, *L'Arabie Saoudite en question, du wahhabisme à Ben Laden, aux origines de la tourmente* (Paris: Perrin, 2002), p. 149.

2. "The Transnational Salafi/Wahhabi Movement Inside the United States," n. d.

3. Gilles Kepel, *Jihad, expansion et déclin de l'islamisme* (Paris: Gallimard, 2000), pp. 72–73.

4. Stephen Schwartz, *The Two Faces of Islam: The House of Saud from Tradition to Terror* (New York: Doubleday, 2002), p. 220.

5. Kepel, *Jihad*, p. 75.

6. http://www.isdb.org/english_docs/idb_home/backgrnd.htm.

7. http://www.alfaadel.com/islam_qa/wamy.html.

8. Judith Miller, *God Has Ninety-Nine Names* (New York: Simon & Schuster, 1996), p. 468.

9. Jean-Charles Brisard and Guillaume Dasquié, *Forbidden Truth: U.S.-Taliban Secret Oil Diplomacy and the Failed Hunt for Bin Laden*, trans. Lucy Rounds (New York: Thunder's Mouth Press/Nation Books, 2002), p. 49.

10. Greg Palast and David Pallisser, "FBI and U.S. Spy Agents Say Bush Spiked Bin Laden Probes before 11 September," *The Guardian*, November 7, 2001.

11. http://www.kingfahdbinabdulaziz.com.

12. J. B. Kelly, *Arabia, the Gulf and the West* (New York: Basic Books, 1980), p. 437.

13. Steven Emerson, *The American House of Saud: The Secret Petrodollar Connection* (New York: Franklin Watts, 1985), pp. 298–299.

14. *Washington Post*, November 5, 1977. Also see http://www.hillary.org/hc/Hillary_Clinton_Forum_873_chat1.cgi; http://www.6thcolumnagainstjihad.com/Rublev_P4.htm; recounted in Seth Cropsey, "Arab Money and the Universities," *Commentary* 67, no. 4 (April 1979), accessible at http://www.commentarymagazine.com/Summaries/V67I4P74-1.htm.

15. Emerson, *American House of Saud*, pp. 303–306.

16. Martin Kramer, "Ivory Towers on Sand: The Failure of Middle Eastern Studies in America," Washington

Institute for Middle East Policy, Washington, D.C., 2001.

Chapter 6

1. http://www.saudiembassy.net/press_release/00_spa/02 16-cult.html.
2. http://www.alazhar.org/english/contact.htm.
3. http://www.ain-al-yaqeen.com/issues/20000602/feat9en .htm.
4. I am paraphrasing the long article by Franklin Foer, "Moral Hazard: The Life of a Liberal Muslim," *The New Republic*, November 14, 2002.
5. I would like to express my appreciation to a number of Arabic journalists who were kind enough to guide me through the labyrinth of the history of the Arab press and the Arab media. It is understandable that they are not particularly eager to have their names mentioned here.

Chapter 7

1. Judith Miller, *God Has Ninety-Nine Names* (New York: Simon & Schuster, 1996), pp. 181ff.; Joseph A. Kechichian, *Succession in Saudi Arabia* (New York: Palgrave, 2001), p. 83; Gilles Kepel, *Jihad, expansion et déclin de l'islamisme* (Paris: Gallimard, 2000), p. 178; Jean-Charles Brisard and Guillaume Dasquié, *Forbidden Truth: U.S.-Taliban Secret Oil Diplomacy and the Failed Hunt for bin Laden*, trans. Lucy Rounds (New York: Thunder's Mouth Press/Nation Books, 2002), p. 80.
2. Strategic Affairs: http://www.stratmag.com/issueFeb1/ page05.htm.
3. See Lucy Komisar, "Shareholders in the Bank of Terror?" Slate online (March 15, 2002), accessible at http://archive

.salon.com/tech/feature/2002/03/15/al_taqwa/. Also see http://www.publiceye.org/fascist/third_position.html.

4. Antoine Basbous, "Les pays du Golfe face à la crise algérienne," *Cahiers de l'Orient*, no. 51 (1998).

5. Stephen Schwartz, *The Two Faces of Islam* (New York: Doubleday, 2002), p. 186.

6. http://www.kff.com/winners/2001/2001winners.htm. Other prizes are attributed for "Islamic studies," "Arabic literature," medicine, and science.

7. Schwartz, *The Two Faces of Islam*, pp. 189–199.

8. Kepel, *Jihad*, p. 142.

9. These details come from Kepel, *Jihad*, pp. 142ff., 184.

10. Ahmed Rashid, *Taliban: Militant Islam, Oil and Fundamentalism in Central Asia* (New Haven, Conn.: Yale University Press, 2000), p. 45.

11. Ahmed Rashid, *Jihad: The Rise of Militant Islam in Central Asia* (New Haven, Conn.: Yale University Press, 2002), pp. 95, 102, 115–117, 139–140, 154, 166 (quotation from p. 154).

12. http://www.tolueislam.com/Bazm/Shahid/SM_001.htm.

13. Some sources mention the figure of forty to fifty thousand *madrasas* not recognized by the authorities and about ten thousand officially recognized. "Madrasas, etc.," Buffalo Networks Pvt. Ltd., May 15, 2001, Tehelka.com.

14. The facts presented here are largely taken from the unpublished article by Alexei Alexiev, "Islamic Extremism and Its Sponsors: Lessons from Pakistan," which I gratefully acknowledge.

15. Maloy Krishna Dhar, "Living in the ISI's shadow," *Kashmir Sentinel* September 1–October 15, 1998, http://hvk.org/articles/1198/0022.html; M. G. Ashok Krishna, "The Inter-Services Intelligence (ISI) of Pakistan," IPCS, May 25, 1999, article no. 191, http://www.ipcs.org/issues/articles/191-ip-krishna.htm.

16. Ralph Braibanti, "Strategic Significance of Pakistan," Pakistan Institute for Air Defense Studies, n. d., http://www.piads.com.pk/users/braibanti1a.html.
17. B. Raman, "Pakistan's Army Within the Army," June 30, 2000, http://www.asiafeatures.com/currentaffairs/0007, 0415,03a.html.
18. Thomas Woodrow, "Saudi Arabia financed Pak nuke program: Ex-U.S. DIA official," Press Trust of India, *Hindustan Times*, November 10, 2001.

Chapter 8

1. January 29, 2002.
2. http://www.arabicnews.com/ansub/Daily/Day/020129/2002012944.html.
3. Joshua Teitelbaum, *Holier Than Thou: Saudi Arabia's Islamic Opposition*, Washington, D.C., Washington Institute for Near East Policy, Policy Papers 2, 2000.
4. Abdulla Muhammad al-Zaid, *Education in Saudi Arabia: A Model with a Difference* (1982), a book published in English in 1995 by the Saudi Cultural Mission in the United States, originally published by the Saudi High Authority for Educational Policy.
5. *Education in Saudi Arabia*, pp. 39–40.
6. *Education in Saudi Arabia*, pp. 39, 42, 45.
7. *Al Hadith*, 2000, for the tenth grade.
8. MEMRI, Special Report 10: "Friday Sermons in Saudi Mosques: Review and Analysis," (September 26, 2002), accessible at http://memri.org/bin/articles.cgi?Page=archives&Area=sr&ID=SR01002.
9. Reported in *Ain al-Yaqeen*, September 20, 2002.
10. *Al-Hayat*, October 22, 2002. Quotations are from MEMRI, Special Report, "Saudi Arabia," no. 12 (December 20, 2002), "Preliminary Overview. Saudi Arabia's Education System: Curriculum, Spreading

Saudi Education to the World and the Official Saudi Position on Education Policy."

11. *Voice of America*, April 25, 2002, editorial number 0-09844.

12. MEMRI, Special Dispatch 400, "Saudi Opposition Sheikhs on America, Bin Laden, and Jihad," (July 18, 2002), accessible at http://memri.org/bin/articles.cgi ?Page=archives&Area=sd&ID=SP40002.

13. Ibid.

14. Taken from Antoine Basbous, *L'Arabie Saoudite en question, du wahhabisme à Ben Laden, aux origines de la tourmente* (Paris: Perrin, 2002), pp. 17–19, and Nicholas Pelham, "Saudi Clerics Issue Edicts against Helping 'Infidels,'" *Christian Science Monitor*, October 12, 2001.

15. I am grateful to Dr. Shmuel Bar for having provided the documents quoted.

16. http://www.kalemat.org/sections.php?so=va$taid=93.

17. http://www.alminbar.net/alkhutab/khutbaa.asp?media URL=2818.

18. Sheikh Ali Abdurrahman al-Hudhaifi, *The Historic Khutba*, n. d., "Published by Ahle Sunnah Wal Jama'at."

19. http://www.alminbar.cc/alkhutab/khutbaa.asp?media URL=5979, February 22, 2002. MEMRI Special Report, "Friday Sermons."

20. http://www.alminbar.cc/alkhutab/khutbaa.asp?media URL=5268, October 6, 2001.

21. MEMRI, Special Dispatch 304, "Saudi Government Efforts to Curtail Incitement in Mosques and Press," (November 28, 2001), accessible at http://memri.org/ bin/articles.cgi?Page=archives&Area=sd&ID=SP30401.

Chapter 9

1. The best introduction to this is the magisterial work by David Pryce-Jones, *The Closed Circle: An Interpretation of the Arabs* (New York: Harper & Row, 1989).

2. *Ain Al-Yaqeen*, December 8, 2000, http://www.ain-al-yaqeen.com/issues/20001208/feat5en.htm.
3. Alexei Alexiev, "The Missing Link in the War on Terror: Confronting Saudi Subversion," *National Review*, October 28, 2002.
4. Jean-Charles Brisard, *Terrorism Financing: Roots and Trends of Saudi Terrorism Financing*, December 19, 2002, UN, 27.
5. Matthew Levitt, "Tackling the Financing of Terrorism in Saudi Arabia," *Policywatch* no. 609 (March 11, 2002), Washington Institute for Near East Policy, http://www.washingtoninstitute.org/watch/Policywatch2002/609.htm.
6. Alexiev, "The Missing Link."
7. Ibid.
8. Judith Miller, *God Has Ninety-Nine Names* (New York: Simon & Schuster, 1996), p. 118.
9. The case is *In Re: Terrorist Attacks on Sept. 11, 2001*, 03- MD-1570, Southern District of New York. Many of the key defendants have been dismissed from the litigation (see http://www.nysd.uscourts.gov/rulings/03MDL 1570_RCC_011905.PDF and http://www.bloomberg .com/apps/news?pid=10000087&sid=aCQwDXe3ae8o &refer=top_world_news).
10. Brisard, *Terrorism Financing*.
11. Brisard, *Terrorism Financing*, p. 17.
12. Sourcing for Zouaydi as financer to al-Qaeda, see page 10 of http://banking.senate.gov/_files/levitt.pdf; and page 24 of http://www.nationalreview.com/document/document-un122002.pdf. For association between Al-Turki and Zouaydi, see page 16 of http://banking.senate .gov/_files/brisard.pdf, which reads in part: "In 1999, in his capacity of advisor-minister to King Fahd of Saudi Arabia, Abdullah al Turki entered in negotiations to become business partner of Muhammad Zouaydi, al-Qaida financier for Europe, for a construction project in

Madrid, Spain, worth $2.3 million. Both agreed to participate as business partners and a contract was written on October 1, 1999 by Muhammad Zouaydi acting as representative of the Spanish company Proyectos y Promociones ISO, stating that both parties will finance 50% of the project and split the incomes 70/30 between Abdullah al Turki and Muhammad Zouaydi. As a guaranty for the operation, Muhammad Zouaydi sent a check of $1.1 million on September 15, 1999 with Abdullah al Turki as beneficiary. Several documents established that both men had business relations on a regular basis until at least year 2000."

For Zouaydi prosecution see http://www.euroatlantic .blogspot.com/, which states in part: "Around April 2002, Spanish authorities searched the home and offices of Muhammad Zouaydi, a senior al-Qaeda financier in Madrid. Investigators found a five-page fax dated October 24, 2001, revealing that Zouaydi was not only financing the Hamburg cell responsible for the September 11 attacks, but also Hamas. In the fax, which Zouaydi kept for his records, the Hebron Muslim Youth Association solicited funds from the Islamic Association of Spain. According to Spanish prosecutors, "the Hebron Muslim Youth Association is an organization known to belong to the Palestinian terrorist organization Hamas which is financed by activists of said organization living abroad." Spanish police also say Zouaydi gave a total of almost $6,600 marked "Gifts for Palestine" to Sheikh Helal Jamal, a Palestinian religious figure in Madrid tied to Hamas."

13. Douglas Farah, "Saudis Face U.S. Demand on Terrorism: Halting Financiers May Be Urged," *Washington Post*, November 26, 2002.
14. Brian Ross, "Secret List: CIA Circulates List of Saudis Accused of Funneling Money to Bin Laden," *ABC News*, November 25, 2002.

15. *Middle East Newsline*, "Saudi Arabia Allows Continued Funding to Al-Qaeda," Washington, November 27, 2002.

16. http://www.cfr.org/publications.php?id=5080.

17. See AFP, Washington, D.C., November 23, 2002, "Saudi Money Linked to Two 9/11 Hijackers: Reports"; Dana Priest and Susan Schmidt, "Congressional Panel Links Hijackers, Saudi Financiers: FBI, Justice Dept. Ask Government Not to Declassify Findings," *Washington Post*, November 23, 2002; Michael Isikoff and Evan Thomas, "The Saudi Money Trail: Rent Payments for 9-11 Hijackers and Mysterious Checks from a Princess's Account. Is There a Saudi Tie to Terror? Inside the Probe the Bush Administration Does Not Want You to Know About," *Newsweek*, December 2, 2002.

18. Reuters, dispatch from Kuwait, October 22, 2001: "Saudi Questions Identity of U.S. Attackers."

19. Complete interview in *Ain Al-Yaqeen*, November 29, 2002, http://www.ain-al-yaqeen.com/issues/20021129/feat6en.htm.

20. *Newsweek*, January 13, 2002, interview with Jonathan Alter.

21. Glenn R. Simpson, "Terror Investigators Followed Funds to a Saudi Businessman," *Wall Street Journal*, November 26, 2002.

22. "Large Sums of Money Transferred by Saudi Arabia to the Palestinians Are Used for Financing Terror Organizations (Particularly Hamas) and Terrorist Activities (Including Suicide Attacks) Inside Israel," Israeli army document, May 6, 2002.

Chapter 10

1. This treatment is largely taken from Yossef Bodansky, *Bin Laden: The Man Who Declared War on America* (Roseville, Calif.: Prima Forum, 1999), whose investiga-

tion, based on intelligence sources, confirms the author's conclusions.

2. Robert Baer, *See No Evil* (New York: Crown, 2001).
3. Bodansky, *Bin Laden*, p. 17.
4. Bodansky, *Bin Laden*, p. 18.
5. Bodansky, *Bin Laden*, p. 24.
6. Bodansky, *Bin Laden*, p. 107.
7. Bodansky, *Bin Laden*, p. 109.
8. Bodansky, *Bin Laden*, pp. 13–14.
9. Bodansky, *Bin Laden*, p. 20.
10. Bodansky, *Bin Laden*, pp. 28–31.
11. See Jean-Charles Brisard and Guillaume Dasquié, *Forbidden Truth: U.S.-Taliban Secret Oil Diplomacy and the Failed Hunt for Bin Laden* (New York: Thunder's Mouth Press/Nation Books, 2002), pp. 103–104.
12. Quoted in Bodansky, *Bin Laden*, p. 194.
13. Bodansky, *Bin Laden*, pp. 280–281.
14. Bodansky, *Bin Laden*, p. 282.
15. Bodansky, *Bin Laden*, p. 301.
16. Bodansky, *Bin Laden*, p. 161.

Chapter 11

1. Patrick E. Tyler, "Explaining Gift, Saudi Envoy Voices Pain for Strained Ties," *New York Times*, November 27, 2002.
2. Robert G. Kaiser and David B. Ottaway, "Saudi Leader's Anger Revealed Shaky Ties," *Washington Post*, February 10, 2002.
3. Steven Emerson, *The American House of Saud: The Secret Petrodollar Connection* (New York: Franklin Watts, 1985), p. 25.
4. Emerson, *American House of Saud*, p. 33.
5. Emerson, *American House of Saud*, p. 34.
6. Emerson, *American House of Saud*, p. 25.
7. Emerson, *American House of Saud*, pp. 267–268.

8. Emerson, *American House of Saud*, pp. 269–280.
9. Emerson, *American House of Saud*, p. 285.
10. Emerson, *American House of Saud*, p. 71.
11. Emerson, *American House of Saud*, p. 72.
12. Emerson, *American House of Saud*, p. 73.
13. J. B. Kelly, *Arabia, the Gulf and the West* (New York: Basic Books, 1980), p. 265.
14. Lawrence F. Kaplan, "Arabian Fights: How the Saudis Lobby Bush," *The New Republic*, December 24, 2001.
15. Robert Baer, *See No Evil* (New York: Crown, 2002), p. 265.
16. "The Mideast Linkage Factor: It's Time to Keep American Promises," *International Herald Tribune*, November 29, 2002.

Chapter 12

1. Matt Welch, "Shilling for the House of Saud," NewsMax.com, August 31, 2002.
2. Robert G. Kaiser and David B. Ottaway, "Oil for Security Fueled Close Ties," *Washington Post*, February 11, 2002.
3. See *Washington Post* columnist, John McCaslin, April 11, 2003, accessible at http://www.townhall.com/columnists/johnmccaslin/printjm20030411.shtml: "It's the 'Kissinger plan,' says former U.S. ambassador to Saudi Arabia James Akins, who served under Secretary of State Henry Kissinger. 'I thought it had been killed but it's back'

In the wake of the oil shocks of the 1970s, Akins says, a 'screwy idea' was floated to American newspapers and magazines outlining a U.S. takeover of Arab oil fields.

'Then I made a fatal mistake,' Akins tells the magazine. 'I said on television that anyone who would propose that is either a madman, a criminal, or an agent of the Soviet Union.'

A short time later, Akins was told that the 'madman' was his own boss, Kissinger, who reportedly had introduced the proposal during a senior background briefing. Akins was fired a short time later."

Also see http://www.axiusnews.com/Dove/2003/mar/dove031103.htm: "Originally, this was the 'Kissinger plan," says James Akins, former U.S. ambassador to Saudi Arabia. He lost his state department job for publicly criticizing administration plans to control Arab oil back in 1975 when Henry Kissinger was secretary of state."

And http://globalfire.tv/nj/03en/politics/the_wmd_lie .htm: "Akins was ambassador to Saudi Arabia before he was fired after a series of conflicts with then Secretary of State Henry Kissinger."

4. Emerson, *American House of Saud*, pp. 258–260.
5. Emerson, *American House of Saud*, pp. 364–366.
6. Emerson, *American House of Saud*, p. 373.
7. Emerson, *American House of Saud*, pp. 407–408.
8. http://www.arabnews.com/Article.asp?ID=21413.
9. David Mulholland, editor of *Jane's Defense Weekly*, quoted by Oliver Burkeman and Julian Borger, "The Ex-presidents' Club," *The Guardian*, October 31, 2001.
10. Maggie Mulvihill, Jackie Meyers, and Jonathan Wells, "Bush Advisers Cashed In on Saudi Gravy Train," *Boston Herald*, December 11, 2001.
11. "Dark Heart of the American Dream," *The Observer*, June 16, 2002.
12. Daniel Golden, James Bandler, and Marcus Walker, "Bin Laden Family Could Profit from a Jump in Defense Spending Due to Ties to U.S. Bank," *Wall Street Journal*, September 27, 2001.
13. Charles Lewis, director of the Center for Public Integrity, quoted by Charles M. Sennott, "Doubts Are Cast on the Viability of the Saudi Monarchy for the Long Term," *Boston Globe*, http://www.boston.com/dailyglobe2, March 5, 2002.

14. Steve Lohr, "Gerstner to Be Chairman of Carlyle Group," *New York Times*, November 22, 2002.
15. Kate Taylor, "Top Stories," Slate.com (October 29, 2002) accessible at http://slate.msn.com/id/2072923/. The article, in part, reads: "Princess Haifa al-Faisal, who is accused of indirectly giving financial support to two of the Sept. 11 hijackers, was at home in McLean, Va., yesterday, nursing her wounds and taking sympathetic calls from Barbara Bush, the president's mother, and Alma Powell, the secretary's wife." Also see the December 12, 2002, *Wall Street Journal* editorial, "Prince Bandar's Wife," which reads in part: "We agree that there is no evidence that the princess had any intention of financing terrorism, though it would be a mistake for Bandar and the Saudi ruling class to conclude that the professions of support from Barbara Bush and Colin and Alma Powell mean that everything is fine with the U.S.-Saudi relationship. The fact that the princess's donations became such a public issue is a sign that the old days of insider understandings and State Department winking are over."
16. "Saudi Timebomb?" Interview with Brent Scowcroft, PBS Frontline (October 2001). The transcript is available at http://www.pbs.org/wgbh/pages/frontline/shows/saudi/interviews/scowcroft.html.
17. Emerson, *American House of Saud*, pp. 77–94; Reagan quotation, p. 80.
18 Newsweek Periscope, "Saudi Close Ties," *Newsweek*, January 5, 2003.
19. "Saudis Spend Big at Qorvis," *O'Dwyer's PR Daily*, December 27, 2002.
20. Adam Daifallah, "Saudis' Lobbyists Claim Immunity," *New York Sun*, November 22, 2002.
21. Philip Shenon, "Three Partners Quit Firm Handling Saudi PR," *New York Times*, December 6, 2002.

22. This account is based on Emerson, *American House of Saud*, pp. 151–160.

Chapter 13

1. Robert Lacey, *The Kingdom: Arabia and the House of Saud* (1981; New York: Avon, 1983), p. 29.
2. Ibn Khaldun, *The Muqaddimah*, trans. Franz Rosenthal, 3 vols. (New York: Pantheon, 1958.), vol. 1, p. 252.
3. *The Muqaddimah*, vol. 1, p. 265.
4. John L. Burckhardt, *Notes on the Bedouins and Wahabys*, quoted in Alexei Vassiliev, *The History of Saudi Arabia* (London: Saqi Books, 1998), p. 45.
5. *The Muqaddimah*, vol. 1, p. 263.
6. *The Muqaddimah*, vol. 1, p. 266.
7. Lacey, *The Kingdom*, p. 292.
8. *The Muqaddimah*, vol. 1, p. 282.
9. *The Muqaddimah*, vol. 1, p. 303.
10. *The Muqaddimah*, vol. 1, p. 295.
11. *The Muqaddimah*, vol. 1, p. 305.
12. Vassiliev, *History of Saudi Arabia*, p. 81.
13. Quoted by Antoine Basbous, *L'Arabie Saoudite en question, du wahhabisme à Ben Laden, aux origines de la tourmente* (Paris: Perrin, 2002), p. 75.
14. Chapter 60 "Les négateurs du destin," in Mohammad ibn Abd al-Wahhab, *L'Unicité de Dieu (Kitab al Tawhid)* (Paris: Al Qalam Éditions, 1992), pp. 135–136, as for other quotations and references.
15. Vassiliev, *History of Saudi Arabia*, p. 77.
16. Vassiliev, *History of Saudi Arabia*, p. 78.
17. David Pryce-Jones, *The Closed Circle: An Interpretation of the Arabs* (New York: Harper & Row, 1989), p. 258.
18. G. P. Badger, *History of the Imams and Seyyids of Oman* (London, 1871), p. lxv, quoted by J. B. Kelly,

Arabia, the Gulf and the West (New York: Basic Books, 1980), p. 226.

19. Harry St. John Philby, *Arabia* (London, 1930), p. 181, quoted in Kelly, *Arabia, the Gulf and the West*, p. 226.
20. *The Archives of Russian Foreign Policy*, 1803, file 2235, pp. 38–40, quoted by Vassiliev, *History of Saudi Arabia*, p. 97.
21. Kelly, *Arabia, the Gulf and the West*, p. 226.
22. Vassiliev, *History of Saudi Arabia*, p. 96.
23. An honorific title indicating respect for age, influence, wisdom, or power.
24. The history of the Wahhabi conquest and subsequent defeat is derived from Vassiliev, *History of Saudi Arabia*, ch. 5, and other sources.

Chapter 14

1. Gertrude Bell, *The Arab War: Confidential Information for General Headquarters from Gertrude Bell* (London: Cockerel Press, 1940), p. 9, quoted by Robert Lacey, *The Kingdom: Arabia and the House of Saud* (1981; New York: Avon, 1983), p. 125.
2. See the analysis by Efraim and Inari Karsh, *Empires of the Sand: The Struggle for Mastery in the Middle East, 1789–1923* (Cambridge: Harvard University Press, 1999).
3. Lacey, *The Kingdom*, p. 78.
4. Alexei Vassiliev, *The History of Saudi Arabia* (London: Saqi Books, 1998), p. 215.
5. J. B. Kelly, *Arabia, the Gulf and the West* (New York: Basic Books, 1980), p. 230.
6. Kelly, *Arabia, the Gulf and the West*, p. 231.
7. Lacey, *The Kingdom*, p. 145.
8. Lacey, *The Kingdom*, p. 127.
9. Kelly, *Arabia, the Gulf and the West*, p. 237.
10. Vassiliev, *History of Saudi Arabia*, p. 263.

11. Kelly, *Arabia, the Gulf and the West*, p. 235.
12. Stephen Schwartz, *The Two Faces of Islam: The House of Saud from Tradition to Terror* (New York: Doubleday, 2002), p. 104.
13. Vassiliev, *History of Saudi Arabia*, p. 271.
14. Vassiliev, *History of Saudi Arabia*, p. 291.
15. The *Sturmabteilungen*, the paramilitary riff-raff Adolf Hitler used to dominate the streets and launch physical attacks against opponents.
16. Lacey, *The Kingdom*, p. 207.
17. Lacey, *The Kingdom*, p. 211.
18. Vassiliev, *History of Saudi Arabia*, p. 273.

Chapter 15

1. J. B. Kelly, *Arabia, the Gulf and the West* (New York: Basic Books, 1980), pp. 258, 260.
2. Quoted by Anthony Cave Brown, *Oil, Gods and Gold: The Story of Aramco and the Saudi Kings* (New York: Houghton Mifflin, 1999), p. 27.
3. Brown, *Oil, Gods and Gold*, p. 28.
4. Robert Lacey, *The Kingdom: Arabia and the House of Saud* (1981; New York: Avon, 1983), p. 238.
5. Lukasz Hirszowicz, *The Third Reich and the Arab East* (London: Routledge & Kegan Paul, 1966), p. 10.
6. This account as a whole is drawn from Hirszowicz, *The Third Reich*, particularly pp. 47–69.
7. Lacey, *The Kingdom*, p. 261.
8. Brown, *Oil, Gods and Gold*, p. 107.
9. Aramco had four shareholders: Socal (30 percent), Texaco (30 percent), Esso (30 percent), and Mobil (10 percent).
10. Alexei Vassiliev, *The History of Saudi Arabia* (London: Saqi Books, 1998), p. 326.
11. Lacey, *The Kingdom*, p. 289.
12. Vassiliev, *History of Saudi Arabia*, table 1, pp. 319–320.

13. Lacey, *The Kingdom*, p. 280.
14. Kelly, *Arabia, the Gulf and the West*, p. 252.
15. See the astute analysis in Kelly, *Arabia, the Gulf and the West*, particularly pp. 252–258.

Chapter 16

1. Quoted in Alexei Vassiliev, *The History of Saudi Arabia* (London: Saqi Books, 1998), pp. 342–343.
2. Vassiliev, *History of Saudi Arabia*, p. 344.
3. Quoted by H. R. P. Dickson, *Kuwait and Her Neighbors* (London: Allen & Unwin, 1956), pp. 389, 391.
4. Robert Lacey, *The Kingdom: Arabia and the House of Saud* (1981; New York: Avon, 1983), p. 197.
5. See Henry Rollin, *L'Apocalypse de notre temps. Les dessous de la propagande allemande d'après des documents inédits* (1939; Paris: Allia, 1991).
6. Quoted by J. B. Schechtman, *The Mufti and the Führer: The Rise and Fall of Haj Amin el-Husseini* (New York: T. Yoseloff, 1965), p. 84.
7. David Holden and Richard Johns, *The House of Saud* (New York: Holt, Rinehart and Winston, 1981), p. 385.
8. May 31, 1960, quoted by Bernard Lewis, *Semites and Anti-Semites* (New York: Norton, 1986), p. 162.
9. Quoted by David K. Shipler, *Arab and Jew: Wounded Spirits in a Promised Land* (New York: Times Books, 1986).
10. Daniel Pipes, "The Politics of Muslim Anti-Semitism," *Commentary*, August 1981.
11. Lacey, *The Kingdom*, p. 386.
12. Anthony Cave Brown, *Oil, Gods and Gold: The Story of Aramco and the Saudi Kings* (New York: Houghton Mifflin, 1999), p. 199.
13. Harry St. John Philby, *Forty Years in the Wilderness* (London: Hale, 1957), p. 37.

14. José Arnold, *Golden Swords and Pots and Pans* (New York: Harcourt, Brace & World, 1963), pp. 44–45, 51–52.
15. Lacey, *The Kingdom*, p. 321.
16. Joseph A. Kechichian, *Succession in Saudi Arabia* (New York: Palgrave, 2001), pp. 40–43.
17. Lacey, *The Kingdom*, p. 305.
18. Joseph Kostiner, "Transforming Dualities: Tribe and State in Saudi Arabia," in Philip S. Khoury and Joseph Kostiner, eds., *Tribes and State Formation in the Middle East* (Berkeley: University of California Press, 1990), p. 241.
19. Quoted by Antoine Basbous, *L'Arabie Saoudite en question, du wahhabisme à Ben Laden, aux origines de la tourmente* (Paris: Perrin, 2002), p. 75.
20. Lacey, *The Kingdom*, p. 374.
21. Lacey, *The Kingdom*, p. 375.

Chapter 17

1. Robert Lacey, *The Kingdom: Arabia and the House of Saud* (1981; New York: Avon, 1983), p. 333.
2. J. B. Kelly, *Arabia, the Gulf and the West* (New York: Basic Books, 1980), p. 328.
3. Kelly, *Arabia, the Gulf and the West*, p. 367.
4. Kelly, *Arabia, the Gulf and the West*, p. 377. I follow Kelly's remarkable analysis very closely in the foregoing account of the "prehistory" of the oil crisis as well as in what follows. I am deeply indebted to his work.
5. Alexei Vassiliev, *The History of Saudi Arabia* (London: Saqi Books, 1998), p. 46.
6. This was James Akins, who was appointed ambassador to Riyadh and quickly dismissed, as we have seen by Secretary of State Henry Kissinger, who reproached him for being more the Saudi ambassador to the United States than the American ambassador to Saudi Arabia.

7. Quoted by Kelly, *Arabia, the Gulf and the West*, p. 383.
8. Kelly, *Arabia, the Gulf and the West*, p. 390.
9. Kelly, *Arabia, the Gulf and the West*, pp. 389–390.
10. Kelly, *Arabia, the Gulf and the West*, pp. 390–392.
11. Kelly, *Arabia, the Gulf and the West*, p. 397.
12. Kelly, *Arabia, the Gulf and the West*, p. 410.
13. Kelly, *Arabia, the Gulf and the West*, p. 423.
14. The other principal beneficiary of the increase in prices was, curiously enough, the USSR of Leonid Brezhnev, for which it provided an unexpected injection of resources, since the country was a major producer and exporter of oil. King Faisal may have delayed the collapse of communism by ten or fifteen years.
15. Lacey, *The Kingdom*, p. 422.

Chapter 18

1. See, for example, the *CIA World Factbook 2002: Saudi Arabia*; online: www.cia.gov/cia/publications/factbook/geos/sa.html; *United Nations Development Report* (New York: Oxford University Press, 2001), p. 179; *World Bank Atlas*, 2001, p. 45; and United Nations, DESA, "Country Profiles on the Situation of Youth."
2. Sandra Mackey, *The Saudis: Inside the Desert Kingdom* (Boston: Houghton Mifflin, 1987), pp. 31–33.
3. Mackey, *The Saudis*, p. 46.
4. Mackey, *The Saudis*, p. 59.
5. All these examples come from Mackey, *The Saudis*, who lived in Saudi Arabia and was a clandestine reporter.
6. Mackey, *The Saudis*, p. 350.
7. Mackey, *The Saudis*, pp. 55–56.
8. Central Department of Statistics, Planning Ministry.
9. CIA, *World Factbook 2002*.
10. Mackey, *The Saudis*, p. 185.
11. Said Eddin Ibrahim, "Oil, Migration and the New Arab Social Order," in Malcolm H. Kerr and El Sayed Yassin,

eds., *Rich and Poor States in the Middle East: Egypt and the New Arab Order* (Boulder, Colo.: Westview, 1982), p. 50.

12. Sir James Craig, *Glasgow Herald*, October 9, 1980, quoted in David Pryce-Jones, *The Closed Circle: An Interpretation of the Arabs* (New York: Harper & Row, 1989), p. 270.

13. Robert Lacey, *The Kingdom: Arabia and the House of Saud* (1981; New York: Avon, 1983), pp. 514–515.

14. Ibn Khaldun, *The Muqaddimah*, trans. Franz Rosenthal, 3 vols. (New York: Pantheon, 1958), vol. 1, p. 303.

15. For Hitler's economic doctrine, see my translation and presentation of the "Mémorandum de Hitler pour le plan de quatre ans," *xxe siècle*, and my forthcoming book *Les Ateliers de Vulcain. Histoire de la planification économique.*

16. Mackey, *The Saudis*, p. 371.

17. Lacey, *The Kingdom*, p. 374.

18. Lacey, *The Kingdom*, p. 419.

19. Lacey, *The Kingdom*, p. 419.

20. *International Herald Tribune*, December 23, 1977.

Conclusion

1. Steven Emerson, *The American House of Saud: The Secret Petrodollar Connection* (New York: Franklin Watts, 1985), pp. 368–370, and 373.

2. Seymour M. Hersh, "King's Ransom: How Vulnerable Are the Saudi Royals?," *The New Yorker*, October 22, 2002.

3. "Frontline," Looking for Answers: Interview with Bandar Bin Sultan, PBS Television, October 9, 2001. The entire transcript of the interview is accessible at http://www.pbs.org/wgbh/pages/frontline/shows/terrorism/interviews/bandarhtml.

4. David Pryce-Jones, *The Closed Circle: An Interpreta-tion of the Arabs* (New York: Harper & Row, 1989), p. 277.
5. Robert G. Kaiser and David B. Ottaway, "Saudi Leader's Anger Revealed Shaky Ties," *Washington Post*, February 10, 2002.
6. Ibn Khaldun, *The Muqaddimah*, trans. Franz Rosenthal, 3 vols. (New York: Pantheon, 1958), vol. 1, pp. 279–280.

Epilogue

1. The author is in possession of this fax.
2. The author is in possession of the e-mail.
3. The author is in possession of the e-mail.
4. "The wages of courage," Caroline Glick, *Jerusalem Post*, January 19, 2005.
5. *The Saudi Gazette* at http://www.iccuk.org/media/ spotlight/prince_turki_wins_label_case.htm; also see http://www.saudi-us-relations.org/newsletter2004/saudi-relations-interest-12-08.html and the BBC News at http://news.bbc.co.uk/1/hi/uk/4072219.stm.
6. *Macbeth*, 2.2.57–60.
7. Don van Natta, Jr., and Timothy L. O'Brien, "Saudis Promising Action on Terror," *New York Times*, September 14, 2003.
8. Saturday June 5, 2004.
9. Reuven Paz, GLORIA, "Arab Volunteers Killed in Iraq: An Analysis," PRISM Occasional Papers Vol. 3 No. 1 (3 March 2005)—Arab Volunteers Killed in Iraq: An Analysis.
10. *Associated Press*, November 7, 2004.
11. Quoted by Barry Rubin, "PR Saudi Style," February 15, 2005, Gloria.idc.ac.il/columns/2005/02_15.html.
12. " Saudi sound bites," *Washington Times*, February 17, 2005.

13. MEMRI, Special Dispatch 834, "Saudi Government Daily Accuses U.S. Army of Harvesting Organs of Iraqis," December 24, 2004, accessible at http://memri.org/bin/articles.cgi?Page=archives&Area=sd&ID=SP83404.

14. MEMRI, Special Report #17, "Saudi Royal Family's Financial Support to the Palestinians 1998–2003: More than 15 Billion Riyals ($4 Billion U.S.) Given to 'Mujahideen Fighters' and 'Families of Martyrs,'" (July 3, 2003), accessible at http://memri.org/bin/articles.cgi?Page=archives&Area=sr&ID=SR1703. For purported connections between Saudis/Saudi Arabia and Al Qaeda, see http://www.cbsnews.com/stories/2002/06/23/attack/main513121.shtml; http://www.nationalreview.com/comment/kohlmann200406180921.asp; and http://www.msnbc.com/news/964663.asp?0sl=-22&cp1=1.

15. Fox News, June 23, 2003, accessible at http://www.foxnews.com/story/0,2933,90174,00.html.

16. Nick Fielding, *The Sunday Times* (London), July 6, 2003.

17. *Maariv*, July 16, 2004. Also see "Can Saudi Arabia Save Itself?" *World Press Review* (vol. 51, no. 2) February 2004 accessible at http://www.worldpress.org/print_article.cfm?article_id=1854&dont=yes. This article mentions that Robert Baer in his *Sleeping with the Devil: How Washington Sold Our Soul for Saudi Crude* makes this assertion.

18. *Al Jazeera*, October 6, 2004.

19. *Arab News*, February 10, 2005.

20. Robin Gedye, "Saudi Boss of Charity in 'terror link' fired," *Daily Telegraph*, January 9, 2004.

21. Geostrategy-Direct, Sept. 25, 2004. URL: http://www.worldnetdaily.com/news/article?ay?ARTICLE...ID=40599.

22. Steven Stalinsky, "PR Coup For Saudi Royals," February 16, 2005, *The New York Sun*, URL: http://www.nysun.com/article/9315.
23. Olivier Guitta, *The Weekly Standard*, April 4, 2005, vol.10, #27.
24. Voice of America, August 16, 2004.
25. MEMRI, Special Dispatch 706, "Saudi Crown Prince on Yunbu' Attack: 'Zionism Is Behind Terrorist Actions In The Kingdom . . . I Am 95% Sure Of That,'" May 3, 2004, from Saudi television on May 2, accessible at http://memri.org/bin/articles.cgi?Page=archives&Area=sd&ID=SP70604.
26. *Washington Times*, February 4, 2004.
27. For instance the publication in the government newspaper *al-Watan*, November 19, 2004, on an insulting cartoon targeting Dr. Rice.
28. MEMRI, Special Dispatch 805, "Saudi Government Newspaper Editorial: 'Bush the Nazi,'" (October 26, 2004), accessible at http://memri.org/bin/articles.cgi?Page=archives&Area=sd&ID=SP80504 and MEMRI, Special Dispatch 806, "Saudi Government Daily: 'U.S. to Invade Pakistan,'" (October 26, 2004), accessible at http://memri.org/bin/articles.cgi?Page=archives&Area=sd&ID=SP80604.
29. Michael Isikoff and Mark Hosenball, "Did Saudis Deceptively Finance Ad Campaign?" *Newsweek*, December 16, 2004.
30. USCIRF, Communique, February 7, 2005.
31. Scott Wilson, "Saudis Tell Syria To Leave Lebanon," *Washington Post*, March 4, 2005.
32. Audio-tape, December 15, 2004.
33. Matthew R. Simmons, "Twilight in the Desert: The Fading of Saudi Arabia's Oil," Hudson Institute, September 9, 2004.
34. Faiza Saleh Ambah, "The Cause the Saudis Can't Make," *Washington Post*, March 27, 2005.

35. Nir Boms and Eric Stakelbeck, "Saudi Promises," *Washington Times*, April 21, 2004.
36. Olivier Guitta, *The Weekly Standard*, February 9, 2005.
37. Fouad Ajami, "Reaping the Whirlwind," *U.S. News & World Report*, June 28, 2004.

Index

Afghanistan, 11, 68, 71–73, 74, 98. See also Taliban
Ain al-Yaqeen, 49, 56–57, 96
Akins, James, 132
Al al-Sheikh family, 13, 31
Al al-Sheikh, Abdulmalik, 164–65, 194
Algeria, 67–70, 112, 201
Ali, Muhammad, 157, 193
al-Qaeda, 45, 47, 69, 79, 97–98, 101–2, 105, 141, 230
Arabian-American Oil Corporation (Aramco), 7, 121–24, 159, 193, 195–96, 199–201, 224; establishment, 175, 178, 181–83; and oil crisis, 204–7
Arafat, Yasser, 104, 223
Aramco. See Arabian-American Oil Company
Armed Islamic Group (GIA), 68–69, 112
Al-Azhar University, 55–59, 62

Baker, James, 135–37
Bangladesh, 75, 216
Al-Banna, Hassan, 40–42, 59
Al-Bayoumi, Omar, 102
Bedouins, 145–49, 153–56, 158, 164–66
Benevolent International Foundation (BIF), 70, 99
Bhutto, Benazir, 77, 111–12
Bhutto, Zulfikar Ali, 75, 77, 110, 223
Bin Baz, Abdulaziz, 16–17, 23–24, 26, 57, 69, 194
Bin Laden family, 32, 99, 114–15, 136
Bin Laden Group, 10, 136
Bin Laden, Abdullah, 47
Bin Laden, Osama, 6, 46, 68, 70, 74, 81–83, 88–89, 98, 230, 235; in Afghanistan, 111, 114, 115. See also Saudi Arabia; September 11, 2001 attacks
Bosnia, 70, 90, 97
Brezhnev, Leonid, 107–8, 189, 231

Bush, Barbara, 134, 137
Bush, George H. W., 134–35, 137–38
Bush, George W., 88, 101, 120, 130, 141

Carlyle Group, 135–37
Carter, Jimmy, 107, 133–34, 143, 225
Casey, William J., 108
Central Intelligence Agency (CIA), 109–10, 127–28
China, 109–11, 131, 138
Christians, 18, 86–87, 90–92
Christopher, Warren, 144
Churchill, Winston, 167, 181
Clinton, Bill, 117, 134, 144
Companie Française des Pétroles, 181
Cox, Percy, 163, 168
Crane, Charles, 174–75, 188
cultural centers, 49–50, 60
Cutler, Walter, 129, 132

Dar al-Mal al-Islamiyya (DMI), 44–45
Death of a Princess, 142–44
Deobandi, 36–38, 72–73, 75, 110
Dulles, John Foster, 195, 202

education, 14–16, 25–26, 37–38, 41, 49–53, 76, 85–87. See also Al-Azhar University; madrasas
Egypt, 35, 56, 132, 156–58, 170, 236, 239. See also Abdel-Nasser, Gamal; Al-Azhar University; Muslim

Brotherhood; Al-Sadat, Anwar; Six-Day War; Yom Kippur War
Eisenhower, Dwight D., 137, 183, 193
Esso, 205

financial institutions, 16, 30, 38, 44, 46, 112
foreigners, 4–5, 14, 20–21, 150, 211–12, 227
France, 162–63, 176, 182, 206–7, 236
Front islamique du salut. See Islamic Salvation Front
FSI. See Islamic Salvation Front

Germany, 143, 163
GIA. See Armed Islamic Group
Grand Mosque, siege, 9–11, 42
Great Britain, 34, 37, 82–83, 156, 158–59, 162–68, 182, 206–7, 236. See also Saudi Arabia
Gul, Hamid, 77, 111

Hamas, 105–6, 134, 142, 235, 242
Hamza, Fuad, 177, 188
Al-Haramayn Islamic Foundation, 70, 96–97
Hasa, 18, 164, 238–39
Hekmatyar, Gulbuddin, 71, 74, 110
Hitler, Adolf, 45–46, 107–8, 154, 170, 173, 221

Hussein, Saddam, 4, 7, 58, 83, 114, 136–37, 139, 224
Al-Husseini, Amin, 104, 177, 189

Ibn Abd al-Wahhab, Muhammad, 31, 60, 85–86, 145, 149–54, 164
Ibn Khaldun, Abu Zayd, 158–60, 1168
Ibn Saud, Abdulaziz, 9–13, 18, 20, 33–34, 134, 190, 196, 222, 228, 243; and Great Britain, 150, 156, 161–68, 171; and Hitler, 176; and Islam, 30; pre-WWII supporters, 173–75; and U.S., 179–83, 185–87; and Zionism, 185–87. See also Ikhwan
Ibn Saud, Muhammad, 145, 149, 153
Ikhwan, 9, 27, 83, 113, 165–71, 195, 234, 241
India, 37, 39, 75, 109–10, 163, 167, 241–42. See also Deobani
International Islamic Relief Organization (IIRO), 45, 47, 96, 98
Inter-Services Intelligence (ISI), 77, 109–12, 115
Iran, 4, 11, 91, 111, 127, 206, 236, 238; revolution, 42, 109, 137, 225. See also Organization of Arab Petroleum Exporting Countries; Organization of Petroleum Exporting Countries; Khomeini, Ruhollah; Kameni, Seyed Ali
Iraq, 105–6, 111, 122, 156, 194, 225, 236, 238, 242; and Kuwait, 69, 83, 167; and media, 63, 64; and oil crisis, 205–6. See also Hussein, Saddam; Organization of Petroleum Exporting Countries
Islam, 4–5, 57, 88, 157–58; and Christianity, 18, 86–87, 90–92; extremism, 39–40, 42, 45, 48–49, 59, 74, 82–85, 88–94; and Judaism, 86–87, 88, 103–5. See also Deobani; Muslim Brotherhood; Saudi Arabia; Wahhabism
Israel, 65, 75, 88, 121–22, 124–25, 180, 197–98, 204, 223–24, 239; and Palestine, 130, 139; and terrorism, 102–4, 134. See also Palestine; Six-Day War; Yom Kippur War

Jews, 18, 39, 86–87, 90–92, 121, 124, 176–79, 188; and Islam, 86–87, 88, 103–5. See also Saudi Arabia; Zionism
jihad, 36–37, 39, 41–42, 88–89, 93, 114, 116, 235
Jordan, 167, 207, 239
Jungers, Frank, 123, 204–5

Kameni, Seyed Ali, 42. See
also Iran
Khashoggi, Adnan, 31,
133–34
Khomeini, Ruhollah, 9, 35,
63. See also Iran
King Faisal Foundation
(KFF), 40, 55, 70
Kissinger, Henry, 132, 138,
206–7
Kosovo, 70–71, 90
Kuwait, 69, 83–84, 114,
158–59, 161, 167. See also
Organization of Arab
Petroleum Exporting
Countries; Organization of
Petroleum Exporting
Countries

Lebanon, 62–63, 207, 242
Lenin, Vladimir Ilyich, 29,
35, 154, 174, 219, 221
Libya, 122, 201. See also
Organization of Arab
Petroleum Exporting
Countries

madrasas, 37–38, 72, 76–77,
79
Mawdudi, Sayyid Abdul-Ala,
39, 71
media, 2, 19, 26, 34, 38,
61–66, 94, 142–44
Middle East Institute (MEI),
123, 129–30, 131
Mobil, 205
Muslim Brotherhood, 36,
40–42, 59, 67–68, 83–84

mutawiyin, 15–16, 120, 169,
227–28

Abdel-Nasser, Gamal, 35,
41–42, 57, 59, 62, 190,
193–94, 197–98, 222
nationalism, Arab, 35, 138,
188, 197
Nazer, Hisham, 124, 215
Nixon, Richard, 138, 202,
206
nuclear weapons, 79, 111

October War. See Yom
Kippur War
oil, 2–3, 35, 137–38,
238–40; embargoes, 2–3,
120–22, 127, 132,
143–44, 191, 195–97,
228–29; revenues, 2–4, 41,
48, 60, 233–34; rise of
industry, 175–76, 179–80.
See also Arabian-American
Oil Corporation;
Organization of Petroleum
Exporting Countries
Oman, 121, 172
Organization of Arab
Petroleum Exporting
Countries (OAPEC),
200–202
Organization of Petroleum
Exporting Countries
(OPEC), 2–3, 48, 195,
199–200, 202–8, 221–22
Organization of the Islamic
Conference (OIC), 43,
45–46, 78, 224

Ottoman Empire, 155–57, 162–63, 164, 166–67, 236

Pakistan, 37, 71–73, 75–79, 98, 111, 212, 223–24, 236, 242. See also United States
Palestine, 45, 104–6, 130, 134, 174, 177, 180. See also Arafat, Yasser; Zionism
Palestinian Liberation Organization (PLO), 122–23, 223
Pasha, Ibrahim, 157, 222
Philby, Harry St. John, 154, 161, 173–75, 191

Qaddafi, Mohmmar, 52, 201
Al-Qadi, Yasin, 71, 105
Al-Qarqani, Khalid al-Hud, 177, 178
Qatar, 172, 206

Reagan, Ronald, 107, 131, 138–39, 140
Roosevelt, Franklin D., 108, 175, 179–80, 182
Russia, 162–63, 174. See also Soviet Union

Al-Sadat, Anwar, 59, 132, 204–5, 222, 224–25
Al-Saud family, 1, 3, 5–6, 11–14, 31–33, 159–60, 227–28, 231–32; finances, 47–53, 60, 135–36, 190–93, 213–15, 229–30, 232–34, 240

Al-Saud, Abdallah bin Abdulaziz, 9, 11, 69, 88, 93–94, 130, 194–95, 225, 228, 231–33; and Osama bin Laden, 117; and U.S., 120–21, 127, 133, 141
Al-Saud, Bandar bin Sultan, 102, 119, 126, 131, 135, 137, 141, 228, 230–31
Al-Saud, Fahd, 11, 61, 97, 100, 131–34, 136, 213–14, 223–25, 228, 231–32, 243; and Islam, 48–51; and Osama bin Laden, 114, 117
Al-Saud, Faisal, 11, 13, 16, 34, 45, 121, 171, 180, 222–24, 243; and anti-Semitism, 189–90; and Islam, 25–26, 30–31, 234; and oil crisis, 128, 200, 202–6, 208–9, 236; and Saudi economy, 191, 193–97
Al-Saud, Khalid, 11, 133, 180, 189, 224, 243
Al-Saud, Khalid bin Sultan, 64, 123
Al-Saud, Nayef bin Abdulaziz, 11, 87, 101, 103, 105, 115, 231–32
Al-Saud, Nawwaf, 85, 127, 194
Al-Saud, Salman bin Abdulaziz, 11, 63, 71, 97, 101, 113, 231–32
Al-Saud, Saud, 155–57, 171, 185, 190–91, 193–95, 243

Al-Saud, Saud al-Faisal, 104,
125, 143
Al-Saud, Sultan bin
Abdulaziz, 11, 68–69, 79,
87, 93, 99–103, 114–15,
133, 135, 231–32
Al-Saud, Turki al-Faisal, 44,
71–72, 84–85, 99, 112–16,
127, 133, 220
Saudi Arabia, 104–6, 112,
130, 175–76, 186–88, 211,
215–17; agriculture, 213,
218; economy, 3–4, 30, 60,
191–93, 196, 208–9, 211,
213–19, 222, 233–34;
embassies, 2, 30, 43,
119–20, 121; financial
contributions, 48–53,
59–61, 99–102, 105–6,
112; and Great Britain,
162–68, 171, 173, 176,
181, 185; history, 1,
33–34, 36–37, 56, 156–59,
161, 168–72, 194–95,
236–37, 241; international
policy, 30–31, 33;
intolerence in, 4–5, 14,
227–28; and Islam, 30–31,
34–36, 85, 241–42; law,
4–5, 14–18, 19, 227–28;
military and defense,
125–26, 131–32, 218, 240;
and Osama bin Laden, 84,
85, 100, 112–17, 139,
172; petrochemical
industry, 215, 218,
221–22; reforms, 237–38,
242–43; and terrorism,

83–84, 103–4, 230; and
U.S., 193, 204–5;
workforce, 212, 219–21.
See also Bedouin; Ibn
Saud, Abdulaziz;
mutawiyin; Organization
of Arab Petroleum
Exporting Countries;
Organization of Petroleum
Exporting Countries;
Organization of the Islamic
Conference (OIC); Al-Saud
family; United States; Yom
Kippur War
Saudi Aramco, 224. See also
Arabian-American Oil
Corporation
Saudi High Commission for
Relief to Bosnia-
Herzegovina, 70, 97–98
Scowcroft, Brent, 136–40,
142
September 11, 2001 attacks,
6, 39, 47, 49, 81, 97,
99–100, 102–3, 127–28,
134, 136
Shiism, Shiites, 9–10, 14,
18–20, 79, 91–92,
136–37, 170–71, 227,
238, 241
Six-Day War, 197, 200–201
Soviet Union, 29–30, 33, 35,
46, 60–61, 98–99, 144,
173; and Afghanistan, 11,
71–73, 107–8, 111;
economy, 215; expansion,
138; and Syria, 222. See
also Russia; Saudi Arabia

Standard Oil of California (SoCal), 121–22, 175, 181–82, 205

Standard Oil of New Jersey, 181

Sudan, 111, 115

Al-Sudairis family, 13, 31, 232

Syria, 63, 90, 111, 156, 194, 222, 236, 242

Tabligh-i Jamaat, 36, 68

Taliban, 38–39, 71–74, 79, 90, 112, 115. See also Afghanistan

technology, 20–21, 38, 59, 92, 150, 171, 175–76, 182, 196

terrorism, 45–47, 81–82, 97–102, 112; and charities, 70, 74, 105, 112, 235–36; and Islam, 48–49, 52–53, 88–90, 93. See also Saudi Arabia

Texaco, 175, 181, 205

Truman, Harry S, 121, 181, 185

United Nations, 30, 46, 48, 207, 223

United States, 34, 38, 44–46, 81–82, 129–33, 200, 202, 206; alliance with Saudi Arabia and Pakistan, 108–10, 112; Americans and terrorism abroad, 81–82, 97, 120; and Arab boycott against Israel, 124–25; opposition to, 88–90, 116; and Saudi Arabia, 7, 93–94, 103, 119–21, 139–40, 228–29, 240; and terrorism financiers, 72, 76, 101–2, 112. See also Arabian-American Oil Corporation; September 11, 2001 attacks; World Trade Center

Venezuela. See Organization of Petroleum Exporting Countries

Wahhabism, 5–7, 18–21, 26–27, 35–36, 41–43, 96–97, 149–54, 234–35, 237–38; doctrine, 23–25, 38, 57, 69–70. See also Bin Baz, Abdulaziz; World Association of Muslim Youth; World Muslim League

West, Westernization, opposition to, 34, 36, 48, 203

"White Guard." See National Guard

women, 11, 14–18, 23–24, 38, 59, 130, 227–28

World Association of Muslim Youth (WAMY), 43, 46–47, 96, 99

World Muslim League (WML), 39, 42, 43–45, 57, 71, 98–99, 101, 123, 224

World Trade Center, 1993 attack, 47. See also September 11, 2001 attacks

Yamani, Zaki, 200, 201, 203–4, 206, 221
Yassin, Yussuf, 177, 188

Yemen, 113–14, 156, 194, 198, 239, 241
Yom Kippur War, 204, 222

Zia ul-Haq, Muhammad, 75–77, 98, 110–11, 224
Zionism, 45–46, 103–4, 143, 186–87, 223

About the Author

Laurent Murawiec is a senior fellow with the Hudson Institute in Washington, D.C. He was a senior international policy analyst with the RAND Corporation until 2002. He was a foreign correspondent in Germany and Central Europe; cofounder of GeoPol Services S.A., a Geneva, Switzerland, consulting company; and an adviser to the French Ministry of Defense. He has taught the history of central economic planning at the prestigious École des Hautes Études en Sciences Sociales in Paris and military analysis and cultural anthropology at the Elliott School of International Affairs at George Washington University. His books include *War in the 21st Century* and *The Spirit of Nations: Cultures and Geopolitics*.